How Do We Know?
Yes, You Can Learn Algebra!

By Ralph E. Magoun

www.trafford.com
North America & international
toll-free: 1 888 232 4444 (USA & Canada)
fax: 812 355 4082

Thanks:

To all my friends for the support and inspiration they have provided during the preparation of this book. To Chris, a friend of my son, who expressed to me his frustration at being unable to perform at the college level in a chemistry class, because he had forgotten the algebra he had learned. I have since had the same conversation with many other students, yet the conversation with Chris was pivotal in formulating my goal of helping students remember how to use numbers. To Miss Mattie Lee Burris who made algebra exciting for me and introduced me to the idea of justifying the algebraic process. To Mary Spafford and Barbara Marden who helped me see that my goal was a dream to be done. To Wanda Kay Perry and Grace Callahan who provided countless hours technical help, without which I would still be trying to figure out how to "Right Click". To Dr. Charles Mullins who tried hard to help me see what mathematics is about. To Loran Termine for reading through the manuscript and remembering the paper in the paper and pencil joke. To Jacob Moore for a review of the manuscript from a student's point of view. To Russ Williams at Cajun Clickers for many hours of computer expertise.

A special thanks to my meditation teacher for teaching me the importance of focused concentration.

The following thanks for Professional help and a disclaimer on my part of their responsibility for what I say in **"How Do We Know?"**. Blaming them for what I have written or what I say words mean would be like blaming gravity for a loose cannon. My thanks are not meant to imply an endorsement by these folks of me or this book. What I learned from these people might well be quite different from what they taught.

Thanks,

To Holly Hamilton who introduced me to the concept of **Precision Teaching**.

At Louisiana State University:
To Dr. R. Kenton Denny for explaining SAFMEDS and Standard Celeration Charts. His explanations were clear and concise.

Dr. Terrie Poehl for explaining the intent of The National Council of Mathematics (NCTM) Standards to me and suggesting that mechanistic approaches were not consistent with the emphasis on developing thinking skills recommended by the NCTM.

Dr. Robert Matthews for sharing his insights into reflexive thinking, metacognition and Cognitive Psychology. He gave me a bunch of new words to use.

At Southern University:
Dr. Maurice Berger who cheerfully critiqued the dialogues between Sunny and Bunny. He reaffirmed for me the importance of humor and archetypical involvement in education.

Valdez Gant who tried to have me ground the book on sound mathematical principals.

Most of all my thanks to all the students who worked with me, I love you all.

The most beautiful thing we can experience is the mysterious. It is the source of all true art and science.
    Einstein, What I Believe, 1930.

HOW DO WE KNOW? presents a system for review of arithmetic and algebra which can remove the "mystery" of arithmetic calculations and enable students to see the beauty of the mystery of mathematics and science.

HOW DO WE KNOW? contains operant conditioning in the form of **Precision Teaching**, and reflexive thinking in the form of justification tables reminiscent of formal geometric proofs.

Precision Teaching is a powerful tool for motivating students to learn. It has found wide acceptance in the field of special education. Extensive research has validated this approach to operant conditioning in educational settings.

Four of Lindsey's Seven Guiding Principals that I have found useful in my class room:
Adapted from West, Young and Spooner, Precision Teaching, An Introduction.
1. The Learner Knows Best.
    Use student behavior as a measure of instructional effectiveness.

2. Focus on directly observable behaviors.
    Evaluation should be from concrete, clearly observable behaviors.

3. Use frequency of correct responses as a measure of performance.
    I find correct responses per minute a convenient measure for students to chart their behaviors.

4. Use a standard chart format for visual display.
    Precision Teaching proposes that graphing this frequency of responses on logarithmic graph paper (Standard Celeration Chart) provides a useful tool to study performance patterns.

A good example of the Standard Celeration Chart is: 3-Cycle Academic Chart from Sopris West, 4093 Specialty Place, Longmont, CO 80504. Telephone number: 303-651-2829.

In The Nature of Proof, Fawcett describes the importance of justification of thought patterns in the learning process. I have found that such a reflexive process leads to retention of material learned. I feel this sort of process is what Chi et al are speaking of as "self talk". To justify the thought processes students need to be given the words to use and SAFEMEDS from the **Precision Teaching** program are a great way to introduce word meaning to students. A free, downloadable, printable business-card size version is available from: www.ralphmagoun.com

Suggestions for using this material:

The **HOW DO WE KNOW?** materials presuppose that students have forgotten the basics of arithmetic and algebra, and need a review.

Precision Teaching Worksheets

Three minute activities on algebraic review in which the students solve worksheets, correct their own papers and graph the results. Correct responses per minute are graphed daily. A sampling of these activities as worksheets is presented. In my experience, students willingly begin class with these sorts of activities and I find the process leads to a focused class ready to move on to the lesson at hand. **Precision Teaching** suggests graphing a frequency of correct answers per minute on a special graph paper that encourages the students' progress with visual success. (Standard Celeration Chart)

The Teaching Process

Post the rules of mathematical operations and principals on poster board around the room and review and modify as you feel inclined. One of the **Precision Teaching** worksheets can be used as an example in an untimed practice session.

Precision Teaching

Copy and distribute the worksheets and allow three minutes for completion. If students finish before three minutes have them record the time they used and use this time to determine correct responses per minute. Post correct responses and allow students to correct their own papers and graph this frequency on a Celeration chart. Students calculate correct responses per minute and graph their own results. I use three work sheets on the same topic as needed over a three day period.

Scoring the Worksheets

I suggest the students score their own papers and that they have the option to decide if their answer is correct or not. Sometimes I suggest a solution path based on the algorithm suggested in the text which might be different from the system the student has previously learned. If the student obtains the correct answer, seems good to me. The question below has a number of different possibilities. I have tried to avoid ambiguity, but many students are quick to obtain the correct answers using a previously learned method. I hope that allowing students to evaluate their own work helps to overcome this challenge.

Example:
Fill in the following table:

Expression	Justification/Operation	Result
$9-(-6)$		
$9 + (+6)$		

My suggested answers:
Fill in the following table:

Expression	Justification/Operation	Result
$9-(-6)$	**To subtract a number, add the opposite.**	**$9 + (+6)$**
$9 + (+6)$	**To combine numbers with the same sign, simply add the numbers and keep the common sign.**	**15**

I am not an authority on Precision Teaching. I have found many of the ideas of Dr. O. R. Lindsley very useful in the classroom. Below are some typical graphs for student performance I have observed. A percent correct graph is pictured, then a frequency graph on regular graph paper, and the frequency graph on Log graph paper. The Celeration Society proposes that frequency is generally a better measure of student performance than percent correct. It took some time and a very patient College Professor, Dr. R. Kenton Denny at Louisiana State University, to convince me that frequency was better. I think you can see that for the sort of work presented here the percent correct seems to show mastery, while a frequency graph indicates continued improvement. I am convinced that frequency of correct response can be an important and useful representation of student progress. The work of Dr. O. R. Lindsley, as currently being furthered by the Standard Celeration Society, suggests that a chart of frequency graphed on special graph paper can lead to exploration of many of the parameters of teaching. The special graph of frequency on a Celeration Chart is at the heart of Precision Teaching.

A good example of the Standard Celeration Chart is: 3-Cycle Academic Chart from Sopris West, 4093 Specialty Place, Longmont, CO 80504. Telephone number: 303-651-2829.

As a chemistry teacher I found that for many calculations, progress was exponential as suggested by the work of Dr. O. R. Lindsley and thus leads to a straight line on the Celeration Chart.

In How Do We Know? I usually ask students to provide a written justification as part of the answer. This writing step slows down the response time and the results are not quiet as pretty as for straight forward calculations.

I find Precision Teaching particularly useful to get students focused at the beginning of a class.

Note: Frequency $= \dfrac{\text{Counts}}{\text{minutes}} = \dfrac{\#\,\text{correct}}{\text{minutes}} = \dfrac{C}{t}$, to calculate the frequency the seconds should be converted to the decimal form of minutes.

Seconds	5	10	15	20	25	30	35	40	45	50	55	60
Minutes	0.08	0.17	0.25	0.33	0.42	0.5	0.58	0.67	0.75	0.84	0.92	1.0

Typical data from routine calculations: These graphs are idealized data for illustration.

Worksheet	Date	Questions	Number correct (C)	Time (min: sec)	Time (min) (t)	Frequency (C/t)
PT 1		12	3	3	3	1
PT 2		12	12	3	3	4
PT 3		12	12	1	1	12

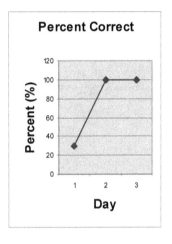
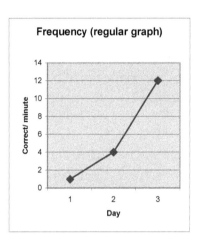
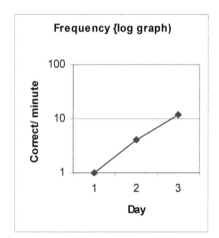

Actual student data from How Do We Know? (Coordinate Plain and Slope)

Worksheet	Date	Questions	Number correct (C)	Time (min: sec)	Time (min) (t)	Frequency (C/t)
PT 1		10	3	3:00	3.00	1
PT 2		10	10	1:00	1.00	10
PT 3		10	10	0:30	0.5	20

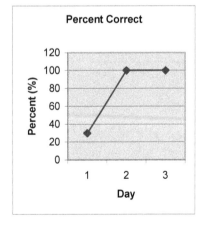
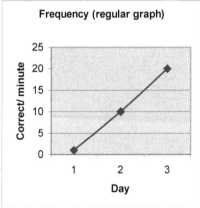
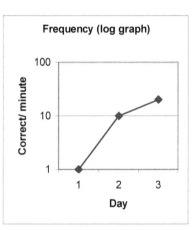

How Do We Know?

For references on Precision Teaching:

Celeration.org, The home page of The Standard Celeration Society for an extensive list of references for Precision Teaching.

Lindsley, O. R. (1990), Precision Teaching. By teachers for children. *Teaching Exceptional Children,* Spring, 10-15.

West, Richard P., K. Richard Young, Fred Spooner (1990), Precision Teaching, An Introduction, *Teaching Exceptional Children,* Spring, 4-9.

White, Owen Roberts (1986), Precision Teaching – Precision Learning, *Exceptional Children,* Vol. 52, No. 6, 522–534.

Other References:

Chi, Michelene T. H., Miriam Bassok, Matthew W. Lewis, Peter Reimann and Robert Glaser (1989), Self-explanations and How Students Study and Use Examples in Learning to Solve Problems. *Cognitive Science* 13,145-182.

Fawcett, Harold P., *The Nature of Proof,* NCTM Thirteenth Yearbook, (1938).

Keedy and Bittinger, *Basic Mathematics,* 6th edition, Addison Wesley Publishing (1992)

How Do We Know?

Table of Contents

How Do We Know?

CHAPTER 1

NUMBER LINE ACTIVITY

-4   -3   -2   -1   0

←——————————————————

0   1   2   3   4

——————————————————→

Overview: In this lesson students will construct a number line and utilize number arrows to represent quantity and as models for combining real numbers.

Mathematical Learning Objectives:	The student will:

Use the number line to develop a basic understanding of real numbers.

Apply appropriate strategies to solve problems combining numbers.

NCTM Standards:

Number and Operations
Understand numbers, ways of representing numbers, relationships among numbers, and number systems.

Geometry
Specify locations and describe spatial relationships using coordinate geometry and other representational systems.

Reasoning and Proof
Recognize reasoning and proof as fundamental aspects of mathematics.

Definitions:

Assume	To take for granted, supposition, arrogance. To believe to be true without proof.
Assumption	A fact or statement taken for granted.
Axiom	A proposition regarded as a self-evident truth.
Definition	A statement of the limits or nature of a word or word group or a sign or symbol.
Truth	Sincerity, honesty, conformity with fact reality, actual existence.
Rule	An established regulation or guide for conduct, procedure or usage.
Real numbers	All the numbers including the integers (which include zero), rational numbers, irrational numbers, and the opposites of all the above.
Opposite of a number	A number that when combined with another number gives a sum of zero. Example: The opposite of 3 is – 3. $3 + (-3) = 0$
Integers	A whole number. Examples -6, -3, 0, 1, 2 ,3
Rational numbers	A number that can be expressed as the ratio of two integers. Terminating and periodic non-terminating decimal fractions are rational numbers. Example of a terminating decimal fraction: $\frac{1}{2} = 0.5$ Example of a periodic non-terminating decimal fraction: $\frac{1}{3} = 0.3333 = 0.\overline{3}...$
Irrational numbers	Non-terminating and non-periodic decimal numbers. Early mathematicians tended to feel that irrational numbers did not follow the rules. Examples: π = 3.141592654… and $\sqrt{2}$ = 1.414213562…
Closed	Follows all the rules. Complete. A term mathematicians use to describe the orderliness of groups of numbers.
Distance	The measure of separation between two points or objects, usually along the shortest path joining them. All distances are positive.
Directed distance	When we speak of positives and negative distances we must create a frame of reference and a reference point. On the number line this reference point is usually zero. Positive to the right and negative to the left.
Zero	The sum of a number and its opposite is zero; the point marked 0 from which quantities are reckoned on a graduated scale; nothing. Zero is a real number.

As we move along the number line in the positive direction from zero, numbers increase and we get larger numbers.

$$0 \quad\quad 1 \quad\quad 2 \quad\quad 3 \quad\quad 4 \longrightarrow$$

This is a <u>Property of Real Numbers</u> (PRN). We are going to call this Property of Real Numbers a "Definition".

If we start counting beans, the more beans we count the larger the pile of beans becomes. Our experience tells us that numbers can get large and that large numbers correspond to more of something. We can think of this as defining addition of real numbers. All the numbers on the number line are Real Numbers.

Example: Add 4 beans, +4 beans
Add 3 more beans, +3 beans
+4 beans +3 beans = +7 beans

Notice that the numbers themselves are just symbols. When we connect numbers to something such as a distance on the number line or objects such as beans, numbers take on a concrete meaning. I have a friend[1] who tells me that mathematics becomes easy for you if you can free your mind to see that numbers do not belong to themselves, they are NOT matter in the universe; they are just symbols.

As we move to the right on the number line we have a directed distance that is positive. Numbers less than zero do exist and are <u>negative numbers</u>. These negative numbers are the opposite of the <u>positive numbers</u>. As we travel to the left on the number line in the negative direction from zero, the value of numbers becomes smaller as the numbers get larger. We can speak of a directed distance that is negative.

$$-4 \quad -3 \quad -2 \quad -1 \quad 0$$
$$\longleftarrow \rule{9cm}{0.4pt}$$

This is a Property of Real Numbers (PRN). We are going to call this property of real numbers a "Definition".

We will discover that a negative means much more than just a" take away". Every real number has an additive opposite and a number and its additive opposite have a sum of zero. This is a Property of Real Numbers (PRN). We are going to call this Property of Real Numbers a "Definition".

> Example: Add 4 beans, +4
> Take away 4 beans = – 4 beans
> +4 beans – 4 beans = 0 beans

As we march up and down the number line combining numbers, we are going to arrive at some numbers that are negative. The idea of counting beans does not work very well. It is rather hard to picture a negative two beans.

> Example: Add 4 beans, +4
> Take away 6 beans, –6
> +4 beans –6 beans = –2 beans

This mystery of what a –2 beans means is part of the adventure of algebra.

Summary: Measuring distances on the number line defines a system of numbers. We can combine these numbers. We are going to call these numbers <u>Real Numbers</u>. A Real positive number has an opposite and it is a Real negative number.

The sum of a number and its opposite is zero. We will justify combining numbers as part of the Properties of Real Numbers (PRN). Is this more than a definition? Do you want more than a definition?

---

[1] **Dr. Charles Mullins, personal communications**

How Do We Know?

Questions for Discussion/Research

1. Some of the synonyms the dictionary lists for assume are: pretend, simulate, feign, counterfeit, and sham. Look up these words in the dictionary and decide how comfortable you feel when you assume.

2. What is the difference between a self evident truth and an assumption?

3. What does the word *truth* mean to you?

4. What would a word like *truthiness*[2] mean?

5. Does Zero have an opposite?

---

[2] **Created by Steven Colbert, Colbert Report, 2003.**

LESSON NOTES

How Do We Know?

NUMBER LINE ACTIVITY

PURPOSE:
We will explore combining of numbers using the number line. This exercise demonstrates using a few examples that the number line gives a reasonable picture for combining numbers. This could be considered an example of an inductive argument.

MATERIALS:
A number line on the board with numbers from –7 to + 7 (1 decimeter divisions).

Seven arrows with lengths from 1 decimeter to 7 decimeters, labeled with positive numbers, 1 to 7, (arrows pointing to the right).

Seven arrows with lengths from 1 decimeter to 7 decimeters, labeled with negative numbers, –1 to – 7, (arrows pointing to the left).

Two sheets of regular poster board will yield arrows that are manageable. A model scaled in centimeters would allow students to construct their own number line and arrows. Colored poster board makes the exercise more dramatic.

The end away from the arrow point is the "base".

PROCEDURE:
1. Assign the number arrows (–7 through +7) to different students.

2. Have the students model the combinations indicated in the table below on the number line; **Remember: positive arrows pointing to the right and negative arrows pointing to the left.**

3. Place the base of one arrow on zero.

4. Place the base of the other arrow on the point of the arrow that has its base on zero; **Remember: positive arrows pointing to the right and negative arrows pointing to the left.**

5. Record the results.

Fill in the following chart:

Expression	Result	Justification
1+2		Distance on the number line
3 + 4		Distance on the number line
+7 +(– 4)		Distance on the number line
6 + (–2)		Distance on the number line
–5 +2		Distance on the number line
+2 +(–5)		Distance on the number line
+2 +5		Distance on the number line
– 7 + 7		Distance on the number line
– 2 + 2		Distance on the number line

See Page 8 for Number Line Activity answers.

NUMBERLINE ACTIVITY ANSWERS

Fill in the following chart:

Expression	Result	Justification
1+2	3	Distance on the number line
3 + 4	7	Distance on the number line
+7 +(– 4)	3	Distance on the number line
6 + (–2)	4	Distance on the number line
–5 +2	-3	Distance on the number line
+2 +(–5)	-3	Distance on the number line
+2 +5	7	Distance on the number line
– 7 + 7	0	Distance on the number line
– 2 + 2	0	Distance on the number line

CHAPTER 2

REAL NUMBER VALUE

$10 > 4$

$-6 < -1$

$|-1| = 1$

$-1 > -16$

$$0 \quad 1 \quad 2 \quad 3 \quad 4 \longrightarrow$$

Overview: The greater than, the less than, and the absolute value signs will be presented and their use with numbers will be practiced.

Mathematical Learning Objective:	The student will: Examine the meanings of positive, negative, and absolute value of numbers in relationship to the size of the numbers.
NCTM Standards:	Reasoning and Proof: Recognize reasoning and proof as fundamental aspects of mathematics.

As we move along the number line in the positive direction from zero, the value of the numbers increase and we get larger numbers.

$$0 \quad 1 \quad 2 \quad 3 \quad 4 \longrightarrow$$

This is a <u>Property of Real Numbers</u> (PRN). We are going to call this Property of Real Numbers a "Definition".

Numbers less than zero do exist and are negative numbers. These negative numbers are the opposite of the positive numbers. As we travel in the negative direction from zero, the value of the numbers become smaller as the numbers get larger.

$$\longleftarrow -4 \quad -3 \quad -2 \quad -1 \quad 0$$

This is a Property of Real Numbers (PRN). We are going to call this property of real numbers a "Definition".

Definitions:

Words	Definition	Symbol
Real numbers	All the positive and negative numbers on the number line including the rational numbers, the irrational numbers and zero.	
Positive numbers	Numbers greater than 0, increasing in value as the numbers get larger. If no sign is written, assume there is a + in front of the number.	+ numbers
Negative numbers	Numbers less than 0, decreasing in value as the numbers get larger. Every real positive number has an opposite that is a real negative number.	– numbers
Opposite numbers	Numbers that are the same distance from zero on the number line, in the opposite direction.	
Absolute value	Magnitude, value or size of a number, without a sign, neither positive nor negative.	| |
Greater than	Number on the left of the sign is larger. larger > smaller	>
Less than	Number on the left of the sign is smaller. smaller < larger	<
Value	A numerical quantity assigned or computed.	
Magnitude	Greatness of size, importance.	
Absolute	Perfect, complete, positive, not doubted, not relative.	
Relative	Meaningful only in relationship (cold to hot).	
Negative	1. Opposite to or lacking in that which is positive. 2. *In Mathematics,* designating a quantity less than zero; or one to be subtracted. 3. *In Electricity,* the place in a battery that has an excess of electrons. 4. The point of view that opposes the positive.	
Positive	1. Showing agreement; affirmative. 2. *In Mathematics,* greater than zero. 3. *In Electricity,* having a deficiency of electrons. 4. Overconfident or dogmatic.	
Opposite	In a contrary direction. The sum of a number and its opposite is zero.	
Justification	To show to be right; to supply grounds for; the reasons for.	
Natural numbers	The number 1 or any number obtained by continually adding 1 to this number.	

Questions for Discussion/Research

1. We have decided that as positive numbers increase, there is more of something. How can the positive part of a battery be deficient in electrons?

2. Does the fact that we have negative numbers for temperature on the Fahrenheit and Celsius temperature scales mean that these negative temperatures are opposites of positive temperatures?

3. If good is the opposite of bad, can you put numbers on "goodness" to measure it relative to "badness"?

Negative numbers do exist. To describe the size of these negative numbers it can be helpful to remember that a negative number is the opposite of a positive number. If a number is large its opposite will be small. The larger the number is with a negative sign in front of it, the smaller the number. The absolute value is not positive or negative. It has size and gets larger as the number gets bigger, but not in relationship to the positives on the number line.

PRECISION TEACHING (PT) SAMPLE ANSWERS:

Expression	Meaning	Justification
$|-3|$	3	Size of a number without a sign.
$-6 < -1$	–6 is less than –1	Number on the left of the sign is smaller. smaller < larger
$2 > 0$	2 is greater than 0	Number on the left of the sign is larger. larger > smaller

Scene: Lunchroom - Chicken Tenders for Lunch

Sunny: Don't they think I know how to count?

Bunny: What do you mean?

Sunny: This stuff is so obvious that it is stupid to even review.

Bunny: Well, I keep forgetting which way the greater and less than signs go.

Sunny: These chicken tenders are good right?

Bunny: Yes.

Sunny: You would eat a big one first, right?

Bunny: Yes.

Sunny: Well, the mouth of the sign goes toward the biggest 'cause it would eat that one first.

Bunny: Maybe that will help me remember.

Sunny: See, I am so smart I don't need to do this stuff again.

Bunny: Well, in math we are supposed to be careful about how we define things, so when we say something we know it will always be right.

Sunny: What do you mean "always right"? That sounds like an absolute to me. My dad says there are no absolutes.

Bunny: Is he sure of that?

Sunny: Absolutely!

LESSON NOTES

SEE PAGE 326 FOR <u>REAL NUMBER VALUE</u>: PRECISION TEACHING (PT) SCORES, FREQUENCY TABLE.

I suggest that students correct their papers, calculate the frequencies and graph their results. Graphing the results on special graph paper (Standard Celeration Chart) can provide visual reinforcement for the students and information about how they are learning. The frequency tables are provided to facilitate this process.

How Do We Know?

PT 1, QUESTIONS

Definitions:

Words	Definition	Symbol
Real numbers	All the positive and negative numbers on the number line including the rational numbers, the irrational numbers and zero.	
Positive numbers	Numbers greater than 0, increasing in value as the numbers get larger. If no sign is written, assume there is a + in front of the number.	+ numbers
Negative numbers	Numbers less than 0, decreasing in value as the numbers get larger. Every real positive number has an opposite that is a real negative number.	– numbers
Absolute value	Magnitude, value or size of a number, without a sign, neither positive nor negative.	| |
Greater than	Number on the left of the sign is larger. larger > smaller	>
Less than	Number on the left of the sign is smaller. smaller < larger	<
Value	A numerical quantity assigned or computed.	
Magnitude	Greatness of size, importance.	

Fill in the following table:

Expression	Meaning	Justification
|–4|		Size of a number without a sign.
6 > 2	6 is greater than 2	
1 < 5		Number on the left of the sign is smaller. smaller < larger
–4 < 0	–4 is less than 0	
|–1|		
–3 < +3		
|5|	5	
10 > 4		
|–9|		Size of a number without a sign.
1 < 9		
–6 < –5	–6 is less than –5	
–1 > –16		

PT 1, ANSWERS

Definitions:

Words	Definition	Symbol
Real numbers	All the positive and negative numbers on the number line including the rational numbers, the irrational numbers and zero.	
Positive numbers	Numbers greater than 0, increasing in value as the numbers get larger. If no sign is written, assume there is a + in front of the number.	+ numbers
Negative numbers	Numbers less than 0, decreasing in value as the numbers get larger. Every real positive number has an opposite that is a real negative number.	– numbers
Absolute value	Magnitude or size of a number, without a sign, neither positive nor negative.	| |
Greater than	Number on the left of the sign is larger. larger > smaller	>
Less than	Number on the left of the sign is smaller. smaller < larger	<
Value	A numerical quantity assigned or computed.	
Magnitude	Greatness of size, importance.	

Fill in the following table:

Expression	Meaning	Justification
|−4|	**4**	Size of a number without a sign.
6 > 2	6 is greater than 2	**Number on the left of the sign is larger. larger > smaller**
1 < 5	**1 is less than 5**	Number on the left of the sign is smaller. smaller < larger
−4 < 0	−4 is less than 0	**Number on the left of the sign is smaller. smaller < larger**
|−1|	**1**	**Size of a number without a sign**
−3 < +3	**−3 is less than +3**	**Number on the left of the sign is smaller. smaller < larger**
|5|	5	**Size of a number without a sign**
10 > 4	**10 is greater than 4**	**Number on the left of the sign is larger. larger > smaller**
|−9|	**9**	Size of a number without a sign.
1 < 9	**1 is less than 9**	**Number on the left of the sign is smaller. smaller < larger**
−6 < −5	−6 is less than −5	**Number on the left of the sign is smaller. smaller < larger**
−1 > −16	**−1 is greater than −16**	**Number on the left of the sign is larger. larger > smaller**

How Do We Know?

PT 2, QUESTIONS

Definitions:

Words	Definition	Symbol
Real numbers	All the positive and negative numbers on the number line including the rational numbers, the irrational numbers and zero.	
Positive numbers	Numbers greater than 0, increasing in value as the numbers get larger. If no sign is written, assume there is a + in front of the number.	+ numbers
Negative numbers	Numbers less than 0, decreasing in value as the numbers get larger. Every real positive number has an opposite that is a real negative number.	– numbers
Absolute value	Magnitude or size of a number, without a sign, neither positive nor negative.	| |
Greater than	Number on the left of the sign is larger. larger > smaller	>
Less than	Number on the left of the sign is smaller. smaller < larger	<
Value	A numerical quantity assigned or computed.	
Magnitude	Greatness of size, importance.	

Fill in the following table:

Expression	Meaning	Justification
|–8|		Size of a number without a sign.
6 >–6	6 is greater than –6	
1 < 2		Number on the left of the sign is smaller. smaller < larger
–4 < –3		
|1|		
–3 < +1		Number on the left of the sign is smaller. smaller < larger
|–15|		Size of a number without a sign.
11 > 4	11 is greater than 4	
|–10|	10	
8 > 6	8 is greater than 6	
8 < 9	8 is less than 9	
–7 < –5		Number on the left of the sign is smaller. smaller < larger
–8 > –16		

PT 2, ANSWERS

Definitions:

Words	Definition	Symbol
Real numbers	All the positive and negative numbers on the number line including the rational numbers, the irrational numbers and zero.	
Positive numbers	Numbers greater than 0, increasing in value as the numbers get larger. If no sign is written, assume there is a + in front of the number.	+ numbers
Negative numbers	Numbers less than 0, decreasing in value as the numbers get larger. Every real positive number has an opposite that is a real negative number.	– numbers
Absolute value	Magnitude or size of a number, without a sign, neither positive nor negative.	| |
Greater than	Number on the left of the sign is larger. larger > smaller	>
Less than	Number on the left of the sign is smaller. smaller < larger	<
Value	A numerical quantity assigned or computed.	
Magnitude	Greatness of size, importance.	

Fill in the following table:

Expression	Meaning	Justification
$\|-8\|$	**8**	Size of a number without a sign.
6 > –6	6 is greater than –6	**Number on the left of the sign is larger. larger > smaller**
1<2	**1 is less than 2**	Number on the left of the sign is smaller. smaller < larger
–4 < –3	**–4 is less than –3**	**Number on the left of the sign is smaller. smaller < larger**
$\|1\|$	**1**	**Size of a number without a sign.**
–3 < +1	**–3 is less than +1**	Number on the left of the sign is smaller. smaller < larger
$\|-15\|$	**15**	Size of a number without a sign.
11 > 4	11 is greater than 4	**Number on the left of the sign is larger. larger > smaller**
$\|-10\|$	10	**Size of a number without a sign.**
8 > 6	8 is greater than 6	**Number on the left of the sign is larger. larger > smaller**
8 < 9	8 is less than 9	**Number on the left of the sign is smaller. smaller < larger**
–7 < –5	**–7 is less than –5**	Number on the left of the sign is smaller. smaller < larger
–8 > –16	**–8 is greater than –16**	**Number on the left of the sign is larger. larger > smaller**

PT 3, QUESTIONS

Definitions:

Words	Definition	Symbol
Real numbers	All the positive and negative numbers on the number line including the rational numbers, the irrational numbers and zero.	
Positive numbers	Numbers greater than 0, increasing in value as the numbers get larger. If no sign is written, assume there is a + in front of the number.	+ numbers
Negative numbers	Numbers less than 0, decreasing in value as the numbers get larger. Every real positive number has an opposite that is a real negative number.	– numbers
Absolute value	Magnitude or size of a number, without a sign, neither positive nor negative.	| |
Greater than	Number on the left of the sign is larger. larger > smaller	>
Less than	Number on the left of the sign is smaller. smaller < larger	<
Value	A numerical quantity assigned or computed.	
Magnitude	Greatness of size, importance.	

Fill in the following table:

Expression	Meaning	Justification
$\|-3\|$	3	
$5 > 2$		Number on the left of the sign is larger. larger > smaller
$1 < 4$	1 is less than 4	
$-4 < -1$		
$\|-10\|$		
$-3 < +3$	–3 is less than +3	
$\|4\|$		Size of a number without a sign.
$10 > 5$	10 is greater than 5	
$\|-7\|$		Size of a number without a sign.
$7 > 2$		
$-6 < -1$	–6 is less than –1	
$-1 > -6$		

PT 3, ANSWERS

Definitions:

Words	Definition	Symbol
Real numbers	All the positive and negative numbers on the number line including the rational numbers, the irrational numbers and zero.	
Positive numbers	Numbers greater than 0, increasing in value as the numbers get larger. If no sign is written, assume there is a + in front of the number.	+ numbers
Negative numbers	Numbers less than 0, decreasing in value as the numbers get larger. Every real positive number has an opposite that is a real negative number.	– numbers
Absolute value	Magnitude or size of a number, without a sign, neither positive nor negative.	| |
Greater than	Number on the left of the sign is larger. larger > smaller	>
Less than	Number on the left of the sign is smaller. smaller < larger	<
Value	A numerical quantity assigned or computed.	
Magnitude	Greatness of size, importance.	

Fill in the following table:

Expression	Meaning	Justification
$|-3|$	3	**Size of a number without a sign.**
$5 > 2$	**5 is greater than 2**	Number on the left of the sign is larger. larger > smaller
$1 < 4$	1 is less than 4	**Number on the left of the sign is smaller. smaller < larger**
$-4 < -1$	**–4 is less than –1**	**Number on the left of the sign is smaller. smaller < larger**
$|-10|$	**10**	**Size of a number without a sign.**
$-3 < +3$	–3 is less than +3	**Number on the left of the sign is smaller. smaller < larger**
$|4|$	**4**	Size of a number without a sign.
$10 > 5$	10 is greater than 5	**Number on the left of the sign is larger. larger > smaller**
$|-7|$	**7**	Size of a number without a sign.
$7 > 2$	**7 is greater than 2**	**Number on the left of the sign is larger. larger > smaller**
$-6 < -1$	–6 is less than –1	**Number on the left of the sign is smaller. smaller < larger**
$-1 > -6$	**–1 is greater than –6**	**Number on the left of the sign is larger. larger > smaller**

How Do We Know?

CHAPTER 3

PROPERTIES OF REAL NUMBERS

$$a \times (b \times c) = (a \times b) \times c$$

$$5 (5 + 2) = 5 \times 5 + 5 \times 2$$

$$(4 + 5) + 6 = 4 + (5 + 6)$$

$$2 \times 3 = 3 \times 2$$

Overview: The properties of real numbers will be presented as a foundation for thinking about numbers and how we can work with them. In this chapter the properties will be introduced as definitions and further exploration of their validity and use will be presented in later chapters. (Chapter 13: Commutation and Distribution, for example)

Mathematical
Learning Objective: The student will:

     Identify and use commutation, distribution, identity, additive and multiplicative inverse in operations with numbers.

NCTM Standards: Number and Operations

     Use the associative and commutative properties of addition and multiplication and the distributive property of multiplication over addition.

For now, we are going to use our experience with the Number Line to justify that we can combine numbers and use properties of real numbers.

Definitions:

Rule	An established regulation or guide for conduct, procedure or usage.
Law	The rules of conduct established by an authority; a sequence of natural events, occurring with unvarying uniformity; the statement of such a sequence.
Associative	Changing the groupings does not change the product of multiplication.
Commute	To change or exchange; to interchange.
Distribute	To spread out.
Property	A characteristic or attribute.
Inductive reasoning	Reasoning based on experimental evidence; often referred to as empirical induction.
Empirical	Based on experiment or evidence.
Mathematical Induction	A concept introduced by G. Peano (1858-1930) to define the number system. A simplistic summation of Mathematical Induction might suggest that: If a statement about integers is true for some integer m and it is possible to show that from the statement for an integer n+ 1 follows from the statement for n, then the statement holds for all integers n greater than or equal to m. It has been proved by formal mathematical logic. Formal mathematical logic is often referred to as deductive reasoning.
Deductive reasoning	Reasoning that uses logic based on rules and definitions and assumptions to establish principles.
Identity element of multiplication and division	There exists an element 1, such that: a x 1 = a, and a ÷ 1 = a.
Identity element of addition and subtraction	There exists an element 0, such that: a + 0 = a, and a - 0 = a.

Associative Property of Addition: Changing the grouping of numbers to be added does not change the sum. $a + (b + c) = (a + b) + c$

> Example: $7 + (3 + 1) = 7 + 4 = 11$
> $(7 + 3) + 1 = 10 + 1 = 11$

Associative Property of Multiplication: Changing the grouping of numbers to be multiplied does not change the product. $a \times (b \times c) = (a \times b) \times c$

> Example: $2 \times (3 \times 4) = 2 \times 12 = 24$
> $(2 \times 3) \times 4 = 6 \times 4 = 24$

Commutative Property of Addition: Changing the order of addition does not matter.

> $a + b = b + a$
> Example: $2 + 4 = 4 + 2 = 6$

Commutative Property of Multiplication: Changing the order of multiplication does not change the answer. $ab = ba$

> Example: $2 \times 3 = 3 \times 2$

Note: Subtraction and division are not commutative

Distributive Property of Multiplication: Multiplication spreads out over addition.

> $a(b + c) = ab + ac$
> Example: $2(3+4) = 2 \times 3 + 2 \times 4 = 14$

Identity Element for Addition and Subtraction: There is a number that can be added to, or subtracted from a number and not change that number. That number is 0.

> $a + 0 = a$, and $a - 0 = a$.
> Examples: $3 + 0 = 3$, and $3 - 0 = 3$

Inverse Property of Addition: There is a number such that it can be combined with another number and the result is 0. This number is called the additive inverse or additive opposite.

> $a - a = 0$
> Example: $3 - 3 = 0$

Identity Element for Multiplication and Division: There is a number that can be multiplied times or divided into another number and not change that number. That number is 1.

> $a \times 1 = a$, and $a \div 1 = a$
> Examples: $5 \times 1 = 5$, and $5 \div 1 = 5$

Multiplicative Inverse Property: Every real number (except zero) has a multiplicative inverse such that the product of the number and its inverse is 1.

> The inverse of a is $\dfrac{1}{a}$ and $a \times \dfrac{1}{a} = 1$
> Example: The inverse of 9 is $\dfrac{1}{9}$, and $9 \times \dfrac{1}{9} = 1$

Questions for further discussion/research:

1. What does closure mean with respect to real numbers?

2. What is the Density Property of real numbers?

3. Can you think of a memory trick (mnemonic device) to help remember what associative, distributive and commutative properties are?

4. Why are division and subtraction not commutative?

PRECISION TEACHING (PT) SAMPLE ANSWERS

Fill in the following table:

Expression	Property	Justification
$4 \times 2 = 2 \times 4$	Commutative	Changing the order of multiplication does not matter.
$x(d + p) = xd + xp$	Distributive	Multiplication spreads out over addition and subtraction.
$Ab = bA$	Commutative	Changing the order of multiplication does not matter.
$6 + 3 = 3 + 6$	Commutative	Changing the order of addition does not matter.
$5(3 + 1) = 5 \times 3 + 5 \times 1$	Distributive	Multiplication spreads out over addition and subtraction.
$3 \times (4 \times 2) = (3 \times 4) \times 2$	Associative	Changing the groupings does not change the product of multiplication.
$W(x - y) = Wx - Wy$	Distributive	Multiplication spreads out over addition and subtraction.
$xy \times 1 = xy$	Identity element of multiplication	Multiplying by one does not change a number.
$14 + 0 = 14$	Identity element of addition	Adding or subtracting zero does not change a number.
$-z\left(\dfrac{1}{-z}\right) = 1$	Multiplicative inverse property	The product of any number (except zero) and its inverse is one.
$Q - Q = 0$	Additive inverse	The sum of a number and its additive inverse is zero.

Scene: Lunchroom - Chef's Surprise for Lunch

Sunny: What a bunch of silliness.

Bunny: This lunch does look pretty bad.

Sunny: No, I mean all those rules and properties of numbers, who needs them?

Bunny: We do, for instance if we started dividing by Zero everything about the number system would be all messed up.

Sunny: You mean more than it already is?

Bunny: Yes.

Sunny: Those Math teachers think all those rules are so neat and cool.

Bunny: They give an order on which to build a beautiful system.

Sunny: (exasperated) Beautiful to who?

Bunny: You should say "to whom". "Whom" is the objective case and the object of the preposition to.

Sunny: (more exasperated) Like I need more rules. How could anybody say math is neat and cool?

Bunny: Well, I think it was Einstein who suggested "Mathematics is the Language of God". And a language has rules.

Sunny: I can suggest a place to put all those rules.

Bunny: Calm down Sunny, life is too important to take seriously.

LESSON NOTES

SEE PAGE 326 FOR <u>PROPERTIES OF REAL NUMBERS</u>: PRECISION TEACHING (PT) SCORES, FREQUENCY TABLE.

I suggest that students correct their papers, calculate the frequencies and graph their results. Graphing the results on special graph paper (Standard Celeration Chart) can provide visual reinforcement for the students and information about how they are learning. The frequency tables are provided to facilitate this process.

PT 1, QUESTIONS

Fill in the following table with the best answer:

Expression	Property	Justification
$x(q - r) = xq - xr$		Multiplication spreads out over addition and subtraction.
$5(5 + 2) = 5 \times 5 + 5 \times 2$	Distributive	
$3 \times 6 = 6 \times 3$	Commutative	
$x(q - r) = xq - xr$	Distributive	
$4 \times 5 \times 6 = 6 \times 5 \times 4$		
$3 \times (4 \times 2) = (3 \times 4) \times 2$	Associative	
$W(x - y) = Wx - Wy$		
$6 \times 1 = 6$	Identity element of multiplication	
$6 + 0 = 6$		Adding or subtracting zero does not change a number
$5\left(\dfrac{1}{5}\right) = 1$	Multiplicative inverse property	
$1 - 1 = 0$		The sum of a number and its additive inverse is zero
$4\left(\dfrac{1}{4}\right) = 1$	Multiplicative inverse property	
$-5 + 5 = 0$		The sum of a number and its additive inverse is zero.
$(4 + 5) + 6 = 4 + (5 + 6)$	Associative	

PT 1, ANSWERS

Fill in the following table with the best answer:

Expression	Property	Justification
$x(q - r) = xq - xr$	**Distributive**	Multiplication spreads out over addition and subtraction.
$5(5 + 2) = 5 \times 5 + 5 \times 2$	Distributive	**Multiplication spreads out over addition and subtraction.**
$3 \times 6 = 6 \times 3$	Commutative	**Changing the order of multiplication does not matter.**
$x(q - r) = xq - xr$	Distributive	**Multiplication spreads out over addition and subtraction.**
$4 \times 5 \times 6 = 6 \times 5 \times 4$	**Commutative**	**Changing the order of multiplication does not matter.**
$3 \times (4 \times 2) = (3 \times 4) \times 2$	Associative	**Changing the groupings does not change the product of multiplication.**
$W(x - y) = Wx - Wy$	**Distributive**	**Multiplication spreads out over addition and subtraction.**
$6 \times 1 = 6$	Identity element of multiplication	**Multiplying by one does not change a number.**
$6 + 0 = 6$	**Identity element of addition**	Adding or subtracting zero does not change a number
$5\left(\dfrac{1}{5}\right) = 1$	Multiplicative inverse property	**The product of any number (except zero) and its' inverse is one.**
$1 - 1 = 0$	**Additive inverse**	The sum of a number and its additive inverse is zero
$4\left(\dfrac{1}{4}\right) = 1$	Multiplicative inverse property	**The product of any number (except zero) and its inverse is one.**
$-5 + 5 = 0$	**Additive inverse**	The sum of a number and its additive inverse is zero.
$(4 + 5) + 6 = 4 + (5 + 6)$	Associative	**Changing the groupings does not change the sum.**

PT 2, QUESTIONS

Fill in the following table:

Expression	Property	Justification
$3 \times 7 = 7 \times 3$		Changing the order of multiplication does not matter.
$x(m + n) = xm + xn$	Distributive	
$5(4 + 2) = 5 \times 4 + 5 \times 2$		Multiplication spreads out over addition and subtraction.
$2 \times 5 \times 6 = 6 \times 5 \times 2$	Commutative	
$7 \times 8 = 8 \times 7$		Changing the order of multiplication does not matter.
$W(x + y) = Wx + Wy$		Multiplication spreads out over addition and subtraction.
$6 + 5 = 5 + 6$		Changing the order of addition does not matter.
$5(3+1) = 5 \times 3 + 5 \times 1$	Distributive	
$2 \times 3 \times 7 = 3 \times 7 \times 2$	Commutative	
$(7 \times 8) \times 9 = 7 \times (8 \times 9)$	Associative	
$3(y + z) = 3y + 3z$	Distributive	
$5 \times 9 = 9 \times 5$		
$y \times 1 = y$	Identity element of multiplication	
$x + 0 = x$	Identity element of addition	
$-5\left(\dfrac{1}{-5}\right) = 1$		The product of any number (except zero) and its' inverse is one.
$3 - 3 = 0$	Additive inverse	
$7\left(\dfrac{1}{7}\right) = 1$	Multiplicative inverse property	
$-8 + 8 = 0$		The sum of a number and its additive inverse is zero.
$(7 + 8) + 9 = 7 + (8 + 9)$	Associative	

PT 2, ANSWERS

Fill in the following table:

Expression	Property	Justification
$3 \times 7 = 7 \times 3$	**Commutative**	Changing the order of multiplication does not matter.
$x(m + n) = xm + xn$	Distributive	**Multiplication spreads out over addition and subtraction.**
$5(4 + 2) = 5 \times 4 + 5 \times 2$	**Distributive**	Multiplication spreads out over addition and subtraction.
$2 \times 5 \times 6 = 6 \times 5 \times 2$	Commutative	**Changing the order of multiplication does not matter.**
$7 \times 8 = 8 \times 7$	**Commutative**	Changing the order of multiplication does not matter.
$W(x + y) = Wx + Wy$	**Distributive**	Multiplication spreads out over addition and subtraction.
$6 + 5 = 5 + 6$	**Commutative**	Changing the order of addition does not matter.
$5(3+1) = 5 \times 3 + 5 \times 1$	Distributive	**Multiplication spreads out over addition and subtraction.**
$2 \times 3 \times 7 = 3 \times 7 \times 2$	Commutative	**Changing the order of multiplication does not matter.**
$(7 \times 8) \times 9 = 7 \times (8 \times 9)$	Associative	**Changing the groupings does not change the product of multiplication.**
$3(y + z) = 3y + 3z$	Distributive	**Multiplication spreads out over addition and subtraction.**
$5 \times 9 = 9 \times 5$	**Commutative**	Changing the order of multiplication does not matter.
$y \times 1 = y$	Identity element of multiplication	**Multiplying by one does not change a number.**
$x + 0 = x$	Identity element of addition	**Adding or subtracting zero does not change a number**
$-5\left(\dfrac{1}{-5}\right) = 1$	**Multiplicative inverse property**	The product of any number (except zero) and its inverse is one.
$3 - 3 = 0$	Additive inverse	**The sum of a number and it's additive inverse is zero**
$7\left(\dfrac{1}{7}\right) = 1$	Multiplicative inverse property	**The product of any number (except zero) and its inverse is one.**
$-8 + 8 = 0$	**Additive inverse**	The sum of a number and its additive inverse is zero.
$(7 + 8) + 9 = 7 + (8 + 9)$	Associative	**Changing the groupings does not change the sum.**

PT 3, QUESTIONS

Fill in the following table:

Expression	Property	Justification
$4 \times 2 = 2 \times 4$		
$x(d + p) = xd + xp$		
$5(7 - 4) = 5 \times 7 - 5 \times 4$	Distributive	
$(3 \times 2) \times 7 = 3 \times (2 \times 7)$		Changing the groupings does not change the product of multiplication.
$3 \times 6 = 6 \times 3$	Commutative	
$Ab = bA$	Commutative	
$6 + 3 = 3 + 6$	Commutative	
$5(3 + 1) = 5 \times 3 + 5 \times 1$	Distributive	
$2 \times 3 \times 5 = 5 \times 2 \times 3$		
$8 \times 9 = 9 \times 8$		
$3 \times (4 \times 2) = (3 \times 4) \times 2$		
$W(x - y) = Wx - Wy$		
$xy \times 1 = xy$		
$14 + 0 = 14$		Adding or subtracting zero does not change a number.
$-z\left(\dfrac{1}{-z}\right) = 1$		The product of any number (except zero) and its inverse is one.
$Q - Q = 0$		The sum of a number and its additive inverse is zero.
$6\left(\dfrac{1}{6}\right) = 1$		
$-9 + 9 = 0$		
$(1 + 2) + 3 = 1 + (2 + 3)$		

PT 3, ANSWERS

Fill in the following table:

Expression	Property	Justification
$4 \times 2 = 2 \times 4$	Commutative	Changing the order of multiplication does not matter.
$x(d + p) = xd + xp$	Distributive	Multiplication spreads out over addition and subtraction.
$5(7 - 4) = 5 \times 7 - 5 \times 4$	Distributive	Multiplication spreads out over addition and subtraction.
$(3 \times 2) \times 7 = 3 \times (2 \times 7)$	Associative	Changing the groupings does not change the product of multiplication.
$3 \times 6 = 6 \times 3$	Commutative	Changing the order of multiplication does not matter.
$Ab = bA$	Commutative	Changing the order of multiplication does not matter.
$6 + 3 = 3 + 6$	Commutative	Changing the order of addition does not matter.
$5(3 + 1) = 5 \times 3 + 5 \times 1$	Distributive	Multiplication spreads out over addition and subtraction.
$2 \times 3 \times 5 = 5 \times 2 \times 3$	Commutative	Changing the order of multiplication does not matter.
$8 \times 9 = 9 \times 8$	Commutative	Changing the order of multiplication does not matter.
$3 \times (4 \times 2) = (3 \times 4) \times 2$	Associative	Changing the groupings does not change the product of multiplication.
$W(x - y) = Wx - Wy$	Distributive	Multiplication spreads out over addition and subtraction.
$xy \times 1 = xy$	Identity element of multiplication	Multiplying by one does not change a number.
$14 + 0 = 14$	Identity element of addition	Adding or subtracting zero does not change a number.
$-z\left(\dfrac{1}{-z}\right) = 1$	Multiplicative inverse property	The product of any number (except zero) and its inverse is one.
$Q - Q = 0$	Additive inverse	The sum of a number and its additive inverse is zero.
$6\left(\dfrac{1}{6}\right) = 1$	Multiplicative inverse property	The product of any number (except zero) and its inverse is one.
$-9 + 9 = 0$	Additive inverse	The sum of a number and its additive inverse is zero.
$(1 + 2) + 3 = 1 + (2 + 3)$	Associative	Changing the groupings does not change the sum.

CHAPTER 4

COMBINING SIGNED NUMBERS

$$5 + (+ 2) = 7$$

$$-4 + (-1) = -5$$

$$|7| - |5| = |2|$$

$$8 - (- 5) = 8 + (+5) = 13$$

Overview: Combining signed numbers will be explored. A series of rules will be presented and the algorithm practiced.

Mathematical
Learning Objective: The student will:

Extend the number line arrow concept to the combining of signed numbers using an absolute value approach.

NCTM Standards: Algebra:

Write equivalent forms of equations, inequalities, and systems of equations and solve them with fluency - mentally or with paper and pencil in simple cases and using technology in all cases.

Reasoning and Proof:

Select and use various types of reasoning and methods of proof.

Definitions:

Induction	Reasoning from particular facts to general conclusions.
Deduction	Reasoning from the general to the specific.
Cite	To mention by way of example, proof, etc.
Assumption	A fact or statement taken for granted.
The identity Element of Addition and Subtraction	There exists an element 0, such that: a + 0 = a, and a - 0 = a.
Opposite Numbers	Numbers that are the same distance from zero on the number line, in the opposite direction. Sometimes the term additive inverse is used. Example: the opposite or additive inverse of -3 is +3
Additive Inverse	Numbers that are the same distance from zero on the number line, in the opposite direction. Sometimes the term opposite is used. Example: the opposite or additive inverse of -3 is +3

We are not always going to have a number line and arrows big enough to use arrows on the number line. For now, let us assume that the results of our number line experience will extend to all the numbers on the number line and describe a set of rules that will allow us to combine these numbers. Let us call these rules <u>Properties of Real Numbers</u> (PRN).

To combine numbers with different signs, it is helpful if we define an idea of a size of a number without a sign, neither positive nor negative. Let us call this number that just has a size or magnitude an <u>absolute value</u> and write it with the number in straight line brackets | |. It is the length on the number line without direction.

Examples: $|+4| = 4$
$|-5| = 5$

Zero is the identity element for addition and subtraction. For any a, a + 0 = a, and a – 0 = a. This leads to: a – a = 0 where –a is an additive opposite of a.

Remember:
Negative numbers are additive opposites of positive numbers and positive numbers are additive opposites of negative numbers.

Example: The opposite of +5 is –5

RULES FOR COMBINING SIGNED NUMBERS

For now let us call these rules **Assumptions**. They are consistent with our experience with the number line.

I. To combine numbers with the same sign simply add the numbers and keep the common sign.

Examples: 5 + (+ 2) = 7
               –4 + (–1) = –5

II. To combine numbers with different signs, find the difference between the absolute values and give the answer the sign of the number that has the largest absolute value.

Example 1:   7 + (–5)
               $|7| - |5| = 2$

Since the sign of 7 was positive and +7 has the larger absolute value, the result will be +2.

               7 + (–5) = +2

Example 2:   (–4) + 3
               $|4| - |3| = 1$

Since the sign of 4 was negative, and –4 has a larger absolute value, the result will be –1.

               (–4) + 3 = –1

III. A number and its additive opposite have a sum of zero. For any a, a + 0 = a, and a – 0 = a.
This leads to: a – a = 0 where –a is an additive opposite of a.

Example: 8 + (–8) = 0

IV. The opposite of an additive opposite is the number itself.[1]

Example: – (–5) = +5

V. To subtract a number, add the opposite.

Example 1:   8 – (– 5) = 8 + (+5) = 13
Example 2:   6 – (+3) = 6 + (–3) = 3

[1]**Keedy and Bittinger, Basic Mathematics, 6th edition, Addison Wesley Publishing (1992)**

Questions for discussion/research

Notice that above, page 35, I snuck in two arguments to justify parts of the process:

III. A number and its additive opposite have a sum of zero. For any a, a + 0 = a, and a – 0 = a.

This leads to: a – a = 0 where –a is an additive opposite of a.

This justification uses some definitions and algebra and is in the form of deductive proof.

IV. The opposite of an additive opposite is the number itself.*

This is justified by a quote from a mathematics text book.

Are these forms of justification equal in believability? Why?

RULES FOR COMBINING SIGNED NUMBERS

I. To combine numbers with the same sign simply add the numbers and keep the common sign.

II. To combine numbers with different signs, find the difference between the absolute values and give the answer the sign of the number that has the largest absolute value.

III. A number and its additive opposite have a sum of zero.

IV. The opposite of an additive opposite is the number itself.

V. To subtract a number, add the opposite

PRECISION TEACHING (PT) SAMPLE ANSWERS:

Fill in the following table:

Expression	Justification/Operation	Result
$-(-6)$	The opposite of an additive opposite is the number itself.	+6
$-4 + (+9)$	To combine numbers with different signs, find the difference between the absolute values and give the answer the sign of the number that has the largest absolute value.	+5
$-9 + 4$	To combine numbers with different signs, find the difference between the absolute values and give the answer the sign of the number that has the largest absolute value.	–5
$-5 + (-6)$	To combine numbers with the same sign, simply add the numbers and keep the common sign.	–11
$+8 + (-8)$	A number and its additive opposite have a sum of zero.	0
$9 - (-6)$	To subtract a number, add the opposite.	9 + (+6) or 15
$9 + (+6)$	To combine numbers with the same sign, simply add the numbers and keep the common sign.	15
$-6 + (-2)$	To combine numbers with the same sign, simply add the numbers and keep the common sign.	–8

Scene: Lunchroom - Corn Dogs for Lunch, Sunny Sitting on the Floor Talking to Bunny

Sunny: What a bunch of BS. Negative numbers! Huh, common sense tells me that zero is
             as low as you go.

Bunny: Well, there are temperatures below zero and anyway negative numbers are defined by
             the number line.

Sunny: And this stuff about minus a minus being a plus. Makes no sense at all.

Bunny: When you take away a distance moved in the negative direction, it's like adding.

Sunny: And they just keep making up rules.

Bunny: The rules define the number system.

Sunny: And absolute value, now whoever dreamed that up you can define as an absolute idiot.

Bunny: It is helpful if we have an ordered system to use to work with signed numbers.

Sunny: I don't understand any of it. Addition and subtraction are enough for me.

Bunny: In algebra we are going to need to use negative numbers.

Sunny: And what do I need to know any of these rules for?

Principal: (approaching Sunny): What are you doing, sitting on the floor eating a corn dog?

Sunny: What do you want me to do, sit on the corn dog and eat the floor?

Principal: (leading Sonny away) Come along to the office with me Sunny.

LESSON NOTES

SEE PAGE 326 FOR <u>COMBINING SIGNED NUMBERS</u> : PRECISION TEACHING (PT) SCORES, FREQUENCY TABLE.

I suggest that students correct their papers, calculate the frequencies and graph their results. Graphing the results on special graph paper (Standard Celeration Chart) can provide visual reinforcement for the students and information about how they are learning. The frequency tables are provided to facilitate this process.

How Do We Know?

PT 1, QUESTIONS

RULES FOR COMBINING SIGNED NUMBERS

I. To combine numbers with the same sign simply add the numbers and keep the common sign.

II. To combine numbers with different signs, find the difference between the absolute values and give the answer the sign of the number that has the largest absolute value.

III. A number and its additive opposite have a sum of zero.

IV. The opposite of an additive opposite is the number itself.

V. To subtract a number, add the opposite.

Fill in the following table:

Expression	Justification/Operation	Result
–5 + (–6)		–11
+8 + (–8)	A number and its additive opposite have a sum of zero.	
5 + 5	To combine numbers with the same sign, simply add the numbers and keep the common sign.	
4 + (–4)		
–7 + 6	To combine numbers with different signs, find the difference between the absolute values and give the answer the sign of the number that has the largest absolute value.	
10 + (–4)		
–5 + (–6)	To combine numbers with the same sign, simply add the numbers and keep the common sign.	
+8 + (–5)		
–9 + (–2)	To combine numbers with the same sign, simply add the numbers and keep the common sign.	
–19 – (–2)		–19 + (+2) or –17
–19 + (+2)	To combine numbers with different signs, find the difference between the absolute values and give the answer the sign of the number that has the largest absolute value.	

PT 1, ANSWERS

RULES FOR COMBINING SIGNED NUMBERS

I. To combine numbers with the same sign simply add the numbers and keep the common sign.

II. To combine numbers with different signs, find the difference between the absolute values and give the answer the sign of the number that has the largest absolute value.

III. A number and its additive opposite have a sum of zero.

IV. The opposite of an additive opposite is the number itself.

V. To subtract a number, add the opposite.

Fill in the following table:

Expression	Justification/Operation	Result
–5 + (–6)	**To combine numbers with the same sign, simply add the numbers and keep the common sign.**	–11
+8 + (–8)	A number and its additive opposite have a sum of zero.	**0**
5 + 5	To combine numbers with the same sign, simply add the numbers and keep the common sign.	**10**
4 + (–4)	**A number and its additive opposite have a sum of zero.**	**0**
–7 + 6	To combine numbers with different signs, find the difference between the absolute values and give the answer the sign of the number that has the largest absolute value.	**–1**
10 + (–4)	**To combine numbers with different signs, find the difference between the absolute values and give the answer the sign of the number that has the largest absolute value.**	**6**
–5 + (–6)	To combine numbers with the same sign, simply add the numbers and keep the common sign.	**–11**
+8 + (–5)	**To combine numbers with different signs, find the difference between the absolute values and give the answer the sign of the number that has the largest absolute value.**	**3**
–9 + (–2)	To combine numbers with the same sign, simply add the numbers and keep the common sign.	**–11**
–19 – (–2)	**To subtract a number, add the opposite.**	–19 + (+2) or –17
–19 + (+2)	To combine numbers with different signs, find the difference between the absolute values and give the answer the sign of the number that has the largest absolute value.	**–17**

PT 2, QUESTIONS

RULES FOR COMBINING SIGNED NUMBERS

I. To combine numbers with the same sign simply add the numbers and keep the common sign.

II. To combine numbers with different signs, find the difference between the absolute values and give the answer the sign of the number that has the largest absolute value.

III. A number and its additive opposite have a sum of zero.

IV. The opposite of an additive opposite is the number itself.

V. To subtract a number, add the opposite.

Fill in the following table:

Expression	Justification/Operation	Result
5 + 4	To combine numbers with the same sign, simply add the numbers and keep the common sign.	
–(–6)		+6
–4 + 9	To combine numbers with different signs, find the difference between the absolute values and give the answer the sign of the number that has the largest absolute value.	
–9 + 4		–5
–5 + (–6)		–11
+8 + (–8)	A number and its additive opposite have a sum of zero.	
–9 + (–2)		
6 + (–6)		0
17 + (–18)		–1
15 – (+12)		15 + (–12) or 3
15 + (–12)		

PT 2, ANSWERS

RULES FOR COMBINING SIGNED NUMBERS

I.   To combine numbers with the same sign simply add the numbers and keep the common sign.

II. To combine numbers with different signs, find the difference between the absolute values and give the answer the sign of the number that has the largest absolute value.

III. A number and its additive opposite have a sum of zero.

IV. The opposite of an additive opposite is the number itself.

V.   To subtract a number, add the opposite.

Fill in the following table:

Expression	Justification/Operation	Result
5 + 4	To combine numbers with the same sign, simply add the numbers and keep the common sign.	**9**
–(–6)	**The opposite of an additive opposite is the number itself.**	+6
–4 + 9	To combine numbers with different signs, find the difference between the absolute values and give the answer the sign of the number that has the largest absolute value.	**+5**
–9 + 4	**To combine numbers with different signs, find the difference between the absolute values and give the answer the sign of the number that has the largest absolute value.**	–5
–5 + (–6)	**To combine numbers with the same sign, simply add the numbers and keep the common sign.**	–11
+8 + (–8)	A number and its additive opposite have a sum of zero.	**0**
–9 + (–2)	**To combine numbers with the same sign, simply add the numbers and keep the common sign.**	**–11**
6 + (–6)	**A number and its additive opposite have a sum of zero.**	0
17 + (–18)	**To combine numbers with different signs, find the difference between the absolute values and give the answer the sign of the number that has the largest absolute value.**	–1
15 – (+12)	To subtract a number, add the opposite.	15 + (–12) or 3
15 + (–12)	**To combine numbers with different signs, find the difference between the absolute values and give the answer the sign of the number that has the largest absolute value.**	3

PT 3, QUESTIONS

RULES FOR COMBINING SIGNED NUMBERS

I.   To combine numbers with the same sign simply add the numbers and keep the common sign.

II. To combine numbers with different signs, find the difference between the absolute values and give the answer the sign of the number that has the largest absolute value.

III. A number and its additive opposite have a sum of zero.

IV. The opposite of an additive opposite is the number itself.

V.   To subtract a number, add the opposite.

Fill in the following table:

Expression	Justification/Operation	Result
5 + 4		
–(–4)		+4
–7 + 6	To combine numbers with different signs, find the difference between the absolute values and give the answer the sign of the number that has the largest absolute value.	
–9 + (– 4)		–13
–5 + (–6)		–11
+8 + (–5)		
–9 + (–2)	To combine numbers with the same sign, simply add the numbers and keep the common sign.	
5 + 4		9
–(–6)		+6
–6 + (–2)	To combine numbers with the same sign, simply add the numbers and keep the common sign.	
5 – (–6)		5 + (+6) or 11
5 + 6		

PT 3, ANSWERS

RULES FOR COMBINING SIGNED NUMBERS

I.   To combine numbers with the same sign simply add the numbers and keep the common sign.

II. To combine numbers with different signs, find the difference between the absolute values and give the answer the sign of the number that has the largest absolute value.

III. A number and its additive opposite have a sum of zero.

IV. The opposite of an additive opposite is the number itself.

V.   To subtract a number, add the opposite.

Fill in the following table:

Expression	Justification/Operation	Result
5 + 4	**To combine numbers with the same sign, simply add the numbers and keep the common sign.**	**9**
–(–4)	**The opposite of an opposite of a number is the number itself.**	+4
–7 + 6	To combine numbers with different signs, find the difference between the absolute values and give the answer the sign of the number that has the largest absolute value.	**–1**
–9 +(– 4)	**To combine numbers with the same sign, simply add the numbers and keep the common sign.**	–13
–5 + (–6)	**To combine numbers with the same sign, simply add the numbers and keep the common sign.**	–11
+8 + (–5)	**To combine numbers with different signs, find the difference between the absolute values and give the answer the sign of the number that has the largest absolute value.**	+3
–9 + (–2)	To combine numbers with the same sign, simply add the numbers and keep the common sign.	**–11**
5 + 4	**To combine numbers with the same sign, simply add the numbers and keep the common sign.**	9
–(–6)	**The opposite of an additive opposite is the number itself.**	+6
–6 + (–2)	To combine numbers with the same sign, simply add the numbers and keep the common sign.	**–8**
5 – (–6)	**To subtract a number, add the opposite.**	5 + (+6) or 11
5 + 6	**To combine numbers with the same sign, simply add the numbers and keep the common sign.**	**11**

CHAPTER 5

MULTIPLICATION TABLES

Number	1	2	3	4	5	6	7	8	9	10	11	12
1	1	2	3	4	5	6	7	8	9	10	11	12
2	2	4	6	8	10	12	14	16	18	20	22	24
3	3	6	9	12	15	18	21	24	27	30	33	36
4	4	8	12	16	20	24	28	32	36	40	44	48
5	5	10	15	20	25	30	35	40	45	50	55	60
6	6	12	18	24	30	36	42	48	54	60	66	72
7	7	14	21	28	35	42	49	56	63	70	77	84
8	8	16	24	32	40	48	56	64	72	80	88	96
9	9	18	27	36	45	54	63	72	81	90	99	108
10	10	20	30	40	50	60	70	80	90	100	110	120
11	11	22	33	44	55	66	77	88	99	110	121	132
12	12	24	36	48	60	72	84	96	108	120	132	144

MULTIPLICATION
TABLES

Overview: Grouping numbers and counting by groups is essential to developing a "number sense", a sense of magnitude and the relationship between numbers. A review of the Multiplication Tables is presented. Division facts will be developed on the basis of the multiplication table.

Mathematical Learning Objective:	The student will: Develop an understanding of combining groups of numbers.
NCTM Standards:	Number and Operations: Understand numbers, way of representing numbers, relationships among numbers, and number systems.

Definitions:

Substitute	To put in place of another. We will assume that if quantities are defined as equal, the number system allows us to substitute the symbols and the numbers for the quantities interchangeably. This assumption will often imply constraints on the substitution. This assumption is essential for the Transitive Property of Equality.
Assume	To take for granted, supposition, to believe to be true without proof.
Transitive Property of Equality	Things equal to the same thing are equal to each other. Example: If a = b and b = c, then a = c.
Identity Element of Multiplication and Division	There exists an element 1, such that: a x 1 = a, and a ÷ 1 = a.
Product	The result obtained when multiplying two or more numbers together.
Multiplication	The process of finding the quantity, obtained by adding a specified quantity to itself a specified number of times. Example: $3(5) = 5+5+5 = 15$
Quotient	The quantity obtained when one number is divided by another.
Division	The inverse of multiplication.
Divisor	The number by which a dividend is divided; the bottom number of a fraction (denominator).
Dividend	The number that is divided; the top number of a fraction (numerator).

Remember:

The slash "/", the fraction bar "—", and the division symbol "÷" all mean division. The capital "X", the parenthesis "( )", the dot "•", a mathematical times sign "×", a vertical line " | ", two variables written together "xy", or a number and a variable written together "5x" all mean multiplication.

PRECISION TEACHING SAMPLE ANSWERS

Fill in the following table:

Number	1	2	3	4	5	6	7	8	9	10	11	12
1	1	2	3	4	5	6	7	8	9	10	11	12
2	2	4	6	8	10	12	14	16	18	20	22	24
3	3	6	9	12	**15**	18	**21**	24	27	**30**	33	36
4	4	8	12	16	20	24	28	32	36	40	44	48
5	5	10	15	20	25	30	35	40	45	50	55	60
6	6	12	18	24	**30**	36	**42**	48	54	**60**	66	72
7	7	14	21	28	35	42	49	56	63	70	77	84
8	8	16	24	32	40	48	56	64	72	80	88	96
9	9	18	27	36	**45**	54	**63**	72	81	90	99	108
10	10	20	30	40	50	60	70	80	90	100	110	120
11	11	22	33	44	55	66	77	88	99	110	121	132
12	12	24	36	48	**60**	72	**84**	96	108	120	132	144

Fill in the following table:

Expression	Result
$42 \div 7$	**6**
12 divided by 3	**4**
$\dfrac{40}{4}$	**10**
$\dfrac{45}{9}$	**5**
48/6	**8**
$49 \div 7$	**7**
36/6	**6**
12 divided by 2	**6**
$42 \div 6$	**7**
12 divided by 4	**3**

Fill in the following table:

Number	Operation	Number	Result
1	×	**9**	9
2	×	**11**	22
7	×	**7**	49
7	×	**8**	56
7	×	**9**	63
8	×	**4**	32
8	×	**5**	40
8	×	**6**	48
10	×	**10**	100

POSTER

Number	1	2	3	4	5	6	7	8	9	10	11	12
1	1	2	3	4	5	6	7	8	9	10	11	12
2	2	4	6	8	10	12	14	16	18	20	22	24
3	3	6	9	12	15	18	21	24	27	30	33	36
4	4	8	12	16	20	24	28	32	36	40	44	48
5	5	10	15	20	25	30	35	40	45	50	55	60
6	6	12	18	24	30	36	42	48	54	60	66	72
7	7	14	21	28	35	42	49	56	63	70	77	84
8	8	16	24	32	40	48	56	64	72	80	88	96
9	9	18	27	36	45	54	63	72	81	90	99	108
10	10	20	30	40	50	60	70	80	90	100	110	120
11	11	22	33	44	55	66	77	88	99	110	121	132
12	12	24	36	48	60	72	84	96	108	120	132	144

SEE PAGE 326 FOR <u>MULTIPLICATION TABLES</u>: PRECISION TEACHING (PT) SCORES, FREQUENCY TABLE.

I suggest that students correct their papers, calculate the frequencies and graph their results. Graphing the results on special graph paper (Standard Celeration Chart) can provide visual reinforcement for the students and information about how they are learning. The frequency tables are provided to facilitate this process.

PT 1, QUESTIONS

Fill in the following table:

Number	1	2	3	4	5	6	7	8	9	10	11	12
1	1	2	3	4	5	6	7	8	9	10	11	12
2	2	4	6	8	10	12	14	16	18	20	22	24
3	3	6	9		15	18	21	24	27	30	33	36
4	4	8	12	16	20	24	28	32	36		44	48
5	5	10	15	20	25	30	35	40	45	50	55	60
6	6	12	18	24	30				54	60	66	72
7	7	14	21	28	35	42		56	63	70	77	84
8	8	16	24	32	40		56		72	80	88	96
9		18	27	36		54	63	72	81	90	99	108
10	10	20	30	40	50	60	70	80	90	100	110	120
11	11	22	33	44	55	66	77	88	99	110	121	132
12	12	24	36	48	60	72	84	96	108	120	132	144

Fill in the following table:

Expression	Result
$42 \div 6$	
12 divided by 4	
$\dfrac{40}{8}$	
$\dfrac{45}{5}$	
$48/8$	
$48 \div 6$	
$36/6$	
12 divided by 6	
$42 \div 7$	
12 divided by 3	

Fill in the following table:

Number	Operation	Number	Result
1	$\times$		8
3	$\times$		33
7	$\times$		28
7	$\times$		35
7	$\times$		42
8	$\times$		16
8	$\times$		24
8	$\times$		32
8	$\times$		40

PT 1, ANSWERS

Fill in the following table:

Number	1	2	3	4	5	6	7	8	9	10	11	12
1	1	2	3	4	5	6	7	8	9	10	11	12
2	2	4	6	8	10	12	14	16	18	20	22	24
3	3	6	9	**12**	15	18	21	24	27	30	33	36
4	4	8	12	16	20	24	28	32	36	**40**	44	48
5	5	10	15	20	25	30	35	40	45	50	55	60
6	6	12	18	24	30	**36**	**42**	**48**	54	60	66	72
7	7	14	21	28	35	42	**49**	56	63	70	77	84
8	8	16	24	32	40	**48**	56	**64**	72	80	88	96
9	**9**	18	27	36	**45**	54	63	72	81	90	99	108
10	10	20	30	40	50	60	70	80	90	100	110	120
11	11	22	33	44	55	66	77	88	99	110	121	132
12	12	24	36	48	60	72	84	96	108	120	132	144

Fill in the following table:

Expression	Result
$42 \div 6$	**7**
12 divided by 4	**3**
$\dfrac{40}{8}$	**5**
$\dfrac{45}{5}$	**9**
48/8	**6**
$48 \div 6$	**8**
36/6	**6**
12 divided by 6	**2**
$42 \div 7$	**6**
12 divided by 3	**4**

Fill in the following table:

Number	Operation	Number	Result
1	×	**8**	8
3	×	**11**	33
7	×	**4**	28
7	×	**5**	35
7	×	**6**	42
8	×	**2**	16
8	×	**3**	24
8	×	**4**	32
8	×	**5**	40

PT 2, QUESTIONS

Fill in the following table:

Number	1	2	3	4	5	6	7	8	9	10	11	12
1	1	2	3	4	5	6		8	9	10	11	12
2	2	4	6	8	10	12		16	18	20	22	24
3	3	6	9	12	15	18		24	27	30	33	36
4	4	8	12	16	20	24	28		36	40	44	48
5	5	10	15	20	25	30	35		45	50	55	60
6	6	12	18	24	30	36			54	60	66	72
7	7	14		28	35					70	77	84
8	8	16	24				56			80	88	96
9	9	18	27	36	45	54		72		90	99	108
10	10	20	30	40	50	60	70	80	90	100	110	120
11	11	22	33	44	55	66	77	88	99	110	121	132
12	12	24	36	48	60	72	84	96	108	120	132	

Fill in the following table:

Expression	Result
$21 \div 7$	
21 divided by 3	
$\dfrac{32}{4}$	
$\dfrac{14}{2}$	
40/8	
$40 \div 5$	
63/7	
63 divided by 9	
$42 \div 6$	
42 divided by 7	

Fill in the following table:

Number	Operation	Number	Result
6	×		48
8	×		48
7	×		49
7	×		56
9	×		81
12	×		144
8	×		72
8	×		64
7	×		56

PT 2, ANSWERS

Fill in the following table:

Number	1	2	3	4	5	6	7	8	9	10	11	12
1	1	2	3	4	5	6	7	8	9	10	11	12
2	2	4	6	8	10	12	14	16	18	20	22	24
3	3	6	9	12	15	18	21	24	27	30	33	36
4	4	8	12	16	20	24	28	32	36	40	44	48
5	5	10	15	20	25	30	35	40	45	50	55	60
6	6	12	18	24	30	36	42	48	54	60	66	72
7	7	14	21	28	35	42	49	56	63	70	77	84
8	8	16	24	32	40	48	56	64	72	80	88	96
9	9	18	27	36	45	54	63	72	81	90	99	108
10	10	20	30	40	50	60	70	80	90	100	110	120
11	11	22	33	44	55	66	77	88	99	110	121	132
12	12	24	36	48	60	72	84	96	108	120	132	144

Fill in the following table:

Expression	Result
$21 \div 7$	3
21 divided by 3	7
$\dfrac{32}{4}$	8
$\dfrac{14}{2}$	7
40/8	5
$40 \div 5$	8
63/7	9
63 divided by 9	7
$42 \div 6$	7
42 divided by 7	6

Fill in the following table:

Number	Operation	Number	Result
6	×	8	48
8	×	6	48
7	×	7	49
7	×	8	56
9	×	9	81
12	×	12	144
8	×	9	72
8	×	8	64
7	×	8	56

How Do We Know?

PT 3, QUESTIONS

Fill in the following table:

Number	1	2	3	4	5	6	7	8	9	10	11	12
1	1	2	3	4	5	6	7	8	9	10	11	12
2	2	4	6	8	10	12	14	16	18		22	24
3	3	6	9	12		18	21	24	27	30	33	36
4	4	8	12	16	20	24	28	32	36		44	48
5	5	10		20	25	30	35	40		50	55	60
6	6	12	18	24		36			54		66	72
7	7	14	21	28	35		49	56	63	70	77	84
8	8	16	24	32		48	56	64	72			96
9	9	18	27	36		54	63	72	81	90	99	108
10	10	20	30	40	50		70		90	100	110	
11	11	22	33	44	55	66	77		99	110	121	132
12	12	24	36	48		72	84	96	108		132	144

Fill in the following table:

Expression	Result
$45 \div 5$	
45 divided by 9	
$\dfrac{80}{10}$	
$\dfrac{80}{8}$	
40/8	
$40 \div 5$	
60/6	
60 divided by 10	
$60 \div 5$	
10 divided by 5	

Fill in the following table:

Number	Operation	Number	Result
6	×		54
8	×		48
6	×		42
10	×		80
9	×		90
5	×		60
5	×		45
3	×		15
11	×		88

PT 3, ANSWERS

Fill in the following table:

Number	1	2	3	4	5	6	7	8	9	10	11	12
1	1	2	3	4	5	6	7	8	9	10	11	12
2	2	4	6	8	10	12	14	16	18	**20**	22	24
3	3	6	9	12	**15**	18	21	24	27	30	33	36
4	4	8	12	16	20	24	28	32	36	**40**	44	48
5	5	10	**15**	20	25	30	35	40	**45**	50	55	60
6	6	12	18	24	**30**	36	**42**	**48**	54	**60**	66	72
7	7	14	21	28	35	**42**	49	56	63	70	77	84
8	8	16	24	32	**40**	48	56	64	72	**80**	**88**	96
9	9	18	27	36	**45**	54	63	72	81	90	99	108
10	10	20	30	40	50	**60**	70	**80**	90	100	110	**120**
11	11	22	33	44	55	66	77	**88**	99	110	121	132
12	12	24	36	48	**60**	72	84	96	108	**120**	132	144

Fill in the following table:

Expression	Result
$45 \div 5$	**9**
45 divided by 9	**5**
$\dfrac{80}{10}$	**8**
$\dfrac{80}{8}$	**10**
$40/8$	**5**
$40 \div 5$	**8**
$60/6$	**10**
60 divided by 10	**6**
$60 \div 5$	**12**
10 divided by 5	**2**

Fill in the following table:

Number	Operation	Number	Result
6	×	**9**	54
8	×	**6**	48
6	×	**7**	42
10	×	**8**	80
9	×	**10**	90
5	×	**12**	60
5	×	**9**	45
3	×	**5**	15
11	×	**8**	88

PT 4, QUESTIONS

Fill in the following table:

Expression	Result
$35 \div 5$	
35 divided by 7	
$\dfrac{27}{3}$	
$\dfrac{27}{9}$	
40/8	
$40 \div 5$	
66/6	
66 divided by 11	
$50 \div 5$	
33/11	
15/5	
$40 \div 5$	
40 divided by 8	
$\dfrac{40}{10}$	
$\dfrac{20}{5}$	

Fill in the following table:

Number	Operation	Number	Result
2	×		12
4	×		24
6	×		30
8	×		48
6	×		60
5	×		25
5	×		45
3	×		15
11	×		55
10	×		80
12	×		96
9	×		72
6	×		48
3	×		24
1	×		8

PT 4, ANSWERS

Fill in the following table:

Expression	Result
35 ÷ 5	7
35 divided by 7	5
$\frac{27}{3}$	9
$\frac{27}{9}$	3
40/8	5
40 ÷ 5	8
66/6	11
66 divided by 11	6
50 ÷ 5	10
33/11	3
15/5	3
40 ÷ 5	8
40 divided by 8	5
$\frac{40}{10}$	4
$\frac{20}{5}$	4

Fill in the following table:

Number	Operation	Number	Result
2	×	6	12
4	×	6	24
6	×	5	30
8	×	6	48
6	×	10	60
5	×	5	25
5	×	9	45
3	×	5	15
11	×	5	55
10	×	8	80
12	×	8	96
9	×	8	72
6	×	8	48
3	×	8	24
1	×	8	8

How Do We Know?

PT 5, QUESTIONS

Fill in the following table:

Expression	Result
$12 \div 12$	
144 divided by 12	
$\dfrac{27}{9}$	
$\dfrac{99}{9}$	
54/6	
$50 \div 5$	
66/6	
66 divided by 11	
$50 \div 5$	
33/11	
45/5	
$48 \div 12$	
96 divided by 8	
$\dfrac{80}{10}$	
$\dfrac{40}{5}$	

Fill in the following table:

Number	Operation	Number	Result
3	$\times$		18
6	$\times$		36
9	$\times$		54
12	$\times$		72
5	$\times$		50
5	$\times$		25
12	$\times$		108
12	$\times$		60
12	$\times$		120
10	$\times$		80
10	$\times$		40
9	$\times$		72
9	$\times$		36
3	$\times$		24
3	$\times$		12

PT 5, ANSWERS

Fill in the following table:

Expression	Result
$12 \div 12$	1
144 divided by 12	12
$\dfrac{27}{9}$	3
$\dfrac{99}{9}$	11
$54/6$	9
$50 \div 5$	10
$66/6$	11
66 divided by 11	6
$50 \div 5$	10
$33/11$	3
$45/5$	9
$48 \div 12$	4
96 divided by 8	12
$\dfrac{80}{10}$	8
$\dfrac{40}{5}$	8

Fill in the following table:

Number	Operation	Number	Result
3	$\times$	6	18
6	$\times$	6	36
9	$\times$	6	54
12	$\times$	6	72
5	$\times$	10	50
5	$\times$	5	25
12	$\times$	9	108
12	$\times$	5	60
12	$\times$	10	120
10	$\times$	8	80
10	$\times$	4	40
9	$\times$	8	72
9	$\times$	4	36
3	$\times$	8	24
3	$\times$	4	12

LET'S TRY SOMETHING DIFFERENT
(A Cooperative Learning Exercise?)

Fill in the following table:

Number	Operation	Number	Result
	÷		2
	÷		3
	÷		4
	÷		5
	÷		6
	÷		7
	÷		8
	÷		9
	÷		10
	÷		11
	÷		12
	÷		12
	÷		11
	÷		10
	÷		1

Fill in the following table:

Number	Operation	Number	Result
	×		25
	×		121
	×		81
	×		64
	×		56
	×		54
	×		33
	×		24
	×		12
	×		63
	×		81
	×		90
	×		99
	×		96
	×		48

LESSON NOTES

How Do We Know?

CHAPTER 6

EQUIVALENT FRACTIONS

$$\frac{1}{2} = \frac{2}{4} = \frac{3}{6} = \frac{4}{8} = \frac{5}{10} = \frac{6}{12} = \frac{50}{100} = \frac{0.5}{1}$$

$$\frac{5}{5} = 1, \; \frac{17}{17} = 1, \; \frac{1000}{1000} = 1$$

$$a \times 1 = a$$
$$1\,a = a$$

$$\frac{2}{3} \times \frac{5}{5} = \frac{10}{15}$$

Overview: The concept of multiplying by one to generate equivalent fractions will be practiced. This will serve as a review of the multiplication table and reinforce the idea that multiplication by one does not change a number.

Mathematical Learning Objective:	The student will:
	Generate equivalent fractions, practice multiplication of fractions, and develop a sense of equivalence of fractions.
NCTM Standards:	Number and operations:
	Understand numbers, ways of representing numbers, relationships among numbers, and number systems.

Definitions:

Term	Definition/comment	Symbol
Fraction	My dictionary says "A numerical representation of two numbers whose quotient is to be determined". Your teacher might well argue irrational numbers need more defining. That is a good thing. For now let us say a fraction is a number that has a numerator and a denominator. Remember, the fraction bar means the top (numerator) is divided by the bottom (denominator). Often the numerator represents a "part", and the bottom represents a "whole".	
Numerator	The term above the line in a fraction.	
Denominator	The term below the line in a fraction.	
Identity Element of Multiplication and Division	There exists an element 1, such that: $a \times 1 = a$ and $a \div 1 = a$.	
Decimal Equivalent *	The form of a fraction obtained by dividing a numerator by a denominator, as from a calculator.	
Equivalent	Equal in quantity or meaning.	
Reciprocal	One of a pair of numbers $\left(\text{as } 7, \frac{1}{7} \right)$ whose product is 1, $\left(7 \times \frac{1}{7} = 1 \right)$. Often the word inverse is used.	Often a negative exponent is used to indicate a reciprocal $7^{-1} = \frac{1}{7}$, $7^{-2} = \frac{1}{7^2}$
Ponder	Think about it.	

*See Addendum II: Decimals, Multiplication and Division

The Identity Property of Multiplication tells us that a number can be multiplied by one and not change the value of the number. If we think of the fraction as a number, then the fraction can be multiplied by one and not change the value of the fraction. Multiplying a fraction by one and creating equivalent fractions is the key to solving problems adding and subtracting fractions. Many other kinds of problems can be solved with this equivalent fraction kind of approach, although some funny looking forms of one can get involved.

I. To multiply fractions, the top numbers (numerators) get multiplied and that becomes a new top number (numerator) and the bottom numbers (denominators) get multiplied and become a new bottom number (denominator).

$$\text{Example: } \frac{2}{3} \times \frac{1}{5} = \frac{2}{15}$$

II. Equivalent fractions are created by multiplying forms of one, usually a number divided by itself, times the fraction.

If we assume the identity property of multiplication is true, then: for any a (a ≠ 0), $\frac{a}{a} = 1$.

Questions for discussion/research

Dividing by a number is the same as multiplying times its reciprocal. As you work through this exercise multiplying fractions by forms of one to create fractions with different denominators, ponder the process you have been taught in the past that allows you to write fractions in lowest terms. Can you use the above definitions to justify such a process?

SEE PAGE 327 FOR EQUIVALENT FRACTIONS: PRECISION TEACHING (PT) SCORES, FREQUENCY TABLE.

I suggest that students correct their papers, calculate the frequencies and graph their results. Graphing the results on special graph paper (Standard Celeration Chart) can provide visual reinforcement for the students and information about how they are learning. The frequency tables are provided to facilitate this process.

PRECISION TEACHING (PT) SAMPLE ANSWERS

Multiplication Table

Number	1	2	3	4	5	6	7	8	9	10	11	12
1	1	2	3	4	5	6	7	8	9	10	11	12
2	2	4	6	8	10	12	14	16	18	20	22	24
3	3	6	9	12	15	18	21	24	27	30	33	36
4	4	8	12	16	20	24	28	32	36	40	44	48
5	5	10	15	20	25	30	35	40	45	50	55	60
6	6	12	18	24	30	36	42	48	54	60	66	72
7	7	14	21	28	35	42	49	56	63	70	77	84
8	8	16	24	32	40	48	56	64	72	80	88	96
9	9	18	27	36	45	54	63	72	81	90	99	108
10	10	20	30	40	50	60	70	80	90	100	110	120
11	11	22	33	44	55	66	77	88	99	110	121	132
12	12	24	36	48	60	72	84	96	108	120	132	144

Remember:

I. To multiply fractions, the top numbers (numerators) get multiplied and that becomes a new top number (numerator) and the bottom numbers (denominators) get multiplied and become a new bottom number (denominator).

$$\text{Example:} \quad \frac{2}{3} \times \frac{1}{5} = \frac{2}{15}$$

II. Any number (except zero) divided by itself is one.

$$\text{Examples:} \quad \frac{5}{5} = 1, \ \frac{17}{17} = 1, \ \frac{1000}{1000} = 1$$

III. Equivalent fractions are created by multiplying forms of one times the fraction.

$$\text{Example:} \quad \frac{1}{2} = \frac{1}{2} \times 1 = \frac{1}{2} \times \frac{5}{5} = \frac{5}{10}$$

IV. $\frac{0}{0} \neq 1$, division by 0 not permitted.

Fill in the following table:

Fraction	$\times \frac{1}{1}$	$\times \frac{2}{2}$	$\times \frac{3}{3}$	$\times \frac{4}{4}$	$\times \frac{5}{5}$	$\times \frac{6}{6}$	$\times \frac{7}{7}$	$\times \frac{8}{8}$	$\times \frac{9}{9}$	$\times \frac{10}{10}$	Decimal
$\frac{2}{5}$	$\frac{2}{5}$	$\frac{4}{10}$	$\frac{6}{15}$	$\frac{8}{20}$	$\frac{10}{25}$	$\frac{12}{30}$	$\frac{14}{35}$	$\frac{16}{40}$	$\frac{18}{45}$	$\frac{20}{50}$	0.4
$\frac{7}{1}$	$\frac{7}{1}$	$\frac{14}{2}$	$\frac{21}{3}$	$\frac{28}{4}$	$\frac{35}{5}$	$\frac{42}{6}$	$\frac{49}{7}$	$\frac{56}{8}$	$\frac{63}{9}$	$\frac{70}{10}$	7
$\frac{1}{2}$	$\frac{1}{2}$	$\frac{2}{4}$	$\frac{3}{6}$	$\frac{4}{8}$	$\frac{5}{10}$	$\frac{6}{12}$	$\frac{7}{14}$	$\frac{8}{16}$	$\frac{9}{18}$	$\frac{10}{20}$	0.5

PT 1, QUESTIONS

Multiplication Table:

Number	1	2	3	4	5	6	7	8	9	10	11	12
1	1	2	3	4	5	6	7	8	9	10	11	12
2	2	4	6	8	10	12	14	16	18	20	22	24
3	3	6	9	12	15	18	21	24	27	30	33	36
4	4	8	12	16	20	24	28	32	36	40	44	48
5	5	10	15	20	25	30	35	40	45	50	55	60
6	6	12	18	24	30	36	42	48	54	60	66	72
7	7	14	21	28	35	42	49	56	63	70	77	84
8	8	16	24	32	40	48	56	64	72	80	88	96
9	9	18	27	36	45	54	63	72	81	90	99	108
10	10	20	30	40	50	60	70	80	90	100	110	120
11	11	22	33	44	55	66	77	88	99	110	121	132
12	12	24	36	48	60	72	84	96	108	120	132	144

Remember:

I. To multiply fractions, the top numbers (numerators) get multiplied and that becomes a new top number (numerator) and the bottom numbers (denominators) get multiplied and become a new bottom number (denominator).

$$\text{Example:} \quad \frac{2}{3} \times \frac{1}{5} = \frac{2}{15}$$

II. Any number (except zero) divided by itself is one.

$$\text{Examples:} \quad \frac{5}{5} = 1, \frac{17}{17} = 1, \frac{1000}{1000} = 1$$

III. Equivalent fractions are created by multiplying forms of one times the fraction.

$$\text{Example:} \quad \frac{1}{2} = \frac{1}{2} \times 1 = \frac{1}{2} \times \frac{5}{5} = \frac{5}{10}$$

IV. $\frac{0}{0} \neq 1$, division by 0 not permitted.

Fill in the following table:

Fraction	$\times \frac{1}{1}$	$\times \frac{2}{2}$	$\times \frac{3}{3}$	$\times \frac{4}{4}$	$\times \frac{5}{5}$	$\times \frac{6}{6}$	$\times \frac{7}{7}$	$\times \frac{8}{8}$	$\times \frac{9}{9}$	$\times \frac{10}{10}$	Decimal
$\frac{3}{2}$	$\frac{3}{2}$	$\frac{6}{4}$		$\frac{12}{8}$			$\frac{21}{14}$		$\frac{27}{18}$		1.5
$\frac{5}{6}$	$\frac{5}{6}$	$\frac{10}{12}$		$\frac{20}{24}$			$\frac{35}{42}$		$\frac{45}{54}$		$0.8\overline{3}$
$\frac{7}{1}$	$\frac{7}{1}$	$\frac{14}{2}$		$\frac{28}{4}$			$\frac{49}{7}$		$\frac{63}{9}$		7

PT 1, ANSWERS

Multiplication Table:

Number	1	2	3	4	5	6	7	8	9	10	11	12
1	1	2	3	4	5	6	7	8	9	10	11	12
2	2	4	6	8	10	12	14	16	18	20	22	24
3	3	6	9	12	15	18	21	24	27	30	33	36
4	4	8	12	16	20	24	28	32	36	40	44	48
5	5	10	15	20	25	30	35	40	45	50	55	60
6	6	12	18	24	30	36	42	48	54	60	66	72
7	7	14	21	28	35	42	49	56	63	70	77	84
8	8	16	24	32	40	48	56	64	72	80	88	96
9	9	18	27	36	45	54	63	72	81	90	99	108
10	10	20	30	40	50	60	70	80	90	100	110	120
11	11	22	33	44	55	66	77	88	99	110	121	132
12	12	24	36	48	60	72	84	96	108	120	132	144

Remember:

I. To multiply fractions, the top numbers (numerators) get multiplied and that becomes a new top number (numerator) and the bottom numbers (denominators) get multiplied and become a new bottom number (denominator).

$$\text{Example:} \quad \frac{2}{3} \times \frac{1}{5} = \frac{2}{15}$$

II. Any number (except zero) divided by itself is one.

$$\text{Examples:} \quad \frac{5}{5} = 1, \frac{17}{17} = 1, \frac{1000}{1000} = 1$$

III. Equivalent fractions are created by multiplying forms of one times the fraction.

$$\text{Example:} \quad \frac{1}{2} = \frac{1}{2} \times 1 = \frac{1}{2} \times \frac{5}{5} = \frac{5}{10}$$

IV. $\frac{0}{0} \neq 1$, division by 0 not permitted.

Fill in the following table:

Fraction	$\times\frac{1}{1}$	$\times\frac{2}{2}$	$\times\frac{3}{3}$	$\times\frac{4}{4}$	$\times\frac{5}{5}$	$\times\frac{6}{6}$	$\times\frac{7}{7}$	$\times\frac{8}{8}$	$\times\frac{9}{9}$	$\times\frac{10}{10}$	Decimal
$\frac{3}{2}$	$\frac{3}{2}$	$\frac{6}{4}$	$\frac{9}{6}$	$\frac{12}{8}$	$\frac{15}{10}$	$\frac{18}{12}$	$\frac{21}{14}$	$\frac{24}{16}$	$\frac{27}{18}$	$\frac{30}{20}$	1.5
$\frac{5}{6}$	$\frac{5}{6}$	$\frac{10}{12}$	$\frac{15}{18}$	$\frac{20}{24}$	$\frac{25}{30}$	$\frac{30}{36}$	$\frac{35}{42}$	$\frac{40}{48}$	$\frac{45}{54}$	$\frac{50}{60}$	$0.8\overline{3}$
$\frac{7}{1}$	$\frac{7}{1}$	$\frac{14}{2}$	$\frac{21}{3}$	$\frac{28}{4}$	$\frac{35}{5}$	$\frac{42}{6}$	$\frac{49}{7}$	$\frac{56}{8}$	$\frac{63}{9}$	$\frac{70}{10}$	7

How Do We Know?

PT 2, QUESTIONS

Multiplication Table:

Number	1	2	3	4	5	6	7	8	9	10	11	12
1	1	2	3	4	5	6	7	8	9	10	11	12
2	2	4	6	8	10	12	14	16	18	20	22	24
3	3	6	9	12	15	18	21	24	27	30	33	36
4	4	8	12	16	20	24	28	32	36	40	44	48
5	5	10	15	20	25	30	35	40	45	50	55	60
6	6	12	18	24	30	36	42	48	54	60	66	72
7	7	14	21	28	35	42	49	56	63	70	77	84
8	8	16	24	32	40	48	56	64	72	80	88	96
9	9	18	27	36	45	54	63	72	81	90	99	108
10	10	20	30	40	50	60	70	80	90	100	110	120
11	11	22	33	44	55	66	77	88	99	110	121	132
12	12	24	36	48	60	72	84	96	108	120	132	144

Remember:

I.   To multiply fractions, the top numbers (numerators) get multiplied and that becomes a new top number (numerator) and the bottom numbers (denominators) get multiplied and become a new bottom number (denominator).

$$\text{Example:} \quad \frac{2}{3} \times \frac{1}{5} = \frac{2}{15}$$

II.   Any number (except zero) divided by itself is one.

$$\text{Examples:} \quad \frac{5}{5} = 1, \ \frac{17}{17} = 1, \ \frac{1000}{1000} = 1$$

III.   Equivalent fractions are created by multiplying forms of one times the fraction.

$$\text{Example:} \quad \frac{1}{2} = \frac{1}{2} \times 1 = \frac{1}{2} \times \frac{5}{5} = \frac{5}{10}$$

IV. $\frac{0}{0} \neq 1$, division by 0 not permitted.

Fill in the following table:

Fraction	$\times \frac{1}{1}$	$\times \frac{2}{2}$	$\times \frac{3}{3}$	$\times \frac{4}{4}$	$\times \frac{5}{5}$	$\times \frac{6}{6}$	$\times \frac{7}{7}$	$\times \frac{8}{8}$	$\times \frac{9}{9}$	$\times \frac{10}{10}$	Decimal
$\frac{3}{4}$	$\frac{3}{4}$	$\frac{6}{8}$	$\frac{9}{12}$	$\frac{12}{16}$	$\frac{15}{20}$	$\frac{18}{24}$	$\frac{21}{28}$	$\frac{24}{32}$	$\frac{27}{36}$	$\frac{30}{40}$	0.75
$\frac{2}{5}$											0.4
$\frac{1}{3}$											$0.\overline{3}$

PT 2, ANSWERS

Multiplication Table:

Number	1	2	3	4	5	6	7	8	9	10	11	12
1	1	2	3	4	5	6	7	8	9	10	11	12
2	2	4	6	8	10	12	14	16	18	20	22	24
3	3	6	9	12	15	18	21	24	27	30	33	36
4	4	8	12	16	20	24	28	32	36	40	44	48
5	5	10	15	20	25	30	35	40	45	50	55	60
6	6	12	18	24	30	36	42	48	54	60	66	72
7	7	14	21	28	35	42	49	56	63	70	77	84
8	8	16	24	32	40	48	56	64	72	80	88	96
9	9	18	27	36	45	54	63	72	81	90	99	108
10	10	20	30	40	50	60	70	80	90	100	110	120
11	11	22	33	44	55	66	77	88	99	110	121	132
12	12	24	36	48	60	72	84	96	108	120	132	144

Remember:

I.   To multiply fractions, the top numbers (numerators) get multiplied and that becomes a new top number (numerator) and the bottom numbers (denominators) get multiplied and become a new bottom number (denominator).

$$\text{Example: } \frac{2}{3} \times \frac{1}{5} = \frac{2}{15}$$

II. Any number (except zero) divided by itself is one.

$$\text{Examples: } \frac{5}{5} = 1, \frac{17}{17} = 1, \frac{1000}{1000} = 1$$

III. Equivalent fractions are created by multiplying forms of one times the fraction.

$$\text{Example: } \frac{1}{2} = \frac{1}{2} \times 1 = \frac{1}{2} \times \frac{5}{5} = \frac{5}{10}$$

IV. $\frac{0}{0} \neq 1$, division by 0 not permitted.

Fill in the following table:

Fraction	$\times \frac{1}{1}$	$\times \frac{2}{2}$	$\times \frac{3}{3}$	$\times \frac{4}{4}$	$\times \frac{5}{5}$	$\times \frac{6}{6}$	$\times \frac{7}{7}$	$\times \frac{8}{8}$	$\times \frac{9}{9}$	$\times \frac{10}{10}$	Decimal
$\frac{3}{4}$	$\frac{3}{4}$	$\frac{6}{8}$	$\frac{9}{12}$	$\frac{12}{16}$	$\frac{15}{20}$	$\frac{18}{24}$	$\frac{21}{28}$	$\frac{24}{32}$	$\frac{27}{36}$	$\frac{30}{40}$	0.75
$\frac{2}{5}$	$\frac{2}{5}$	$\frac{4}{10}$	$\frac{6}{15}$	$\frac{8}{20}$	$\frac{10}{25}$	$\frac{12}{30}$	$\frac{14}{35}$	$\frac{16}{40}$	$\frac{18}{45}$	$\frac{20}{50}$	0.4
$\frac{1}{3}$	$\frac{1}{3}$	$\frac{2}{6}$	$\frac{3}{9}$	$\frac{4}{12}$	$\frac{5}{15}$	$\frac{6}{18}$	$\frac{7}{21}$	$\frac{8}{24}$	$\frac{9}{27}$	$\frac{10}{30}$	$0.\overline{3}$

How Do We Know?

PT 3, QUESTIONS

Multiplication Table:

Number	1	2	3	4	5	6	7	8	9	10	11	12
1	1	2	3	4	5	6	7	8	9	10	11	12
2	2	4	6	8	10	12	14	16	18	20	22	24
3	3	6	9	12	15	18	21	24	27	30	33	36
4	4	8	12	16	20	24	28	32	36	40	44	48
5	5	10	15	20	25	30	35	40	45	50	55	60
6	6	12	18	24	30	36	42	48	54	60	66	72
7	7	14	21	28	35	42	49	56	63	70	77	84
8	8	16	24	32	40	48	56	64	72	80	88	96
9	9	18	27	36	45	54	63	72	81	90	99	108
10	10	20	30	40	50	60	70	80	90	100	110	120
11	11	22	33	44	55	66	77	88	99	110	121	132
12	12	24	36	48	60	72	84	96	108	120	132	144

Remember:

I. To multiply fractions, the top numbers (numerators) get multiplied and that becomes a new top number (numerator) and the bottom numbers (denominators) get multiplied and become a new bottom number (denominator).

$$\text{Example: } \frac{2}{3} \times \frac{1}{5} = \frac{2}{15}$$

II. Any number (except zero) divided by itself is one.

$$\text{Examples: } \frac{5}{5} = 1, \frac{17}{17} = 1, \frac{1000}{1000} = 1$$

III. Equivalent fractions are created by multiplying forms of one times the fraction.

$$\text{Example: } \frac{1}{2} = \frac{1}{2} \times 1 = \frac{1}{2} \times \frac{5}{5} = \frac{5}{10}$$

IV. $\frac{0}{0} \neq 1$, division by 0 not permitted.

Fill in the following table:

Fraction	$\times \frac{1}{1}$	$\times \frac{2}{2}$	$\times \frac{3}{3}$	$\times \frac{4}{4}$	$\times \frac{5}{5}$	$\times \frac{6}{6}$	$\times \frac{7}{7}$	$\times \frac{8}{8}$	$\times \frac{9}{9}$	$\times \frac{10}{10}$	Decimal
$\frac{3}{2}$											
$\frac{0.4}{1}$											
$\frac{1}{2}$											

PT 3, ANSWERS

Multiplication Table:

Number	1	2	3	4	5	6	7	8	9	10	11	12
1	1	2	3	4	5	6	7	8	9	10	11	12
2	2	4	6	8	10	12	14	16	18	20	22	24
3	3	6	9	12	15	18	21	24	27	30	33	36
4	4	8	12	16	20	24	28	32	36	40	44	48
5	5	10	15	20	25	30	35	40	45	50	55	60
6	6	12	18	24	30	36	42	48	54	60	66	72
7	7	14	21	28	35	42	49	56	63	70	77	84
8	8	16	24	32	40	48	56	64	72	80	88	96
9	9	18	27	36	45	54	63	72	81	90	99	108
10	10	20	30	40	50	60	70	80	90	100	110	120
11	11	22	33	44	55	66	77	88	99	110	121	132
12	12	24	36	48	60	72	84	96	108	120	132	144

Remember:

I. To multiply fractions, the top numbers (numerators) get multiplied and that becomes a new top number (numerator) and the bottom numbers (denominators) get multiplied and become a new bottom number (denominator).

$$\text{Example: } \frac{2}{3} \times \frac{1}{5} = \frac{2}{15}$$

II. Any number (except zero) divided by itself is one.

$$\text{Examples: } \frac{5}{5} = 1, \frac{17}{17} = 1, \frac{1000}{1000} = 1$$

III. Equivalent fractions are created by multiplying forms of one times the fraction.

$$\text{Example: } \frac{1}{2} = \frac{1}{2} \times 1 = \frac{1}{2} \times \frac{5}{5} = \frac{5}{10}$$

IV. $\frac{0}{0} \neq 1$, division by 0 not permitted.

Fill in the following table:

Fraction	$\times \frac{1}{1}$	$\times \frac{2}{2}$	$\times \frac{3}{3}$	$\times \frac{4}{4}$	$\times \frac{5}{5}$	$\times \frac{6}{6}$	$\times \frac{7}{7}$	$\times \frac{8}{8}$	$\times \frac{9}{9}$	$\times \frac{10}{10}$	Decimal
$\frac{3}{2}$	$\frac{3}{2}$	$\frac{6}{4}$	$\frac{9}{6}$	$\frac{12}{8}$	$\frac{15}{10}$	$\frac{18}{12}$	$\frac{21}{14}$	$\frac{24}{16}$	$\frac{27}{18}$	$\frac{30}{20}$	1.5
$\frac{0.4}{1}$	$\frac{0.4}{1}$	$\frac{0.8}{2}$	$\frac{1.2}{3}$	$\frac{1.6}{4}$	$\frac{2}{5}$	$\frac{2.4}{6}$	$\frac{2.8}{7}$	$\frac{3.2}{8}$	$\frac{3.6}{9}$	$\frac{4}{10}$	0.4
$\frac{1}{2}$	$\frac{1}{2}$	$\frac{2}{4}$	$\frac{3}{6}$	$\frac{4}{8}$	$\frac{5}{10}$	$\frac{6}{12}$	$\frac{7}{14}$	$\frac{8}{16}$	$\frac{9}{18}$	$\frac{10}{20}$	0.5

CHAPTER 7

OPERATIONS WITH FRACTIONS

÷

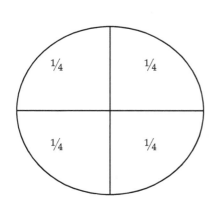

Overview: Operations with fractions are fundamental to routine calculations. For our purposes, we will present algorithms for operations with fractions and call these definitions.

Mathematical
Learning Objective: The student will:

Develop an understanding of fractions and mathematical operations on fractions.

NCTM Standards: Number and Operations:

Understand numbers, ways of representing numbers, relationships among numbers, and number systems.

Definitions:

Word	Definition	Symbol
Ratio	A comparison of two numbers by division.	$-, \div, /, :$
Rational number	A number that can be expressed as a ratio, where the two numbers are integers (whole numbers).	
Proportion	An equation stating the equality of two ratios.	
Equivalent fractions	Ratios that have the same value but have different bottom numbers. (denominators).	
Least common multiple (LCM)	The (LCM) of two numbers is the smallest number that is a multiple of both. The (LCM) of 3 and 5 is 15. The (LCM) of 4 and 6 is 12.	(LCM)
Substitute	To put in place of another. We will assume that if quantities are defined as equal, the number system allows us to substitute the symbols and the numbers for the quantities interchangeably. This assumption will often imply constraints on the substitution.	
Mixed number	A number that has a part that is an integer and a part that is a fraction. Example: $2\dfrac{1}{3}$	
Proper fraction	Any number that can be written as a ratio of real numbers that have a value between 1 and 0 and 0 and -1.	
Improper fraction	A fraction whose top (numerator) is larger or of higher degree than its bottom (denominator). Examples: $\dfrac{7}{2}$, or $\dfrac{2x^2}{3x}$	
Reciprocal	One of a pair of numbers $\left(\text{as } \dfrac{2}{3}, \dfrac{3}{2}\right)$ whose product is 1, $\left(\dfrac{2}{3} \times \dfrac{3}{2} = 1\right)$. Often the word inverse is used.	
Invert	The process of forming a reciprocal. The reciprocal 2/3 is 3/2.	
Division	The inverse of multiplication. Dividing by a number is the same as multiplying by the reciprocal of that number.	$/, -, \div, \overline{)}$

I. To multiply fractions, the top numbers (numerators) get multiplied and that product becomes a new top number (numerator) and the bottom numbers (denominators) get multiplied and that product becomes a new bottom number (denominator).

$$\text{Example: } \frac{2}{3} \times \frac{1}{5} = \frac{2}{15}$$

II. Equivalent fractions are created by multiplying forms of one, usually a number divided by itself, times the fraction.

$$\text{Example: } \frac{1}{2} \times \frac{5}{5} = \frac{5}{10}$$

III. Without making too big a deal out of it, let us just say that while we can multiply the numerator and denominator by the same number, we can divide both the numerator and denominator by the same number and get smaller numerators. Usually this is called reducing to lowest terms.

$$\text{Example: } \frac{5}{10} = \frac{5/5}{10/5} = \frac{1}{2}$$

IV. To divide fractions, the rule that is usually given says invert (find the reciprocal) the divisor (second number) and multiply. Dividing by a number is the same as multiplying by the reciprocal of a number.

$$\text{Example: } \frac{3}{5} \div \frac{2}{3} = \frac{3}{5} \times \frac{3}{2} = \frac{9}{10}$$

V. To add or subtract fractions the bottom numbers (denominators) of the fractions must be the same. To perform the addition or subtraction, perform the indicated operation using the top numbers and leave the bottom numbers the same.

$$\text{Example: } \frac{3}{5} - \frac{1}{5} = \frac{2}{5}$$

All fractions we might want to add or subtract will not have the same bottom numbers (denominators), so how in the world can we make this happen?

$$\text{Example: } \frac{1}{2} + \frac{1}{5} = ?$$

If we look at the multiplication table below we find that the product of 2 and 5 is 10 (2 x 5 = 10). Therefore, 10 is a common multiple of 2 and 5. If we look at the table we find that there is no number smaller than 10 that is a common multiple. Therefore 10 is the Least Common Multiple (LCM) of 2 and 5. Ten will be a convenient number to select as a common denominator (bottom number).

Remember:
Identity Property of Multiplication: Multiplying a number by 1 does not change the value of the number.

$$\text{Example 1: } \frac{1}{2} \times 1 = \frac{1}{2} \times \frac{5}{5} = \frac{5}{10}$$

$$\text{Example 2: } \frac{1}{5} \times 1 = \frac{1}{5} \times \frac{2}{2} = \frac{2}{10}$$

Notice:

$$\frac{1}{2} = \frac{5}{10}, \text{ and } \frac{1}{5} = \frac{2}{10} \text{ So, } \frac{1}{2} + \frac{1}{5} = \frac{5}{10} + \frac{2}{10} = \frac{7}{10}$$

Multiplication Table

Number	1	2	3	4	5	6	7	8	9	10	11	12
1	1	2	3	4	5	6	7	8	9	10	11	12
2	2	4	6	8	10	12	14	16	18	20	22	24
3	3	6	9	12	15	18	21	24	27	30	33	36
4	4	8	12	16	20	24	28	32	36	40	44	48
5	5	10	15	20	25	30	35	40	45	50	55	60
6	6	12	18	24	30	36	42	48	54	60	66	72
7	7	14	21	28	35	42	49	56	63	70	77	84
8	8	16	24	32	40	48	56	64	72	80	88	96
9	9	18	27	36	45	54	63	72	81	90	99	108
10	10	20	30	40	50	60	70	80	90	100	110	120
11	11	22	33	44	55	66	77	88	99	110	121	132
12	12	24	36	48	60	72	84	96	108	120	132	144

Questions for discussion/research

Fill in the following table:

Numbers	Product	Common multiples	Least common multiple (LCM)
6, 9	54	18, 36, 54, 72, 90, 108	18
4, 8	32	8, 16, 24, 32, 40, 48	
3, 9	27		
2, 12			
4, 5			

1. Can any of the numbers that are common multiples be used to form the equivalent fractions used to add and subtract fractions?

2. What reasons can you think of for using the least common multiple (LCM) to form the equivalent fractions?

3. Do you see any patterns in the common multiples of the two numbers?

PRECISION TEACHING (PT) SAMPLE ANSWERS

Fill in the following table:

Expression	Operation	Result	Justification
$\dfrac{3}{5} \times \dfrac{1}{10}$	Multiply top times top and bottom times bottom.	$\dfrac{3}{50}$	To multiply fractions, the top numbers (numerators) get multiplied and that product becomes a new top number (numerator) and the bottom numbers (denominators) get multiplied and that product becomes a new bottom number (denominator).

Fill in the following table:

Expression	Operation	Result	Justification
$\dfrac{2}{3} \div \dfrac{1}{7}$	Find the reciprocal of $\dfrac{1}{7}$.	$\dfrac{7}{1}$	One of a pair of numbers whose product is 1: $\dfrac{1}{7} \times \dfrac{7}{1} = 1$
$\dfrac{2}{3} \div \dfrac{1}{7}$	Invert the divisor and multiply.	$\dfrac{2}{3} \times \dfrac{7}{1}$	Division by a number is the same as multiplying by the reciprocal of that number.
$\dfrac{2}{3} \times \dfrac{7}{1}$	Perform multiplication of fractions.	$\dfrac{14}{3}$	To multiply fractions, the top numbers (numerators) get multiplied and that product becomes a new top number (numerator) and the bottom numbers (denominators) get multiplied and that product becomes a new bottom number (denominator).
$\dfrac{14}{3}$	Write an improper fraction as a mixed number.	$4\dfrac{2}{3}$	$\dfrac{14}{3} = \dfrac{12}{3} + \dfrac{2}{3} = 4\dfrac{2}{3}$

Fill in the following table:

Expression	Operation	Result	Justification
$1\dfrac{1}{3} - \dfrac{2}{3}$	■■■■■■	■■■■■■	Given.
$1\dfrac{1}{3} - \dfrac{2}{3}$	Change the 1 to $\dfrac{3}{3}$ because $\dfrac{3}{3} = 1$.	$\dfrac{3}{3} + \dfrac{1}{3}$	Any number divided by itself is one.
$\dfrac{3}{3} + \dfrac{1}{3}$	Combine the fractions.	$\dfrac{4}{3}$	To perform the addition or subtraction with fractions, perform the indicated operation using the top numbers and leave the bottom numbers the same.
$1\dfrac{1}{3} - \dfrac{2}{3}$	Substitute $\dfrac{4}{3}$ for $1\dfrac{1}{3}$.	$\dfrac{4}{3} - \dfrac{2}{3}$	If quantities are defined as equal, the number system allows us to substitute the symbols and the numbers for the quantities interchangeably.
$\dfrac{4}{3} - \dfrac{2}{3}$	Combine the fractions.	$\dfrac{2}{3}$	To perform the addition or subtraction with fractions, perform the indicated operation using the top numbers and leave the bottom numbers the same.

Fill in the following table:

Expression	Operation	Result	Justification
$\dfrac{1}{3} - \dfrac{1}{5} = ?$	Decide on least common multiple of 3 and 5.	15	From multiplication table.
$\dfrac{1}{3} \times \dfrac{5}{5}$	Change $\dfrac{1}{3}$ to a fraction with 15 as denominator.	$\dfrac{1}{3} \times \dfrac{5}{5} = \dfrac{5}{15}$	Multiplying a number by one does not change the value of the number.
$\dfrac{1}{5} \times \dfrac{3}{3}$	Change $\dfrac{1}{5}$ to a fraction with 15 as denominator.	$\dfrac{1}{5} \times \dfrac{3}{3} = \dfrac{3}{15}$	Multiplying a number by one does not change the value of the number.
$\dfrac{1}{3} - \dfrac{1}{5} =$	Substitution	$\dfrac{5}{15} - \dfrac{3}{15}$	If quantities are defined as equal, the number system allows us to substitute the symbols and the numbers for the quantities interchangeably.
$\dfrac{5}{15} - \dfrac{3}{15}$	Combine fractions	$\dfrac{2}{15}$	To perform the addition or subtraction with fractions, perform the indicated operation using the top numbers and leave the bottom numbers the same. The bottom numbers must be the same for both fractions.

Scene: School Lunchroom - Meatloaf for Lunch

Sunny: I hate meatloaf.

Bunny: My mother makes a meatloaf that tastes great.

Sunny: Meatloaf cannot be made that tastes great.

Bunny: Meatloaf is very nutritious, lots of protein.

Sunny: I hate meatloaf almost as much as I hate math class.

Bunny: I thought it was neat the way we used changing the quantities in recipes to study fractions.

Sunny: I hate fractions!!!

Bunny: We can't do math if we can't solve fraction problems.

Sunny: Did you hear about the study they did on fractions?

Bunny: No.

Sunny: They took a survey and found that $\dfrac{7}{5}$ of the people in America could not solve fraction problems.

Number	1	2	3	4	5	6	7	8	9	10	11	12
1	1	2	3	4	5	6	7	8	9	10	11	12
2	2	4	6	8	10	12	14	16	18	20	22	24
3	3	6	9	12	15	18	21	24	27	30	33	36
4	4	8	12	16	20	24	28	32	36	40	44	48
5	5	10	15	20	25	30	35	40	45	50	55	60
6	6	12	18	24	30	36	42	48	54	60	66	72
7	7	14	21	28	35	42	49	56	63	70	77	84
8	8	16	24	32	40	48	56	64	72	80	88	96
9	9	18	27	36	45	54	63	72	81	90	99	108
10	10	20	30	40	50	60	70	80	90	100	110	120
11	11	22	33	44	55	66	77	88	99	110	121	132
12	12	24	36	48	60	72	84	96	108	120	132	144

LESSON NOTES

SEE PAGE 327 FOR <u>OPERATIONS WITH FRACTIONS</u>: PRECISION TEACHING (PT) SCORES, FREQUENCY TABLE.

I suggest that students correct their papers, calculate the frequencies and graph their results. Graphing the results on special graph paper (Standard Celeration Chart) can provide visual reinforcement for the students and information about how they are learning. The frequency tables are provided to facilitate this process.

PT 1, QUESTIONS

Fill in the following table:

Expression	Operation	Result	Justification
$\dfrac{3}{4} \times \dfrac{1}{11}$	Multiply top times top and bottom times bottom.		To multiply fractions, the top numbers (numerators) get multiplied and that product becomes a new top number (numerator) and the bottom numbers (denominators) get multiplied and that product becomes a new bottom number (denominator).

Fill in the following table:

Expression	Operation	Result	Justification
$\dfrac{1}{2} + \dfrac{1}{6}$	Decide on least common multiple of 2 and 6.		From multiplication table.
$\dfrac{1}{2} \times \dfrac{3}{3}$	Change $\dfrac{1}{2}$ to a fraction with 6 as denominator.	$\dfrac{1}{2} \times \dfrac{3}{3} = \dfrac{3}{6}$	
$\dfrac{1}{2} + \dfrac{1}{6}$	Substitution.		If quantities are defined as equal, the number system allows us to substitute the symbols and the numbers for the quantities interchangeably.
$\dfrac{3}{6} + \dfrac{1}{6}$	Combine fractions.	$\dfrac{4}{6}$	
$\dfrac{4}{6}$	Reduce to lowest terms.	$\dfrac{2}{3}$	

Fill in the following table:

Expression	Operation	Result	Justification
$\dfrac{1}{4} \div \dfrac{3}{1}$	Find the reciprocal of $\dfrac{3}{1}$.	$\dfrac{1}{3}$	
$\dfrac{1}{4} \div \dfrac{3}{1}$	Invert the divisor and multiply.	$\dfrac{1}{4} \times \dfrac{1}{3}$	
$\dfrac{1}{4} \times \dfrac{1}{3}$	Perform multiplication of fractions.		To multiply fractions, the top numbers (numerators) get multiplied and that product becomes a new top number (numerator) and the bottom numbers (denominators) get multiplied and that product becomes a new bottom number (denominator).

PT 1, ANSWERS

Fill in the following table:

Expression	Operation	Result	Justification
$\dfrac{3}{4} \times \dfrac{1}{11}$	Multiply top times top and bottom times bottom.	$\dfrac{3}{44}$	To multiply fractions, the top numbers (numerators) get multiplied and that product becomes a new top number (numerator) and the bottom numbers (denominators) get multiplied and that product becomes a new bottom number (denominator).

Fill in the following table:

Expression	Operation	Result	Justification
$\dfrac{1}{2} + \dfrac{1}{6}$	Decide on least common multiple of 2 and 6.	6	From multiplication table.
$\dfrac{1}{2} \times \dfrac{3}{3}$	Change $\dfrac{1}{2}$ to a fraction with 6 as denominator.	$\dfrac{1}{2} \times \dfrac{3}{3} = \dfrac{3}{6}$	**Multiplying a number by one does not change the value of the number.**
$\dfrac{1}{2} + \dfrac{1}{6}$	Substitution.	$\dfrac{3}{6} + \dfrac{1}{6}$	If quantities are defined as equal, the number system allows us to substitute the symbols and the numbers for the quantities interchangeably.
$\dfrac{3}{6} + \dfrac{1}{6}$	Combine fractions.	$\dfrac{4}{6}$	**To perform the addition or subtraction with fractions, perform the indicated operation using the top numbers and leave the bottom numbers the same. The bottom numbers must be the same for both fractions.**
$\dfrac{4}{6}$	Reduce to lowest terms.	$\dfrac{2}{3}$	**The numerator and denominator of a fraction can both be multiplied or divided by the same number without changing the value of the fraction.**

Fill in the following table:

Expression	Operation	Result	Justification
$\dfrac{1}{4} \div \dfrac{3}{1}$	Find the reciprocal of $\dfrac{3}{1}$.	$\dfrac{1}{3}$	**One of a pair of numbers whose product is 1; $\dfrac{3}{1} \times \dfrac{1}{3} = 1$.**
$\dfrac{1}{4} \div \dfrac{3}{1}$	Invert the divisor and multiply.	$\dfrac{1}{4} \times \dfrac{1}{3}$	**Division by a number is the same as multiplying by the reciprocal of that number.**
$\dfrac{1}{4} \times \dfrac{1}{3}$	Perform multiplication of fractions.	$\dfrac{1}{12}$	To multiply fractions, the top numbers (numerators) get multiplied and that product becomes a new top number (numerator) and the bottom numbers (denominators) get multiplied and that product becomes a new bottom number (denominator).

PT 2, QUESTIONS

Fill in the following table:

Expression	Operation	Result	Justification
$1\dfrac{1}{4} - \dfrac{3}{4}$			Given.
$1\dfrac{1}{4}$	Change the 1 to $\dfrac{4}{4}$ because $\dfrac{4}{4} = 1$.		Any number divided by itself is one.
$\dfrac{4}{4} + \dfrac{1}{4}$	Combine the fractions.	$\dfrac{5}{4}$	
$1\dfrac{1}{4} - \dfrac{3}{4}$	Substitute $\dfrac{5}{4}$ for $1\dfrac{1}{4}$.	$\dfrac{5}{4} - \dfrac{3}{4}$	If quantities are defined as equal, the number system allows us to substitute the symbols and the numbers for the quantities interchangeably.
$\dfrac{5}{4} - \dfrac{3}{4}$	Combine the fractions.	$\dfrac{2}{4}$	
$\dfrac{2}{4}$	Reduce to lowest terms.		The numerator and denominator of a fraction can be multiplied or divided by the same number without changing the value of the fraction.

Fill in the following table:

Expression	Operation	Result	Justification
$\dfrac{1}{5} \div \dfrac{1}{2}$	Find the reciprocal of $\dfrac{1}{2}$.		One of a pair of numbers whose product is 1: $\dfrac{1}{2} \times \dfrac{2}{1} = 1$.
$\dfrac{1}{5} \div \dfrac{1}{2}$	Invert the divisor and multiply.	$\dfrac{1}{5} \times \dfrac{2}{1}$	
$\dfrac{1}{5} \times \dfrac{2}{1}$	Perform multiplication of fractions.		To multiply fractions, the top numbers (numerators) get multiplied and that product becomes a new top number (numerator) and the bottom numbers (denominators) get multiplied and that product becomes a new bottom number (denominator).

PT 2, ANSWERS

Fill in the following table:

Expression	Operation	Result	Justification
$1\dfrac{1}{4} - \dfrac{3}{4}$			Given.
$1\dfrac{1}{4}$	Change the 1 to $\dfrac{4}{4}$ because $\dfrac{4}{4} = 1$.	$\dfrac{4}{4} + \dfrac{1}{4}$	Any number divided by itself is one.
$\dfrac{4}{4} + \dfrac{1}{4}$	Combine the fractions.	$\dfrac{5}{4}$	**To perform the addition or subtraction with fractions, perform the indicated operation using the top numbers and leave the bottom numbers the same.**
$1\dfrac{1}{4} - \dfrac{3}{4}$	Substitute $\dfrac{5}{4}$ for $1\dfrac{1}{4}$.	$\dfrac{5}{4} - \dfrac{3}{4}$	If quantities are defined as equal, the number system allows us to substitute the symbols and the numbers for the quantities interchangeably.
$\dfrac{5}{4} - \dfrac{3}{4}$	Combine the fractions.	$\dfrac{2}{4}$	**To perform the addition or subtraction with fractions, perform the indicated operation using the top numbers and leave the bottom numbers the same.**
$\dfrac{2}{4}$	Reduce to lowest terms.	$\dfrac{1}{2}$	The numerator and denominator of a fraction can be multiplied or divided by the same number without changing the value of the fraction.

Fill in the following table:

Expression	Operation	Result	Justification
$\dfrac{1}{5} \div \dfrac{1}{2}$	Find the reciprocal of $\dfrac{1}{2}$.	$\dfrac{2}{1}$	One of a pair of numbers whose product is 1 $\dfrac{1}{2} \times \dfrac{2}{1} = 1$.
$\dfrac{1}{5} \div \dfrac{1}{2}$	Invert the divisor and multiply.	$\dfrac{1}{5} \times \dfrac{2}{1}$	**Division by a number is the same as multiplying by the reciprocal of that number.**
$\dfrac{1}{5} \times \dfrac{2}{1}$	Perform multiplication of fractions.	$\dfrac{2}{5}$	To multiply fractions, the top numbers (numerators) get multiplied and that product becomes a new top number (numerator) and the bottom numbers (denominators) get multiplied and that product becomes a new bottom number (denominator).

PT 3, QUESTIONS

Fill in the following table:

Expression	Operation	Result	Justification
$\dfrac{1}{3} - \dfrac{1}{4}$	Decide on least common multiple of 3 and 4.		From multiplication table.
$\dfrac{1}{3} \times \dfrac{4}{4}$	Change $\dfrac{1}{3}$ to a fraction with 12 as denominator.	$\dfrac{4}{12}$	
$\dfrac{1}{4} \times \dfrac{3}{3}$	Change $\dfrac{1}{4}$ to a fraction with 12 as denominator.		Multiplying a number by one does not change the value of the number.
$\dfrac{1}{3} - \dfrac{1}{4}$	Substitution.	$\dfrac{4}{12} - \dfrac{3}{12}$	
$\dfrac{4}{12} - \dfrac{3}{12}$	Combine fractions.		To perform the addition or subtraction with fractions, perform the indicated operation using the top numbers and leave the bottom numbers the same. The bottom numbers must be the same for both fractions.

Fill in the following table:

Expression	Operation	Result	Justification
$\dfrac{2}{5} \div \dfrac{7}{4}$	Find the reciprocal of $\dfrac{7}{4}$.		One of a pair of numbers whose product is 1: $\dfrac{7}{4} \times \dfrac{4}{7} = 1$.
$\dfrac{2}{5} \div \dfrac{7}{4}$	Invert the divisor and multiply.	$\dfrac{2}{5} \times \dfrac{4}{7}$	
$\dfrac{2}{5} \times \dfrac{4}{7}$	Perform multiplication of fractions.		To multiply fractions, the top numbers (numerators) get multiplied and that product becomes a new top number (numerator) and the bottom numbers (denominators) get multiplied and that product becomes a new bottom number (denominator).

PT 3, ANSWERS

Fill in the following table:

Expression	Operation	Result	Justification
$\dfrac{1}{3} - \dfrac{1}{4}$	Decide on least common multiple of 3 and 4.	**12**	From multiplication table.
$\dfrac{1}{3} \times \dfrac{4}{4}$	Change $\dfrac{1}{3}$ to a fraction with 12 as denominator.	$\dfrac{4}{12}$	**Multiplying a number by one does not change the value of the number.**
$\dfrac{1}{4} \times \dfrac{3}{3}$	Change $\dfrac{1}{4}$ to a fraction with 12 as denominator.	$\dfrac{3}{12}$	Multiplying a number by one does not change the value of the number.
$\dfrac{1}{3} - \dfrac{1}{4}$	Substitution.	$\dfrac{4}{12} - \dfrac{3}{12}$	**If quantities are defined as equal, the number system allows us to substitute the symbols and the numbers for the quantities interchangeably.**
$\dfrac{4}{12} - \dfrac{3}{12}$	Combine fractions.	$\dfrac{1}{12}$	To perform the addition or subtraction with fractions, perform the indicated operation using the top numbers and leave the bottom numbers the same. The bottom numbers must be the same for both fractions.

Fill in the following table:

Expression	Operation	Result	Justification
$\dfrac{2}{5} \div \dfrac{7}{4}$	Find the reciprocal of $\dfrac{7}{4}$.	$\dfrac{4}{7}$	One of a pair of numbers whose product is 1: $\dfrac{7}{4} \times \dfrac{4}{7} = 1$.
$\dfrac{2}{5} \div \dfrac{7}{4}$	Invert the divisor and multiply.	$\dfrac{2}{5} \times \dfrac{4}{7}$	**Division by a number is the same as multiplying by the reciprocal of that number.**
$\dfrac{2}{5} \times \dfrac{4}{7}$	Perform multiplication of fractions.	$\dfrac{8}{35}$	To multiply fractions, the top numbers (numerators) get multiplied and that product becomes a new top number (numerator) and the bottom numbers (denominators) get multiplied and that product becomes a new bottom number (denominator).

CHAPTER 8

MULTIPLICATION AND DIVISION OF SIGNED NUMBERS

$$+2 \times +6 = +12$$

$$-1 \times -5 = +5$$

$$-10 \div +2 = -5$$

$$+9 \div -3 = -3$$

Overview: Algorithms for multiplying and dividing signed numbers will be presented as rules and the appropriateness of the rules evaluated.

Mathematical
Learning Objective: The student will:

Practice multiplying and dividing signed numbers.

Consider arguments for the validity of the algorithms provided.

NCTM Standards: Number and Operation
Understand patterns, relations and functions.

Definitions:

Algorithm	Any special way of solving a mathematical problem.
Rule	An established regulation or guide for conduct, procedure, etc.
Opposite	In a contrary direction; the sum of a number and its opposite is zero.
Converse	Reversed in position, order, etc.
Contrary	Opposite in nature order, etc.
Combine	To join into one using some defined pattern or rule.
Etc.	Abbreviation for etcetera.
Etcetera	And others, and so forth, etc.
Product	The result obtained when multiplying two or more numbers together.
Multiplication	The process of finding the quantity, obtained by adding a specified quantity a specified number of times. Example: $3(5) = 5 + 5 + 5 = 15$.
Quotient	The quantity obtained when one number is divided by another.
Divide	The inverse of multiplication. Dividing by a number is the same as multiplying by the reciprocal of that number.
Divisor	The number by which a dividend is divided; the bottom number of a fraction (denominator).
Dividend	The part of a fraction that is above the line (numerator); the part that is to be divided in a division problem.

NOTE:

Understood +1: If no sign is written in front of a number it can be assumed that the coefficient is +1.   Example: $x = +x = +1x = +1(x)$

Negative: A negative sign can represent multiplication by -1
Example: $-x = -1x = -1(x)$

RULES FOR MULTIPLICATION AND DIVISION OF SIGNED NUMBERS

For now we will call these rules "Assumptions" and not attempt to validate them more than stating that "The opposite of an opposite is the number itself", and that the number line defines negative numbers, and that negative numbers can be multiplied and divided in the same manner as positive numbers.

I. If the signs are the same the product or quotient will be positive.

$+ \times + = +$

$- \times - = +$

$+ \div + = +$

$- \div - = +$

Examples:

$+2 \times +6 = +12$

$-1 \times -5 = +5$

$+10 \div +2 = +5$

$-9 \div -3 = +3$

II. If the signs are different the product or quotient will be negative.

$+ \times - = -$

$- \times + = -$

$+ \div - = -$

$- \div + = -$

Examples:

$+2 \times -3 = -6$

$-1 \times +4 = -4$

$+8 \div -2 = -4$

$-12 \div +3 = -4$

A + sign in front of a parenthesis can be thought of as a +1.

$+(-3) = +1(-3) = -3$

A – sign in front of a parenthesis can be thought of as -1.

$-(-3) = -1(-3) = +3$

Scene: Lunchroom - Nacho's for Lunch

Bunny: You just got to have jalapenos with these nachos.

Sunny: I just like the chili sauce.

Bunny: You are supposed to eat Nachos with jalapenos.

Sunny: Your rules make just about as much sense as those math sign rules make.
Rules, rules, rules everywhere!

Bunny: Experience shows us that as we move up and down the number line the sign rules
are true.

Sunny: Those rules make about as much sense as my father's rules. Be in by 10:00,
don't smoke, blah, blah, blah.

Bunny: Are you mad about the algebra rules or about your father's rules?

PRECISION TEACHING (PT) SAMPLE ANSWERS:

Remember:

Often when multiplying by a +1 the positive sign and/or the 1 are not written:

Example: $+1(6) = +(6) = 6$

Often when multiplying by a –1 the 1 is not written:

Example: $-1(6) = -(6) = -6$

If no sign is written, it is assumed that there is a positive sign there:

Example: $5 = +(5) = +1 \times 5 = +5.$

The slash "/", the fraction bar "—", and the division symbol "÷" all mean division. The capital "X", the parenthesis "( )", the dot "•", a mathematical times sign "×", a vertical line "|", two variables written together "xy", or a number and a variable written together "5x" all mean multiplication.

RULES FOR MULTIPLICATION AND DIVISION OF SIGNED NUMBERS

   I. If the signs are the same the product or quotient will be positive.

  II. If the signs are different the product or quotient will be negative.

Fill in the following table:

Expression	Simplified	Justification
–(–3)	+3	Signs are the same, the result will be positive.
–1/(–4)	+0.25	Signs are the same, the result will be positive.
+7 | (–3)	–21	Signs are different, the result will be negative.
(+3) ÷ (–1)	–3	Signs are different, the result will be negative.
+(+9)	+9	Signs are the same, the result will be positive.
+(–8)	–8	Signs are different, the result will be negative.

LESSON NOTES

SEE PAGE 327 FOR <u>MULTIPLICATION AND DIVISION OF SIGNED NUMBERS</u>: PRECISION TEACHING (PT) SCORES, FREQUENCY TABLE.

I suggest that students correct their papers, calculate the frequencies and graph their results. Graphing the results on special graph paper (Standard Celeration Chart) can provide visual reinforcement for the students and information about how they are learning. The frequency tables are provided to facilitate this process.

PT 1, QUESTIONS

Remember:

Often when multiplying by a +1 the positive sign and/or the 1 are not written:

Example: $+1(6) = +(6) = 6$

Often when multiplying by a –1 the 1 is not written:

Example: $-1(6) = -(6) = -6$

If no sign is written, it is assumed that there is a positive sign there:

Example: $5 = +(5) = +1 \ X \ 5 = +5.$

The slash "/", the fraction bar "—", and the division symbol "÷" all mean division. The capital "X", the parenthesis "( )", the dot "•", a mathematical times sign "×", a vertical line " | ", two variables written together "xy", or a number and a variable written together "5x" all mean multiplication.

RULES FOR MULTIPLICATION AND DIVISION OF SIGNED NUMBERS

I.   If the signs are the same the product or quotient will be positive.

II. If the signs are different the product or quotient will be negative.

Fill in the following table:

Expression	Simplified	Justification
–(–7)	+7	
–1/(–5)		Signs are the same, the result will be positive.
+(–5)	–5	
(+18) ÷ –1		Signs are different, the result will be negative.
+(+4)		
+(–3)	–3	
$\dfrac{-8}{-2}$		Signs are the same, the result will be positive.
+3 × +4	+12	
–(–2)		Signs are the same, the result will be positive.
+5 | –3		
–12/+3	–4	
+3 X +8		Signs are the same, the result will be positive.
–5(–3)	+15	
–8 ÷ –2		Signs are the same, the result will be positive.
+7 × –5	–35	
-5 × +3		
$\dfrac{-36}{+3}$		Signs are different, the result will be negative.
–6/(–6)	+1	
–(–16)		Signs are the same, the result will be positive.

PT 1, ANSWERS

Remember:

Often when multiplying by a +1 the positive sign and/or the 1 are not written:

Example: $+1(6) = +(6) = 6$

Often when multiplying by a –1 the 1 is not written:

Example: $-1(6) = -(6) = -6$

If no sign is written, it is assumed that there is a positive sign there:

Example: $5 = +(5) = +1 \times 5 = +5.$

The slash "/", the fraction bar "—", and the division symbol "÷" all mean division. The capital "X", the parenthesis "( )", the dot "•", a mathematical times sign "×", a vertical line " | ", two variables written together "xy", or a number and a variable written together "5x" all mean multiplication.

RULES FOR MULTIPLICATION AND DIVISION OF SIGNED NUMBERS

I.   If the signs are the same the product or quotient will be positive.

II. If the signs are different the product or quotient will be negative.

Fill in the following table:

Expression	Simplified	Justification
$-(-7)$	+7	**Signs are the same, the result will be positive.**
$-1/(-5)$	**+0.2**	Signs are the same, the result will be positive.
$+(-5)$	–5	**Signs are different, the result will be negative.**
$(+18) \div -1$	**–18**	Signs are different, the result will be negative.
$+(+4)$	**+4**	**Signs are the same, the result will be positive.**
$+(-3)$	–3	**Signs are different, the result will be negative.**
$\dfrac{-8}{-2}$	**+4**	Signs are the same, the result will be positive.
$+3 \times +4$	+12	**Signs are the same, the result will be positive.**
$-(-2)$	**+2**	Signs are the same, the result will be positive.
$+5 \mid -3$	–15	**Signs are different, the result will be negative.**
$-12/+3$	–4	**Signs are different, the result will be negative.**
$+3 \times +8$	**24**	Signs are the same, the result will be positive.
$-5(-3)$	+15	**Signs are the same, the result will be positive.**
$-8 \div -2$	**+4**	Signs are the same, the result will be positive.
$+7 \times -5$	–35	**Signs are different, the result will be negative.**
$-5 \times +3$	–15	**Signs are different, the result will be negative.**
$\dfrac{-36}{+3}$	**–12**	Signs are different, the result will be negative.
$-6/(-6)$	+1	**Signs are the same, the result will be positive.**
$-(-16)$	**+16**	Signs are the same, the result will be positive.

PT 2, QUESTIONS

Remember:
Often when multiplying by a +1 the positive sign and/or the 1 are not written:
$$\text{Example:} \qquad +1(6) = +(6) = 6$$

Often when multiplying by a –1 the 1 is not written:
$$\text{Example:} \qquad -1(6) = -(6) = -6$$

If no sign is written, it is assumed that there is a positive sign there:
$$\text{Example:} \qquad 5 = +(5) = +1 \text{ X } 5 = +5.$$

The slash "/", the fraction bar "—", and the division symbol "÷" all mean division. The capital "X", the parenthesis "( )", the dot "•", a mathematical times sign "×", a vertical line "|", two variables written together "xy", or a number and a variable written together "5x" all mean multiplication.

RULES FOR MULTIPLICATION AND DIVISION OF SIGNED NUMBERS

I.   If the signs are the same the product or quotient will be positive.

II. If the signs are different the product or quotient will be negative.

Fill in the following table:

Expression	Simplified	Justification
–(–4)		Signs are the same, the result will be positive.
+7 × –3		
–(+3)		Signs are different, the result will be negative.
+3 × +1	+3	
–8 ÷ –2		
–1(–6)		Signs are the same, the result will be positive.
+(–8)	–8	
$\dfrac{-6}{-2}$		
+3 | +2		Signs are the same, the result will be positive.
–(–4)	+4	
+7 X –3		Signs are different, the result will be negative.
–9/+3		
+3 X +9		
–5(–3)	+15	
–8 ÷ –4		Signs are the same, the result will be positive.
+7 × –3	–21	
–5 X +2		Signs are different, the result will be negative.
$\dfrac{-9}{+3}$	–3	

PT 2, ANSWERS

Remember:
Often when multiplying by a +1 the positive sign and/or the 1 are not written:

Example: $+1(6) = +(6) = 6$

Often when multiplying by a –1 the 1 is not written:

Example: $-1(6) = -(6) = -6$

If no sign is written, it is assumed that there is a positive sign there:

Example: $5 = + (5) = +1 \times 5 = +5.$

The slash "/", the fraction bar "—", and the division symbol "÷" all mean division. The capital "X", the parenthesis "( )", the dot "•", a mathematical times sign "×", a vertical line "|", two variables written together "xy", or a number and a variable written together "5x" all mean multiplication.

RULES FOR MULTIPLICATION AND DIVISION OF SIGNED NUMBERS

I.   If the signs are the same the product or quotient will be positive.

II. If the signs are different the product or quotient will be negative.

Fill in the following table:

Expression	Simplified	Justification
–(–4)	+4	Signs are the same, the result will be positive.
+7 × –3	–21	**Signs are different, the result will be negative.**
–(+3)	–3	Signs are different, the result will be negative.
+3 × +1	+3	**Signs are the same, the result will be positive.**
–8 ÷ –2	+4	**Signs are the same, the result will be positive.**
–1(–6)	+6	Signs are the same, the result will be positive.
+(–8)	–8	**Signs are different, the result will be negative.**
$\dfrac{-6}{-2}$	+3	**Signs are the same, the result will be positive.**
+3 | +2	+6	Signs are the same, the result will be positive.
–(–4)	+4	**Signs are the same, the result will be positive.**
+7 × –3	–21	Signs are different, the result will be negative.
–9/+3	–3	**Signs are different, the result will be negative.**
+3 × +9	+27	**Signs are the same, the result will be positive.**
–5(–3)	+15	**Signs are the same, the result will be positive.**
–8 ÷ –4	+2	Signs are the same, the result will be positive.
+7 × –3	–21	**Signs are different, the result will be negative.**
–5 × +2	–10	Signs are different, the result will be negative.
$\dfrac{-9}{+3}$	–3	**Signs are different, the result will be negative.**

PT 3, QUESTIONS

Remember:

Often when multiplying by a +1 the positive sign and/or the 1 are not written:

Example: +1(6) = +(6) = 6

Often when multiplying by a –1 the 1 is not written:

Example: –1(6) = –(6) = –6

If no sign is written, it is assumed that there is a positive sign there:

Example: 5 = +(5) = +1 X 5 = +5.

The slash "/", the fraction bar "–", and the division symbol "÷" all mean division. The capital "X", the parenthesis "( )", the dot "•", a mathematical times sign" × ", a vertical line " | ", two variables written together "xy", or a number and a variable written together "5x" all mean multiplication.

RULES FOR MULTIPLICATION AND DIVISION OF SIGNED NUMBERS

I.   If the signs are the same the product or quotient will be positive.

II. If the signs are different the product or quotient will be negative.

Fill in the following table:

Expression	Simplified	Justification
–(–3)		Signs are the same, the result will be positive.
–1/–4	+0.25	
+(–3)		
+3 ÷ –1		
+(+9)		Signs are the same, the result will be positive.
+(–8)	–8	
$\dfrac{-6}{-2}$		
+3 × +2	+6	
–(–4)		Signs are the same, the result will be positive.
+7 | –3		
–9/+3		
+3 × +9		
–5(–3)		Signs are the same, the result will be positive.
–8 ÷ –4		Signs are the same, the result will be positive.
+7 × –3	–21	
$\dfrac{-9}{+3}$		
–6/–1	+6	
–(–4)		Signs are the same, the result will be positive.

PT 3, ANSWERS

Remember:
Often when multiplying by a +1 the positive sign and/or the 1 are not written:

Example: $+1(6) = +(6) = 6$

Often when multiplying by a –1 the 1 is not written:

Example: $-1(6) = -(6) = -6$

If no sign is written, it is assumed that there is a positive sign there:

Example: $5 = +(5) = +1 \text{ X } 5 = +5.$

The slash "/", the fraction bar "−", and the division symbol "÷" all mean division. The capital "X", the parenthesis "( )", the dot "•", a mathematical times sign"×", a vertical line " | ", two variables written together "xy", or a number and a variable written together "5x" all mean multiplication.

RULES FOR MULTIPLICATION AND DIVISION OF SIGNED NUMBERS

I.   If the signs are the same the product or quotient will be positive.

II. If the signs are different the product or quotient will be negative.

Fill in the following table:

Expression	Simplified	Justification
$-(-3)$	**+3**	Signs are the same, the result will be positive.
$-1/-4$	**+0.25**	**Signs are the same, the result will be positive.**
$+(-3)$	**–3**	**Signs are different, the result will be negative**
$+3 \div -1$	**–3**	**Signs are different, the result will be negative.**
$+(+9)$	**+9**	Signs are the same, the result will be positive.
$+(-8)$	**–8**	**Signs are different, the result will be negative.**
$\dfrac{-6}{-2}$	**+3**	**Signs are the same, the result will be positive.**
$+3 \times +2$	**+6**	**Signs are the same, the result will be positive.**
$-(-4)$	**+4**	Signs are the same, the result will be positive.
$+7 \mid -3$	**–21**	**Signs are different, the result will be negative.**
$-9/+3$	**–3**	**Signs are different, the result will be negative.**
$+3 \times +9$	**27**	**Signs are the same, the result will be positive.**
$-5(-3)$	**+15**	Signs are the same, the result will be positive.
$-8 \div -4$	**+2**	Signs are the same, the result will be positive.
$+7 \times -3$	**–21**	**Signs are different, the result will be negative.**
$\dfrac{-9}{+3}$	**–3**	**Signs are different, the result will be negative.**
$-6/-1$	**+6**	**Signs are the same, the result will be positive.**
$-(-4)$	**+4**	Signs are the same, the result will be positive.

CHAPTER 9

$$E^XP^ON^EN^TS = E^XP^ON^{(E+T)}S$$

$$\sqrt{x} \cdot \sqrt{x} = \sqrt{x \cdot x} = \sqrt{x^2} = x$$

$$\frac{\sqrt{x}}{\sqrt{y}} = \sqrt{\frac{x}{y}}$$

$$x^6 x^{-5} = x^{(6+(-5))} = x^1 = x$$

Overview: The rules for combining exponents will be presented. Operations involving exponents and radicals will be practiced.

Mathematical
Learning Objective: The student will:
                                     Simplify exponential expressions.

NCTM Standards: Number and operations:
                                     Understand numbers, ways of representing numbers,
                                     relationships among numbers, and number systems.

RULES FOR COMBINING EXPONENTS

$$x^a x^b = x^{(a+b)},$$

$$\frac{x^a}{x^b} = x^{(a-b)},$$

$$\frac{x^a}{x^a} = x^{(a-a)} = x^0 = 1, \text{ any number (except zero) raised to the 0 power is 1.}$$

$$\left(x^a\right)^b = x^{ab},$$

$$\left(x^a \cdot y^b\right)^c = x^{ac} \cdot y^{bc}$$

Definitions:

Term	Definition/comment	Symbol/Example
Addition	Used to indicate combining things or numbers.	+
Subtraction	Finding the difference between things, numbers; sometimes thinking "take away" is useful.	-
Multiplication	It is often easier than addition, if groups of things are counted, $3(5) = 5 + 5 + 5 = 15$.	$X, (), \times, \cdot$
Factor	Any of the quantities which when multiplied together form a product. In the sentence $3(5) = 15$, the 3 and the 5 are factors of 15.	
Product	The number obtained by multiplying two or more numbers together.	
Division	The inverse of multiplication. Dividing by a number is the same as multiplying by the reciprocal of that number.	$/, -, \div, \overline{)}$ Note: $a\!/\!b = \dfrac{a}{b} = a \div b = b\overline{)a}$
Exponent	A superscript after a number (base) indicates how many times the number (base) is taken as a factor. Example: in x^3 the three is an exponent and x is a base.	x^3
Raising to an exponent	Writing a number with a superscript indicates how many times the number (base) is multiplied times itself. Example: $x^3 = x \cdot x \cdot x$.	x^3
Raising to the zero power	By definition, any number (except zero) raised to the zero power is 1.	$x^0 = 1$
Base	The number that is raised to an exponent.	$X^2 \bullet x^3 = x^5$ $x^3 \times y^4 = x^3y^4$
Reciprocal	One of a pair of numbers, $\left(\text{as } 7, \dfrac{1}{7}\right)$ whose product is 1, $\left(7 \times \dfrac{1}{7} = 1\right)$. Often the word inverse is used.	Often a negative exponent is used to indicate a reciprocal. $7^{-1} = \dfrac{1}{7}$
Negative exponent	Negative exponents indicate reciprocals.	$7^{-2} = \dfrac{1}{7^2}$
Decimal	The form of a number you get when you divide a numerator by a denominator, as from a calculator.	$\dfrac{3}{4} = 3 \div 4 = 0.75$
Rational number	A number that can be expressed as a ratio, where the two numbers are integers (whole numbers).	
Irrational number	Non-terminating, non-repeating decimal number; a number that cannot be expressed as a quotient of two integers.	π and $\sqrt{2}$
Rationalizing a denominator	Removing an irrational number from the denominator (bottom number) of a fraction.	$\dfrac{1}{\sqrt{3}} = \dfrac{1}{\sqrt{3}} \times \dfrac{\sqrt{3}}{\sqrt{3}} = \dfrac{\sqrt{3}}{3}$

If you get serious about mathematics, you can begin to experience a poetic beauty about numbers. Many math teachers are enthralled by numbers that can be expressed as the ratio of two whole numbers. These are called rational numbers. Numbers that cannot be expressed as a ratio of two whole numbers are called irrational numbers. Whether you gain an appreciation for these numbers or not, getting irrational numbers out of the bottom (denominator) of a fraction is of great practical importance in many calculations. Getting these messy irrational numbers out of denominators is referred to as rationalization. Rationalizing denominators is a form of simplification. In many calculations irrational numbers cause approximations to be necessary. Approximations are guesses. Irrational numbers are messy.

For all numbers $x \geq 0$ and $y \geq 0$, $\sqrt{x} \cdot \sqrt{y} = \sqrt{x \cdot y}$, and $\sqrt{x \cdot y} = \sqrt{x} \cdot \sqrt{y}$

For each number $x \geq 0$, $\sqrt{x} \cdot \sqrt{x} = \sqrt{x \cdot x} = \sqrt{x^2} = x$

For all positive numbers x and y, $\dfrac{\sqrt{x}}{\sqrt{y}} = \sqrt{\dfrac{x}{y}}$. Notice that y is a positive number so $y \neq 0$

Scene: Lunch Room - Chicken Pot Pie for Lunch

Bunny: Irrational numbers seem so messy.

Sunny: Irrational is what my mom gets when she tells me to clean my room.

Bunny: Well, I bet it is because your room is so messy.

Sunny: And what's so great about order and these rational numbers?

Bunny: Rational numbers let you deal with exact numbers, not decimals.

Sunny: Calculators and computers don't care about decimals.

PRECISION TEACHING (PT) SAMPLE ANSWERS

Fill in the following table:

Expression	Simplified	Result	Justification
$x^6 x^{-5}$	$x^6 x^{-5} = x^{(6+(-5))} = x^1 = x$	x	$x^a x^b = x^{(a+b)}$
$\left(x^3\right)^{-5}$	$\left(x^3\right)^{-5} = x^{(3 \cdot -5)} = x^{-15} = \dfrac{1}{x^{15}}$	$x^{-15} = \dfrac{1}{x^{15}}$	$\left(x^a\right)^b = x^{ab}$
$\dfrac{xy^3}{x}$	$\dfrac{xy^3}{x} = x^{(1-1)}y^3 = 1 \times y^3 = y^3$	y^3	$\dfrac{x^a}{x^a} = x^{(a-a)} = x^0 = 1$
$x^5 \cdot y^4$	$x^5 \cdot y^4$	$x^5 \cdot y^4$	Cannot be simplified, bases not the same.
$\left(x^5 \cdot y^4\right)^3$	$\left(x^5 \cdot y^4\right)^3 = x^{5 \cdot 3} y^{4 \cdot 3} = x^{15} \cdot y^{12}$	$x^{15} \cdot y^{12}$	$\left(x^a \cdot y^b\right)^c = x^{ac} \cdot y^{bc}$

Rationalize the denominator: $\dfrac{1}{\sqrt{y^3}}$

Fill in the following table:

Expression	Change	Result	Justification
$\dfrac{1}{\sqrt{y^3}}$	Multiply times 1	$\dfrac{1}{\sqrt{y^3}} \cdot 1$	Multiplication by 1 does not change a number.
$\dfrac{1}{\sqrt{y^3}} \cdot 1$	Substitute $\dfrac{\sqrt{y}}{\sqrt{y}}$ for 1, because $\dfrac{\sqrt{y}}{\sqrt{y}} = 1$	$\dfrac{1}{\sqrt{y^3}} \cdot \dfrac{\sqrt{y}}{\sqrt{y}}$	Expressions defined as equal may be substituted for each other.
$\dfrac{1}{\sqrt{y^3}} \cdot \dfrac{\sqrt{y}}{\sqrt{y}}$	Multiply the two fractions	$\dfrac{\sqrt{y}}{\sqrt{y^4}}$	To multiply fractions, the top numbers (numerators) get multiplied and that product becomes a new top number (numerator) and the bottom numbers (denominators) get multiplied and that product becomes a new bottom number (denominator).
$\dfrac{\sqrt{y}}{\sqrt{y^4}}$	simplify	$\dfrac{\sqrt{y}}{y^2}$	$\dfrac{\sqrt{y}}{\sqrt{y^4}} = \dfrac{\sqrt{y}}{\sqrt{(y^2)^2}} = \dfrac{\sqrt{y}}{y^2}$

LESSON NOTES

SEE PAGE 327 FOR <u>EXPONENTS</u>: PRECISION TEACHING (PT) SCORES, FREQUENCY TABLE.

I suggest that students correct their papers, calculate the frequencies and graph their results. Graphing the results on special graph paper (Standard Celeration Chart) can provide visual reinforcement for the students and information about how they are learning. The frequency tables are provided to facilitate this process.

PT 1, QUESTIONS

Fill in the following table:

Expression	Simplified	Result	Justification
$x^3 x^2$	$x^3 x^2 = x^{3+2} = x^5$		
$\left(x^3\right)^{-5}$			$\left(x^a\right)^b = x^{ab}$
$\dfrac{y^3}{y^{-2}}$	$\dfrac{y^3}{y^{-2}} = y^{3-(-2)} = y^{3+2} = y^5$		
$x^5 \cdot y^4$	$x^5 \cdot y^4$	$x^5 \cdot y^4$	
$\left(x^5 \cdot y^4\right)^3$	$\left(x^5 \cdot y^4\right)^3 = x^{5\cdot3} y^{4\cdot3} = x^{15} \cdot y^{12}$		
$x^5 \cdot x^{-5}$		1	

Rationalize the denominator: $\dfrac{1}{\sqrt{y}}$

Fill in the following table:

Expression	Change	Result	Justification
$\dfrac{1}{\sqrt{y}}$	Multiply times 1	$\dfrac{1}{\sqrt{y}} \cdot 1$	Multiplication by 1 does not change a number.
$\dfrac{1}{\sqrt{y}} \cdot 1$	Substitute $\dfrac{\sqrt{y}}{\sqrt{y}}$ for 1, because $\dfrac{\sqrt{y}}{\sqrt{y}} = 1$	$\dfrac{1}{\sqrt{y}} \cdot \dfrac{\sqrt{y}}{\sqrt{y}}$	
$\dfrac{1}{\sqrt{y}} \cdot \dfrac{\sqrt{y}}{\sqrt{y}}$	Multiply the two fractions		
$\dfrac{1 \cdot \sqrt{y}}{\sqrt{y} \cdot \sqrt{y}}$	simplify	$\dfrac{1 \cdot \sqrt{y}}{\sqrt{y} \cdot \sqrt{y}} = \dfrac{\sqrt{y}}{y}$	

PT 1, ANSWERS

Fill in the following table:

Expression	Simplified	Result	Justification
$x^3 x^2$	$x^3 x^2 = x^{3+2} = x^5$	x^5	$x^a x^b = x^{(a+b)}$
$\left(x^3\right)^{-5}$	$\left(x^3\right)^{-5} = x^{(3 \cdot -5)} = x^{-15} = \dfrac{1}{x^{15}}$	$x^{-15} = \dfrac{1}{x^{15}}$	$\left(x^a\right)^b = x^{ab}$
$\dfrac{y^3}{y^{-2}}$	$\dfrac{y^3}{y^{-2}} = y^{3-(-2)} = y^{3+2} = y^5$	y^5	$\dfrac{x^a}{x^b} = x^{(a-b)}$
$x^5 \cdot y^4$	$x^5 \cdot y^4$	$x^5 \cdot y^4$	**Cannot be simplified, Bases not the same**
$\left(x^5 \cdot y^4\right)^3$	$\left(x^5 \cdot y^4\right)^3 = x^{5 \cdot 3} y^{4 \cdot 3} = x^{15} \cdot y^{12}$	$x^{15} \cdot y^{12}$	$\left(x^a \cdot y^b\right)^c = x^{ac} \cdot y^{bc}$
$x^5 \cdot x^{-5}$	$x^5 \cdot x^{-5} = x^{5+(-5)} = x^0 = 1$	1	$\dfrac{x^a}{x^a} = x^{(a-a)} = x^0 = 1$

Rationalize the denominator: $\dfrac{1}{\sqrt{y}}$

Fill in the following table:

Expression	Change	Result	Justification
$\dfrac{1}{\sqrt{y}}$	Multiply times 1	$\dfrac{1}{\sqrt{y}} \cdot 1$	Multiplication by 1 does not change a number.
$\dfrac{1}{\sqrt{y}} \cdot 1$	Substitute $\dfrac{\sqrt{y}}{\sqrt{y}}$ for 1, because $\dfrac{\sqrt{y}}{\sqrt{y}} = 1$	$\dfrac{1}{\sqrt{y}} \cdot \dfrac{\sqrt{y}}{\sqrt{y}}$	**Expressions defined as equal may be substituted for each other.**
$\dfrac{1}{\sqrt{y}} \cdot \dfrac{\sqrt{y}}{\sqrt{y}}$	Multiply the two fractions	$\dfrac{\sqrt{y}}{\sqrt{y} \cdot \sqrt{y}}$	**To multiply fractions, the top numbers (numerators) get multiplied and that product becomes a new top number (numerator) and the bottom numbers (denominators) get multiplied and that product becomes a new bottom number (denominator).**
$\dfrac{\sqrt{y}}{\sqrt{y} \cdot \sqrt{y}}$	simplify	$\dfrac{\sqrt{y}}{y}$	$\dfrac{\sqrt{y}}{\sqrt{y} \cdot \sqrt{y}} = \dfrac{\sqrt{y}}{\sqrt{y \cdot y}} = \dfrac{\sqrt{y}}{\sqrt{y^2}} = \dfrac{\sqrt{y}}{y}$

PT 2, QUESTIONS

Fill in the following table:

Expression	Simplified	Result	Justification
$x^6 x^0$			$x^a x^b = x^{(a+b)}$
$(x^2)^5$		x^{10}	
$\dfrac{x^3 y^2}{x}$	$\dfrac{x^3 y^2}{x} = x^{3-1} y^2 = x^2 y^2$		
$2x^2 \cdot 3y^3$		$6x^2 y^3$	Exponential terms cannot be simplified, bases not the same.
$\left(\dfrac{y}{x}\right)^5$		$\dfrac{y^5}{x^5}$	
$\left(x^{-3} \cdot y^{-4}\right)^{-2}$	$\left(x^{-3} \cdot y^{-4}\right)^{-2} = x^{-3 \cdot -2} y^{-4 \cdot -2} = x^6 \cdot y^8$		$\left(x^a \cdot y^b\right)^c = x^{ac} \cdot y^{bc}$

Rationalize the denominator: $\dfrac{1}{\sqrt{2}}$

Fill in the following table:

Expression	Change	Result	Justification
$\dfrac{1}{\sqrt{2}}$	Multiply times 1	$\dfrac{1}{\sqrt{2}} \cdot 1$	
$\dfrac{1}{\sqrt{2}} \cdot 1$	Substitute $\dfrac{\sqrt{2}}{\sqrt{2}}$ for 1, because $\dfrac{\sqrt{2}}{\sqrt{2}} = 1$		
$\dfrac{1}{\sqrt{2}} \cdot \dfrac{\sqrt{2}}{\sqrt{2}}$	Multiply the two fractions		To multiply fractions, the top numbers (numerators) get multiplied and that product becomes a new top number (numerator) and the bottom numbers (denominators) get multiplied and that product becomes a new bottom number (denominator).
$\dfrac{\sqrt{2}}{\sqrt{2} \cdot \sqrt{2}}$	simplify		$\dfrac{\sqrt{2}}{\sqrt{2} \cdot \sqrt{2}} = \dfrac{\sqrt{2}}{\sqrt{2} \cdot 2} = \dfrac{\sqrt{2}}{\sqrt{2^2}} = \dfrac{\sqrt{2}}{2}$

PT 2, ANSWERS

Fill in the following table:

Expression	Simplified	Result	Justification
$x^6 x^0$	$x^6 x^0 = x^{6+0} = x^6$	x^6	$x^a x^b = x^{(a+b)}$
$(x^2)^5$	$(x^2)^5 = x^{2 \cdot 5} = x^{10}$	x^{10}	$(x^a)^b = x^{ab}$
$\dfrac{x^3 y^2}{x}$	$\dfrac{x^3 y^2}{x} = x^{3-1} y^2 = x^2 y^2$	$x^2 y^2$	$\dfrac{x^a}{x^b} = x^{(a-b)}$
$2x^2 \cdot 3y^3$	$2x^2 \cdot 3y^3 = 6x^2 y^3$	$6x^2 y^3$	Exponential terms cannot be simplified, bases not the same.
$\left(\dfrac{y}{x}\right)^5$	$\left(\dfrac{y}{x}\right)^5 = \dfrac{y^{1 \cdot 5}}{x^{1 \cdot 5}} = \dfrac{y^5}{x^5}$	$\dfrac{y^5}{x^5}$	$(x^a \cdot y^b)^c = x^{ac} \cdot y^{bc}$
$(x^{-3} \cdot y^{-4})^{-2}$	$(x^{-3} \cdot y^{-4})^{-2} = x^{-3 \cdot -2} y^{-4 \cdot -2} = x^6 \cdot y^8$	$x^6 \cdot y^8$	$(x^a \cdot y^b)^c = x^{ac} \cdot y^{bc}$

Rationalize the denominator: $\dfrac{1}{\sqrt{2}}$

Fill in the following table:

Expression	Change	Result	Justification
$\dfrac{1}{\sqrt{2}}$	Multiply times 1	$\dfrac{1}{\sqrt{2}} \cdot 1$	**Multiplication by 1 does not change a number.**
$\dfrac{1}{\sqrt{2}} \cdot 1$	Substitute $\dfrac{\sqrt{2}}{\sqrt{2}}$ for 1, because $\dfrac{\sqrt{2}}{\sqrt{2}} = 1$	$\dfrac{1}{\sqrt{2}} \cdot \dfrac{\sqrt{2}}{\sqrt{2}}$	**Expressions defined as equal may be substituted for each other.**
$\dfrac{1}{\sqrt{2}} \cdot \dfrac{\sqrt{2}}{\sqrt{2}}$	Multiply the two fractions	$\dfrac{\sqrt{2}}{\sqrt{2} \cdot \sqrt{2}}$	To multiply fractions, the top numbers (numerators) get multiplied and that product becomes a new top number (numerator) and the bottom numbers (denominators) get multiplied and that product becomes a new bottom number (denominator).
$\dfrac{\sqrt{2}}{\sqrt{2} \cdot \sqrt{2}}$	simplify	$\dfrac{\sqrt{2}}{2}$	$\dfrac{\sqrt{2}}{\sqrt{2} \cdot \sqrt{2}} = \dfrac{\sqrt{2}}{\sqrt{2 \cdot 2}} = \dfrac{\sqrt{2}}{\sqrt{2^2}} = \dfrac{\sqrt{2}}{2}$

How Do We Know?

PT 3, QUESTIONS

Fill in the following table:

Expression	Simplified	Result	Justification
$x^{-6}x^{-5}$	$x^{-6}x^{-5} = x^{(-6+(-5))} = \mathbf{x}^{-11} = \dfrac{1}{x^{11}}$		
$\left(x^3\right)^5$		x^{15}	
$\dfrac{xy^3}{y^7}$			$\dfrac{x^a}{x^b} = x^{(a-b)}$
$x^2 \cdot y^2$			
$(x \cdot y)^3$			
$\dfrac{y^5}{x^5}$			Cannot be simplified, Bases not the same

Rationalize the denominator: $\dfrac{1}{\sqrt{3}}$

Fill in the following table:

Expression	Change	Result	Justification
$\dfrac{1}{\sqrt{3}}$	Multiply times 1		
$\dfrac{1}{\sqrt{3}} \cdot 1$	Substitute $\dfrac{\sqrt{3}}{\sqrt{3}}$ for 1, because $\dfrac{\sqrt{3}}{\sqrt{3}} = 1$		
$\dfrac{1}{\sqrt{3}} \cdot \dfrac{\sqrt{3}}{\sqrt{3}}$	Multiply the two fractions	$\dfrac{\sqrt{3}}{\sqrt{3} \cdot \sqrt{3}}$	To multiply fractions, the top numbers (numerators) get multiplied and that product becomes a new top number (numerator) and the bottom numbers (denominators) get multiplied and that product becomes a new bottom number (denominator).
$\dfrac{\sqrt{3}}{\sqrt{3} \cdot \sqrt{3}}$	simplify	$\dfrac{\sqrt{3}}{3}$	

PT 3, ANSWERS

Fill in the following table:

Expression	Simplified	Result	Justification
$x^{-6}x^{-5}$	$x^{-6}x^{-5} = x^{(-6+(-5))} = x^{-11} = \dfrac{1}{x^{11}}$	$x^{-11} = \dfrac{1}{x^{11}}$	$x^a x^b = x^{(a+b)}$
$\left(x^3\right)^5$	$\left(x^3\right)^5 = x^{(3 \cdot 5)} = x^{15}$	x^{15}	$\left(x^a\right)^b = x^{ab}$
$\dfrac{xy^3}{y^7}$	$\dfrac{xy^3}{y^7} = xy^{3-7} = xy^{-4} = \dfrac{x}{y^4}$	$\dfrac{x}{y^4}$	$\dfrac{x^a}{x^b} = x^{(a-b)}$
$x^2 \cdot y^2$	$x^2 \cdot y^2$	$x^2 \cdot y^2$	**Cannot be simplified, bases not the same.**
$\left(x \cdot y\right)^3$	$\left(x \cdot y\right)^3 = x^{1 \cdot 3} y^{1 \cdot 3} = x^3 \cdot y^3$	$x^3 \cdot y^3$	$\left(x^a \cdot y^b\right)^c = x^{ac} \cdot y^{bc}$
$\dfrac{y^5}{x^5}$	$\dfrac{y^5}{x^5}$	$\dfrac{y^5}{x^5}$	**Cannot be simplified, bases not the same.**

Rationalize the denominator: $\dfrac{1}{\sqrt{3}}$

Fill in the following table:

Expression	Change	Result	Justification
$\dfrac{1}{\sqrt{3}}$	Multiply times 1	$\dfrac{1}{\sqrt{3}} \cdot 1$	**Multiplication by 1 does not change a number.**
$\dfrac{1}{\sqrt{3}} \cdot 1$	Substitute $\dfrac{\sqrt{3}}{\sqrt{3}}$ for 1, because $\dfrac{\sqrt{3}}{\sqrt{3}} = 1$	$\dfrac{1}{\sqrt{3}} \cdot \dfrac{\sqrt{3}}{\sqrt{3}}$	**Expressions defined as equal may be substituted for each other.**
$\dfrac{1}{\sqrt{3}} \cdot \dfrac{\sqrt{3}}{\sqrt{3}}$	Multiply the two fractions	$\dfrac{\sqrt{3}}{\sqrt{3} \cdot \sqrt{3}}$	To multiply fractions, the top numbers (numerators) get multiplied and that product becomes a new top number (numerator) and the bottom numbers (denominators) get multiplied and that product becomes a new bottom number (denominator).
$\dfrac{\sqrt{3}}{\sqrt{3} \cdot \sqrt{3}}$	simplify	$\dfrac{\sqrt{3}}{3}$	$\dfrac{\sqrt{3}}{\sqrt{3} \cdot \sqrt{3}} = \dfrac{\sqrt{3}}{\sqrt{3} \cdot 3} = \dfrac{\sqrt{3}}{\sqrt{3^2}} = \dfrac{\sqrt{3}}{3}$

CHAPTER 10

PROPERTIES OF 0

$$0(4) = 0$$

$$\frac{0}{-4} = 0$$

$\frac{5}{0}$ is undefined, division by zero is not permitted.

$$-3 + 0 = -3$$

$$2 - 0 = 2$$

$$-9 + (+9) = 0$$

$$5 + (-5) = 0$$

Overview: Realizing what we can and cannot do with zero as a manipulative in mathematical situations helps students solve equations and reinforce the concept of quantity.

| **Mathematical Learning Objective:** | The student will: |
| | Explore creating zeros as a strategy for simplifying mathematical expressions. |

| **NCTM Standards:** | Number and Operations |
| | <u>Understand meanings</u> of operations and how they relate to one another. |

Definitions:

Zero	The sum of a number and its opposite is zero; the point marked 0 from which quantities are reckoned on a graduated scale; nothing. Zero is a real number.
Identity Element of Addition and Subtraction	There exists an element 0, such that: a + 0 = a, and a - 0 = a.
Defined	To determine the limits or nature of; to describe exactly.
Undefined	The opposite of defined; not possible to describe exactly.
Nothing	A thing that does not exist.
Conundrum	A riddle whose answer is often a pun; any puzzling problem (see paradox).
Limit	The point, line, etc. at which something ends.
Paradox	2MDs.
Opposite	In a contrary direction; the sum of a number and its opposite is zero.
Additive inverse	The sum of a number and its additive inverse is zero.

Questions for Discussions Research

1. If something has a word to describe it, can we say it does not exist?

2. What is the difference between something that is very small and nothing?

3. Are there numbers between 0 and 1?

4. If there are numbers between 0 and 1, do they get bigger or smaller as we get closer to zero?

Scene: School Lunchroom - Pizza for Lunch

Sunny: So much to try to remember - all these rules.

Bunny: (taking a piece of pepperoni off Sunny's pizza): They are just definitions and if you think about them, they really aren't that complicated.

Sunny: Maybe for you.

Bunny: (taking a piece of pepperoni off Sunny's pizza): If somebody gives you nothing five times, what you got?

Sunny: Well, uh, nothing.

Bunny: (taking a piece of pepperoni off Sunny's pizza): And what's half of nothing?

Sunny: Well, uh, nothing. But why can't you divide by zero?

Bunny: (taking a piece of pepperoni off Sunny's pizza): Well, any number close to zero is going to be very little, right?

Sunny: I guess.

Bunny: And how many little bitty things are going to be in a big thing?

Sunny: Lots.

Bunny: (taking a piece of pepperoni off Sunny's pizza): And maybe even too many to count, and too many to count would be undefined wouldn't it?

Sunny: Yeah.

Bunny: And a number plus its opposite equals zero.

Sunny: (noticing that all the pepperoni is gone): And even I know that when you eat my five pieces of pepperoni, I ain't got none left.

Bunny: You are so bright; it's no wonder your mom calls you Sunny.

For now we are going to accept these properties of zero as "Assumptions".

1. Zero times any number yields zero. Example: $0 \cdot 5 = 0$
2. Division by zero is not permitted.   Example: $\dfrac{6}{0}$ = undefined
3. Zero divided by any number (except zero) is zero. Example: $\dfrac{0}{2} = 0$
4. Zero added to, or subtracted from a number does not change the number.
        Examples: $3 + 0 = 3$ $2 - 0 = 2$
5. The sum of a number and its additive inverse is zero.   Example: $5 + (-5) = 0$

PRECISION TEACHING (PT) SAMPLE ANSWERS:

Remember:
The slash "/", the fraction bar "—", and the division symbol "÷" all mean division. The capital "X", the parenthesis "( )", the dot "●", a mathematical times sign" × ", a vertical line " | ", two variables written together "xy", or a number and a variable written together "5x" all mean multiplication.

If no sign is written in front of a number it is considered to be positive. Example: $1 = +1$

PROPERTIES OF ZERO

1. Zero times any number yields zero.
2. Division by zero is not permitted.
3. Zero divided by any number (except zero) is zero.
4. Zero added to, or subtracted from a number does not change the number.
5. The sum of a number and its additive inverse is zero.

Fill in the following table:

Expression	Simplified	Justification
5/0	undefined	Division by zero is not permitted.
$3 \div 0$	undefined	Division by zero is not permitted.
$0 \div 6$	0	Zero divided by any number (except zero) is zero.
$0 \cdot 6$	0	Zero times any number yields zero.
$-9 + (+9)$	0	The sum of a number and its additive inverse is zero.
$\dfrac{1}{0}$	undefined	Division by zero is not permitted.
$-3 + 0$	-3	Zero added to or subtracted from a number does not change the number.
$0(4)$	0	Zero times any number yields zero.

PT 1, QUESTIONS

Remember:

The slash "/", the fraction bar "—", and the division symbol "÷" all mean division. The capital "X", the parenthesis "( )", the dot "•", a mathematical times sign" × ", a vertical line " | ", two variables written together "xy", or a number and a variable written together "5x" all mean multiplication.

If no sign is written in front of a number it is considered to be positive. Example: 1 = +1

PROPERTIES OF ZERO

1. Zero times any number yields zero.
2. Division by zero is not permitted.
3. Zero divided by any number (except zero) is zero.
4. Zero added to, or subtracted from a number does not change the number.
5. The sum of a number and its additive inverse is zero.

Fill in the following table:

Expression	Simplified	Justification
5/0	undefined	Division by zero is not permitted.
0 · 6		Zero times any number is zero.
0 + 8	+8	
3 ÷ 0	undefined	
–4 +(+4)		The sum of a number and its additive inverse is zero.
$\dfrac{11}{0}$		
5 ÷ 0	undefined	
0 ÷ 6		Zero divided by any number (except zero) is zero.
–3 + 0	–3	
0 + 4	+4	

SEE PAGE 328 FOR <u>PROPERTIES OF 0</u>: PRECISION TEACHING (PT) SCORES, FREQUENCY TABLE.

I suggest that students correct their papers, calculate the frequencies and graph their results. Graphing the results on special graph paper (Standard Celeration Chart) can provide visual reinforcement for the students and information about how they are learning. The frequency tables are provided to facilitate this process.

PT 1, ANSWERS

Remember:

The slash "/", the fraction bar "—", and the division symbol "÷" all mean division. The capital "X", the parenthesis "( )", the dot "•", a mathematical times sign "×", a vertical line " | ", two variables written together "xy", or a number and a variable written together "5x" all mean multiplication.

If no sign is written in front of a number it is considered to be positive. Example: 1 = +1

PROPERTIES OF ZERO

1. Zero times any number yields zero.
2. Division by zero is not permitted.
3. Zero divided by any number (except zero) is zero.
4. Zero added to, or subtracted from a number does not change the number.
5. The sum of a number and its additive inverse is zero.

Fill in the following table:

Expression	Simplified	Justification
5/0	undefined	Division by zero is not permitted.
$0 \cdot 6$	**0**	Zero times any number is zero.
$0 + 8$	+8	**Zero added to or subtracted from a number does not change the number.**
$3 \div 0$	undefined	**Division by zero is not permitted.**
$-4 + (+4)$	**0**	The sum of a number and its additive inverse is zero.
$\dfrac{11}{0}$	**undefined**	**Division by zero is not permitted.**
$5 \div 0$	undefined	**Division by zero is not permitted.**
$0 \div 6$	**0**	Zero divided by any number (except zero) is zero.
$-3 + 0$	−3	**Zero added to or subtracted from a number does not change the number.**
$0 + 4$	+4	**Zero added to or subtracted from a number does not change the number.**

PT 2, QUESTIONS

Remember:

The slash "/", the fraction bar "—", and the division symbol "÷" all mean division. The capital "X", the parenthesis "( )", the dot " • ", a mathematical times sign" × ", a vertical line " | ", two variables written together "xy", or a number and a variable written together "5x" all mean multiplication.

If no sign is written in front of a number it is considered to be positive. Example: 1 = +1

PROPERTIES OF ZERO

1. Zero times any number yields zero.
2. Division by zero is not permitted.
3. Zero divided by any number (except zero) is zero.
4. Zero added to, or subtracted from a number does not change the number.
5. The sum of a number and its additive inverse is zero.

Fill in the following table:

Expression	Simplified	Justification
3/0		Division by zero is not permitted.
0×8	0	
$-9 +(+9)$		
$\dfrac{1}{0}$	undefined	
$3 \div 0$		Division by zero is not permitted.
$0 \div 6$	0	
$-3 + 0$		
$0(4)$		Zero times any number is zero.
$\dfrac{18}{0}$		
$3(0)$	0	

PT 2, ANSWERS

Remember:
The slash "/", the fraction bar "—", and the division symbol "÷" all mean division. The capital "X", the parenthesis "( )", the dot "•", a mathematical times sign "×", a vertical line "|", two variables written together "xy", or a number and a variable written together "5x" all mean multiplication.

If no sign is written in front of a number it is considered to be positive. Example: 1 = +1

PROPERTIES OF ZERO

1. Zero times any number yields zero.
2. Division by zero is not permitted.
3. Zero divided by any number (except zero) is zero.
4. Zero added to, or subtracted from a number does not change the number.
5. The sum of a number and its additive inverse is zero.

Fill in the following table:

Expression	Simplified	Justification
3/0	**undefined**	Division by zero is not permitted.
0×8	0	**Zero times any number is zero.**
–9 +(+9)	**0**	**The sum of a number and its additive inverse is zero.**
$\dfrac{1}{0}$	undefined	**Division by zero is not permitted.**
$3 \div 0$	**undefined**	Division by zero is not permitted.
$0 \div 6$	0	**Zero divided by any number (except zero) is zero.**
–3 + 0	**–3**	**Zero added to or subtracted from a number does not change the number.**
0(4)	**0**	Zero times any number is zero.
$\dfrac{18}{0}$	**undefined**	**Division by zero is not permitted.**
3(0)	0	**Zero times any number is zero.**

PT 3, QUESTIONS

Remember:

The slash "/", the fraction bar "—", and the division symbol "÷" all mean division. The capital "X", the parenthesis "( )", the dot "•", a mathematical times sign" × ", a vertical line " | ", two variables written together "xy", or a number and a variable written together "5x" all mean multiplication.

If no sign is written in front of a number it is considered to be positive. Example: 1 = +1

PROPERTIES OF ZERO

1. Zero times any number yields zero.
2. Division by zero is not permitted.
3. Zero divided by any number (except zero) is zero.
4. Zero added to, or subtracted from a number does not change the number.
5. The sum of a number and its additive inverse is zero.

Fill in the following table:

Expression	Simplified	Justification
5/0		Division by zero is not permitted.
3 ÷ 0		
0 ÷ 6	0	
0 X 6		
–9 +(+9)	0	
$\dfrac{1}{0}$	undefined	
–3 + 0	–3	
0(4)		Zero times any number is zero.
0 + 7		Zero added to or subtracted from a number does not change the number.
0 ÷ 18		

PT 3, ANSWERS

Remember:
The slash "/", the fraction bar "—", and the division symbol "÷" all mean division. The capital "X", the parenthesis "( )", the dot "•", a mathematical times sign "×", a vertical line "|", two variables written together "xy", or a number and a variable written together "5x" all mean multiplication.

If no sign is written in front of a number it is considered to be positive. Example: 1 = +1

PROPERTIES OF ZERO

1. Zero times any number yields zero.
2. Division by zero is not permitted.
3. Zero divided by any number (except zero) is zero.
4. Zero added to, or subtracted from a number does not change the number.
5. The sum of a number and its additive inverse is zero.

Fill in the following table:

Expression	Simplified	Justification
5/0	**undefined**	Division by zero is not permitted.
3 ÷ 0	**undefined**	**Division by zero is not permitted.**
0 ÷ 6	0	**Zero divided by any number (except zero) is zero.**
0 X 6	**0**	**Zero times any number is zero.**
–9 +(+9)	0	**The sum of a number and its additive inverse is zero.**
$\dfrac{1}{0}$	undefined	**Division by zero is not permitted.**
–3 + 0	–3	**Zero added to or subtracted from a number does not change the number.**
0(4)	**0**	Zero times any number is zero.
0 + 7	7	Zero added to or subtracted from a number does not change the number.
0 ÷ 18	**0**	**Zero divided by any number (except zero) is zero.**

CHAPTER 11

PROPERTIES OF

1

$$6 \times \frac{1}{6} = \frac{6}{6} = 1 \text{ and } 10 \times \frac{1}{10} = \frac{10}{10} = 1$$

$$\frac{1 \text{ yard}}{3 \text{ feet}} = 1$$

$$\frac{12 \text{ inches}}{1 \text{ foot}} = 1$$

$$\frac{1 \text{ pound}}{16 \text{ ounces}} = 1$$

Overview: In this lesson, students will use daily timed tasks to become fluent using the properties of one to manipulate mathematical expressions.

Mathematical Learning Objectives: The student will:

Develop fluency using the properties of one to change the appearance of numbers.

Utilize the defined properties of one to justify the results of the manipulation.

NCTM Standards: Number and Operations

Understand meanings and operations and how they relate to one another.

Algebra

Represent and analyze mathematical situations and structures using algebraic symbols.

Definitions:

One	The first of the counting numbers; the identity element of multiplication and division.
Identity Element of Multiplication and Division.	There exists an element 1, such that: a x 1 = a, and a ÷ 1 = a.
Quantity	A number or symbol expressing a thing that can be measured.
Transitive Property of Equality	Things equal to the same thing are equal to each other. For any quantities a, b, and c, if a = b and b = c, then a = c.
Substitute	To put in place of another. We will assume that if quantities are defined as equal, the number system allows us to substitute the symbols and the numbers for the quantities interchangeably. This assumption will often imply constraints on the substitution. This assumption is essential for the Transitive Property of Equality.
Reciprocal	One of a pair of numbers $\left(\text{as } 7, \dfrac{1}{7}\right)$ whose product is 1, $\left(7 \times \dfrac{1}{7} = 1\right)$. Often the word inverse is used. Often a negative exponent is used to indicate a reciprocal, $7^{-1} = \dfrac{1}{7}$, $7^{-2} = \dfrac{1}{7^2}$. The product of a number and its reciprocal is 1.
Equivalent quantities	The following quantities are defined as being equivalent: 1 meter = 100 centimeters, 1 yard = 3 feet, 1 pound = 16 ounces, 12 inches = 1 foot.

For now, we are going to call these Properties of One "Assumptions".

PROPERTIES OF ONE

1. Multiplying any number by 1 does not change the number.
    Example: $1 \times 5 = 5$

2. Dividing any number by 1 does not change the number.
    Example: $\dfrac{16}{1} = 16$

3. Any number (except zero) divided by itself is 1.
    Example: $\dfrac{5}{5} = 1$

4. Any quantity (except zero) divided by itself is 1.
    Example: $\dfrac{1 \text{ second}}{1 \text{ second}} = 1, \dfrac{1 \text{ meter}}{1 \text{ meter}} = 1, \dfrac{1 \text{ yard}}{3 \text{ feet}} = 1$

5. The product of any number and its reciprocal is one.
    Example: $6 \times \dfrac{1}{6} = \dfrac{6}{6} = 1$ and $10 \times \dfrac{1}{10} = \dfrac{10}{10} = 1$

Scene: Lunchroom - Tuna Casserole for Lunch

Sunny: Sure don't look like no one to me. How do we know it is?

Bunny: What's that?

Sunny: One yard divided by three feet - how can that equal one?

Bunny: The rule says any number divided by itself equals one.

Sunny: Yeah, well, three feet ain't a number.

Bunny: It's just a definition.

Sunny: I just don't understand.

Bunny: Why didn't you ask the teacher to explain it?

Sunny: What, and look stupid?

Bunny: I bet a lot of other students didn't understand either. But no one stopped him and asked questions.

Sunny: Well, it's his fault, he goes too fast.

Bunny: Maybe when we use it, it will make more sense.

Sunny: Now you and me together, that makes sense.

Bunny: (With mock excitement): OH! Sunny!

How Do We Know?

PRECISION TEACHING (PT) SAMPLE ANSWERS

Remember:
The slash "/", the fraction bar "—", and the division symbol "÷" all mean division. The capital "X", the parenthesis "( )", the dot "•", a mathematical times sign"×", a vertical line " | ", two variables written together "xy", or a number and a variable written together "5x" all mean multiplication.

PROPERTIES OF ONE

1. Multiplying any number by 1 does not change the number.

2. Dividing any number by 1 does not change the number.

3. Any number (except zero) divided by itself is 1.

4. Any quantity (except zero) divided by itself is 1.

5. The product of any number and its reciprocal is one.

Fill in the following table:

Expression	Result	Justification
5/1	5	Dividing any number by one does not change the number.
1X6	6	Multiplying any number by 1 does not change the number.
9 /9	1	Any number (except zero) divided by itself is 1.
$\dfrac{1}{1}$	1	Any number (except zero) divided by itself is 1.
inches/ inches	1	Any quantity (except zero) divided by itself is 1.
6 ÷ 1	6	Dividing any number by one does not change the number.
$\dfrac{12 \text{ inches}}{1 \text{ foot}}$	1	Any quantity (except zero) divided by itself is 1.
1(4)	4	Multiplying any number by 1 does not change the number.

LESSON NOTES

SEE PAGE 328 FOR <u>PROPERTIES OF 1</u>: PRECISION TEACHING (PT) SCORES, FREQUENCY TABLE.

I suggest that students correct their papers, calculate the frequencies and graph their results. Graphing the results on special graph paper (Standard Celeration Chart) can provide visual reinforcement for the students and information about how they are learning. The frequency tables are provided to facilitate this process.

PT 1, QUESTIONS

Remember:
The slash "/", the fraction bar "—", and the division symbol "÷" all mean division. The capital "X", the parenthesis "( )", the dot "•", a mathematical times sign "×", a vertical line " | ", two variables written together "xy", or a number and a variable written together "5x" all mean multiplication.

PROPERTIES OF ONE

1. Multiplying any number by 1 does not change the number.

2. Dividing any number by 1 does not change the number.

3. Any number (except zero) divided by itself is 1.

4. Any quantity (except zero) divided by itself is 1.

5. The product of any number and its reciprocal is one.

Fill in the following table:

Expression	Result	Justification
5/1		Dividing any number by one does not change the number.
1 X 14	14	
9 / 9		
$\dfrac{1}{1}$		Dividing any number by one does not change the number.
12 inches/ 12 inches	1	
6 ÷ 1		
3 X 1		Multiplying any number by 1 does not change the number.
1(9)	9	
$\dfrac{15}{15}$		Any number (except zero) divided by itself is 1.
12 eggs/1 dozen eggs		

PT 1, ANSWERS

Remember:
The slash "/", the fraction bar "−", and the division symbol "÷" all mean division. The capital "X", the parenthesis "( )", the dot "•", a mathematical times sign "×", a vertical line " | ", two variables written together "xy", or a number and a variable written together "5x" all mean multiplication.

PROPERTIES OF ONE

1. Multiplying any number by 1 does not change the number.

2. Dividing any number by 1 does not change the number.

3. Any number (except zero) divided by itself is 1.

4. Any quantity (except zero) divided by itself is 1.

5. The product of any number and its reciprocal is one.

Fill in the following table:

Expression	Result	Justification
5/1	5	Dividing any number by one does not change a number.
1 X 14	14	**Multiplying any number by 1 does not change the number.**
9 /9	1	**Any number (except zero) divided by itself is 1.**
$\dfrac{1}{1}$	1	Dividing any number by one does not change the number.
12 inches/ 12 inches	1	**Any quantity (except zero) divided by itself is 1.**
6 ÷ 1	6	**Dividing any number by 1 does not change the number.**
3 X 1	3	Multiplying any number by 1 does not change the number.
1(9)	9	**Multiplying any number by 1 does not change the number.**
$\dfrac{15}{15}$	1	Any number (except zero) divided by itself is 1.
12 eggs/1 dozen eggs	1	**Any quantity (except zero) divided by itself is 1.**

PT 2, QUESTIONS

Remember:

The slash "/", the fraction bar "—", and the division symbol "÷" all mean division. The capital "X", the parenthesis "( )", the dot "•", a mathematical times sign "×", a vertical line "|", two variables written together "xy", or a number and a variable written together "5x" all mean multiplication.

PROPERTIES OF ONE

1. Multiplying any number by 1 does not change the number.

2. Dividing any number by 1 does not change the number.

3. Any number (except zero) divided by itself is 1.

4. Any quantity (except zero) divided by itself is 1.

5. The product of any number and its reciprocal is one.

Fill in the following table:

Expression	Result	Justification
6/1	6	
1 X 6		Multiplying any number by 1 does not change the number.
9 / 9	1	
$\dfrac{7}{7}$		
5 meters/5 meters		Any quantity (except zero) divided by itself is 1.
71 ÷ 71	1	
3z X 1	3z	
1(18)		
$\dfrac{100 \text{ centimeters}}{1 \text{ meter}}$	1	
100/100		

PT 2, ANSWERS

Remember:

The slash "/", the fraction bar "—", and the division symbol "÷" all mean division. The capital "X", the parenthesis "( )", the dot "•", a mathematical times sign" × ", a vertical line " | ", two variables written together "xy", or a number and a variable written together "5x" all mean multiplication.

PROPERTIES OF ONE

1. Multiplying any number by 1 does not change the number.

2. Dividing any number by 1 does not change the number.

3. Any number (except zero) divided by itself is 1.

4. Any quantity (except zero) divided by itself is 1.

5. The product of any number and its reciprocal is one.

Fill in the following table:

Expression	Result	Justification
6/1	6	**Dividing any number by 1 does not change the number.**
1 X 6	**6**	Multiplying any number by 1 does not change the number.
9 /9	1	**Any number (except zero) divided by itself is 1.**
$\dfrac{7}{7}$	1	**Any number (except zero) divided by itself is 1.**
5 meters/5 meters	**1**	Any quantity (except zero) divided by itself is 1.
71 ÷ 71	1	**Any number (except zero) divided by itself is 1.**
3z X 1	3z	**Multiplying any number by 1 does not change the number.**
1(18)	**18**	**Multiplying any number by 1 does not change the number.**
$\dfrac{100 \text{ centimeters}}{1 \text{ meter}}$	1	**Any quantity (except zero) divided by itself is 1.**
100/100	**1**	**Any number (except zero) divided by itself is 1.**

PT 3, QUESTIONS

Remember:

The slash "/", the fraction bar "—", and the division symbol "÷" all mean division. The capital "X", the parenthesis "( )", the dot "•", a mathematical times sign "×", a vertical line " | ", two variables written together "xy", or a number and a variable written together "5x" all mean multiplication.

PROPERTIES OF ONE

1. Multiplying any number by 1 does not change the number.

2. Dividing any number by 1 does not change the number.

3. Any number (except zero) divided by itself is 1.

4. Any quantity (except zero) divided by itself is 1.

5. The product of any number and its reciprocal is one.

Fill in the following table:

Expression	Result	Justification
4x/4x		
1 X 2	2	
7 /1		Dividing any number by 1 does not change the number.
$\dfrac{\sqrt{2}}{\sqrt{2}}$		
5 seconds/ 5 seconds	1	
60 ÷ 1		Dividing any number by 1 does not change the number.
y X 1		
6/6		Any number (except zero) divided by itself is 1.
$\dfrac{12\ inches}{1\ foot}$	1	
18/1		

PT 3, ANSWERS

Remember:
The slash "/", the fraction bar " — ", and the division symbol "÷" all mean division. The capital "X", the parenthesis "( )", the dot "•", a mathematical times sign "×", a vertical line " | ", two variables written together "xy", or a number and a variable written together "5x" all mean multiplication.

PROPERTIES OF ONE

1. Multiplying any number by 1 does not change the number.

2. Dividing any number by 1 does not change the number.

3. Any number (except zero) divided by itself is 1.

4. Any quantity (except zero) divided by itself is 1.

5. The product of any number and its reciprocal is one.

Fill in the following table:

Expression	Result	Justification
4x/4x	1	**Any number (except zero) divided by itself is 1.**
1 X 2	2	**Multiplying any number by 1 does not change the number.**
7 /1	7	Dividing any number by 1 does not change the number.
$\dfrac{\sqrt{2}}{\sqrt{2}}$	1	**Any number (except zero) divided by itself is 1.**
5 seconds/ 5 seconds	1	**Any quantity (except zero) divided by itself is 1.**
60 ÷ 1	60	Dividing any number by 1 does not change the number.
y X 1	y	**Multiplying any number by 1 does not change the number.**
6/6	1	Any number (except zero) divided by itself is 1.
$\dfrac{12 \text{ inches}}{1 \text{ foot}}$	1	**Any quantity (except zero) divided by itself is 1.**
18/1	18	**Dividing any number by 1 does not change the number.**

CHAPTER 12

THE
COORDINATE
PLANE
AND

$$\frac{\text{RISE}}{\text{RUN}} = \text{SLOPE}$$

Overview: Points in the plane will be defined in terms of ordered pairs of values for x and y. Combining signed numbers will be practiced calculating the change in x and y for straight lines in the coordinate plane. Division of signed numbers will be practiced by calculating the slope.

**Mathematical
Learning Objective:**   The student will:

Practice graphing points in the coordinate plane. Calculate the change in the horizontal and vertical direction.

NCTM Standards: Algebra

Use mathematical models to understand quantitative relationships.

Definitions:

Word	Meaning	Symbol
Straight	Having the same direction throughout its length; not crooked or bent.	
Axis	A central line around which things are evenly arranged.	
x-axis	The horizontal line on a graph, usually indicating an independent variable; the line $y = 0$.	
y-axis	The vertical line on a graph, usually indicating a dependent variable; the line $x = 0$.	
Length	Distance between two points. Often measured in centimeters (cm).	
Rise	Change in the vertical direction (Δy).	$\Delta y = y_2 - y_1$
Run	Change in the horizontal direction (Δx).	$\Delta x = x_2 - x_1$
Line	A thin threadlike mark, a row of things, as of number points across a page.	
Variable	A letter or symbol that stands for a number that can be changed.	Sometimes x or y
Slope	$m = \text{Rise/run}, \dfrac{\text{change in y}}{\text{change in x}} = \dfrac{\Delta y}{\Delta x} = \dfrac{y_2 - y_1}{x_2 - x_1}$, where (x_1, y_1) and (x_2, y_2) represent an ordered pair of coordinates, indicating points in the plane.	m
Slope of any line parallel to the y-axis	Undefined because $\Delta x = x_2 - x_1 = 0$ and division by 0 is not permitted.	
Substitution	Using a number for a variable or using a variable for a number. We will assume that if quantities are defined as equal, the number system allows us to substitute the symbols and the numbers for the quantities interchangeably.	
Substitution Assumption	If quantities are defined as equal, they may be substituted for each other.	

To describe a point on an *x,y* coordinate axis an ordered pair of numbers is written in parenthesis, and separated by a comma. The first number of the pair indicates a value for the "x", and the second number indicates a value for the "y". By convention to the right is considered positive for x and to the left is considered negative for the x. Up is considered positive for the y and down is considered negative for y. For instance the ordered pairs (–6,1) and (2,–4) are graphed below.

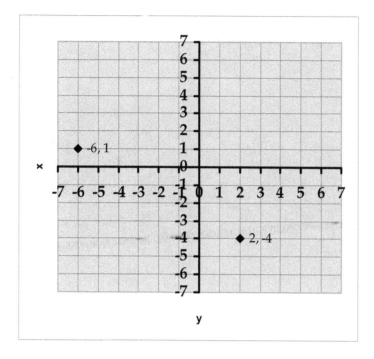

The slope for the line connecting these points can be calculated by substituting into the equation for slope.

Note that describing points as an ordered pair defines the values for the variables so the numbers can be substituted for the variables.

Example:

$$\text{slope} = \frac{y_2 - y_1}{x_2 - x_1}, \text{ for the points, } (x_1, y_1) = (-6, +1) \text{ and } (x_2, y_2) = (2, -4)$$

Substituting these values into the equation for slope

$$\text{slope} = \frac{y_2 - y_1}{x_2 - x_1} = \frac{-4 - (+1)}{2 - (-6)} = \frac{-4 + (-1)}{2 + (+6)} = \frac{-5}{8} = -\frac{5}{8}$$

Notice that to subtract a number, we add the opposite.

Questions for further discussion/research:

1. Plot the points and draw the connecting line in the following Precision Teaching exercises.
2. Write an essay or poem to describe what you observe about rise/run.
   Example:

> Climbing the slope gets harder by the number
> But if I stay with it and just don't slumber
> I might get over my plight
> Contemplating the Infinite

GRAPHING EXERCISE

Locate and connect the following points in order using a **BLACK** marker:
(0,5), (–2,4), (–4,2), (–5,0), (–4,–2), (–2,–4), (0,–5), (2,–4), (4,–2), (5,0), (4,2), (2,4), (0,5)

On the same graph, locate and connect the following points in order, using a **BLUE** marker:
(–3,2), (–2,1), (–1,1), (0,2), (1,1), (2,1), (3,2)

On the same graph, locate and connect the following points in order, using a **RED** marker:
(–3,–1), (–1,–3), (1,–3), (3,–1)

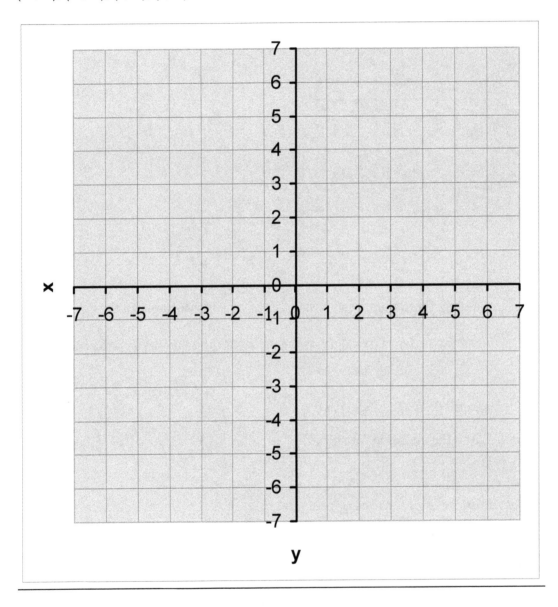

Scene: Lunchroom - Jambalaya and Red Beans for Lunch

Sunny: Who in the world ever dreamed up this coordinate crap?

Bunny: A French philosopher named Rene Descartes is usually given credit for
     inventing it.

Sunny: What did he want to do that for?

Bunny: It gives us a system for locating things.

Sunny: Who cares?

Bunny: Everything has got to be somewhere.

Sunny: What else did this guy Descartes do?

Bunny: Well, he was a soldier and he would join the army in the winter and quit in the
     spring, because armies usually did not fight in winter.

Sunny: Well, that's pretty smart.

Bunny: Descartes also said, "I think, therefore I am".

Sunny: That doesn't make any sense.

Bunny: It is one way of defining what things in the world are all about.

Sunny: Did you know that things are more like they are now, than they have ever been
     before?

**SEE PAGE 328 FOR <u>COORDINATE PLANE AND SLOPE</u>: PRECISION TEACHING (PT)
SCORES, FREQUENCY TABLE.**

I suggest that students correct their papers, calculate the frequencies and graph their results.
Graphing the results on special graph paper (Standard Celeration Chart) can provide visual
reinforcement for the students and information about how they are learning. The frequency tables
are provided to facilitate this process.

PRECISION TEACHING (PT) SAMPLE ANSWERS:

Remember:
Any number (except zero) divided by itself is one.
Division by zero is not permitted.
Zero divided by any number (except zero) is zero.

RULES FOR MULTIPLICATION AND DIVISION OF SIGNED NUMBERS

I. If the signs are the same the product/quotient will be positive.
$$+\times+=+, \quad -\times-=+, \quad +\div+=+, \quad -\div-=+$$

II. If the signs are different the product/quotient will be negative.
$$+\times-=-, \quad -\times+=-, \quad +\div-=-, \quad -\div+=-$$

RULES FOR COMBINING SIGNED NUMBERS

I. To combine numbers with the same sign simply add the numbers and keep the common sign.
Examples: $5 + (+2) = 7$ and $-4 + (-1) = -5$

II. To combine numbers with different signs, find the difference between the absolute values and give the answer the sign of the number that has the largest absolute value.
Example 1: $7 + (-5); |7| - |5| = 2$. Since the sign of 7 was positive and +7 has the larger absolute value, the result will be +2. $7 + (-5) = +2$
Example 2: $5 + (-7); |5| - |7| = 2$. Since the sign of 7 was negative, and –7 has the larger absolute value, the result will be –2. $5 + (-7) = -2$

III. A number and its additive opposite have a sum of zero.
Example: $+8 + (-8) = 0$

IV. The opposite of an additive opposite is the number itself.
Examples: $-(-5) = +5$ and $-(+5) = +(-5) = -5$.

V. To subtract a number, add the opposite.
Example: $8 - (-5) = 8 + (+5) = 13$

Fill in the following table:

(x_1, y_1)	(x_2, y_2)	$\Delta y = y_2 - y_1$	Δy	$\Delta x = x_2 - x_1$	Δx	$\dfrac{\Delta y}{\Delta x}$	Slope $= \dfrac{\Delta y}{\Delta x}$
$(0,5)$	$(-2,4)$	$4 - (+5)$	-1	$-2 - 0$	-2	$\dfrac{-1}{-2}$	$\dfrac{1}{2}$
$(-4,2)$	$(2,1)$	$1 - (+2)$	-1	$2 - (-4)$	$+6$	$\dfrac{-1}{+6}$	$-\dfrac{1}{6}$
$(3,6)$	$(1,2)$	$2 - (+6)$	-4	$1 - (+3)$	-2	$\dfrac{-4}{-2}$	2

PT 1, QUESTIONS

Remember:
Any number (except zero) divided by itself is one.
Division by zero is not permitted.
Zero divided by any number (except zero) is zero.

RULES FOR MULTIPLICATION AND DIVISION OF SIGNED NUMBERS

I. If the signs are the same the product/quotient will be positive.
$$+\times+=+, \quad -\times-=+, \quad +\div+=+, \quad -\div-=+$$

II. If the signs are different the product/quotient will be negative.
$$+\times-=-, \quad -\times+=-, \quad +\div-=-, \quad -\div+=-$$

RULES FOR COMBINING SIGNED NUMBERS

I. To combine numbers with the same sign simply add the numbers and keep the common sign.
Examples: $5 + (+ 2) = 7$ and $-4 + (-1) = -5$

II. To combine numbers with different signs, find the difference between the absolute values and give the answer the sign of the number that has the largest absolute value.
Example 1: $7 + (-5)$; $|7| - |5| = 2$. Since the sign of 7 was positive and +7 has the larger absolute value, the result will be +2. $7 + (-5) = +2$
Example 2: $5 + (-7)$; $|5| - |7| = 2$. Since the sign of 7 was negative, and –7 has the larger absolute value, the result will be –2. $5 + (-7) = -2$

III. A number and its additive opposite have a sum of zero.
Example: $+8 + (-8) = 0$

IV. The opposite of an additive opposite is the number itself.
Examples: $- (-5) = +5$ and $- (+5) = -5.$

V. To subtract a number, add the opposite.
Example: $8 - (- 5) = 8 + (+5) = 13$

Fill in the following table:

(x_1, y_1)	(x_2, y_2)	$\Delta y = y_2 - y_1$	Δy	$\Delta x = x_2 - x_1$	Δx	$\dfrac{\Delta y}{\Delta x}$	Slope $= \dfrac{\Delta y}{\Delta x}$
(0,5)	(1,0)			1 – (0)	+1	$\dfrac{-5}{1}$	
(–2,4)	(–1,0)	0 –(+4)	–4			$\dfrac{-4}{+1}$	
(–2,4)	(–4,2)			–4 – (–2)	–2	$\dfrac{-2}{-2}$	1
(–4,2)	(–2,4)		+2		+2	$\dfrac{+2}{+2}$	1

PT 1, ANSWERS

Remember:
Any number (except zero) divided by itself is one.
Division by zero is not permitted.
Zero divided by any number (except zero) is zero.

RULES FOR MULTIPLICATION AND DIVISION OF SIGNED NUMBERS

I.   If the signs are the same the product/quotient will be positive.
$$+ \times + = +, \quad - \times - = +, \quad + \div + = +, \quad - \div - = +$$

II. If the signs are different the product/quotient will be negative.
$$+ \times - = -, \quad - \times + = -, \quad + \div - = -, \quad - \div + = -$$

RULES FOR COMBINING SIGNED NUMBERS

I.   To combine numbers with the same sign simply add the numbers and keep the common sign.
Examples: $5 + (+ 2) = 7$ and $-4 + (-1) = -5$

II. To combine numbers with different signs, find the difference between the absolute values and give the answer the sign of the number that has the largest absolute value.
Example 1: $7 + (-5); |7| - |5| = 2$. Since the sign of 7 was positive and +7 has the larger absolute value, the result will be +2. $7 + (-5) = +2$
Example 2: $5 + (-7); |5| - |7| = 2$. Since the sign of 7 was negative, and –7 has the larger absolute value, the result will be –2. $5 + (-7) = -2$

III. A number and its additive opposite have a sum of zero.
Example: $+8 + (-8) = 0$

IV. The opposite of an additive opposite is the number itself.
Examples: $- (-5) = +5$ and $- (+5) = -5$.

V.   To subtract a number, add the opposite.
Example: $8 - (- 5) = 8 + (+5) = 13$

Fill in the following table:

(x_1, y_1)	(x_2, y_2)	$\Delta y = y_2 - y_1$	Δy	$\Delta x = x_2 - x_1$	Δx	$\dfrac{\Delta y}{\Delta x}$	$Slope = \dfrac{\Delta y}{\Delta x}$
(0,5)	(1,0)	**0 – (+5)**	**–5**	1 – (0)	+1	$\dfrac{-5}{+1}$	–5
(–2,4)	(–1,0)	0 –(+4)	–4	**–1 – (–2)**	+1	$\dfrac{-4}{+1}$	–4
(–2,4)	(–4,2)	**2 –(+4)**	–2	–4 – (–2)	–2	$\dfrac{-2}{-2}$	1
(–4,2)	(–2,4)	**4 –(+ 2)**	+2	**–2 – (–4)**	+2	$\dfrac{+2}{+2}$	1

PT 2, QUESTIONS

Remember:
Any number (except zero) divided by itself is one.
Division by zero is not permitted.
Zero divided by any number (except zero) is zero.

RULES FOR MULTIPLICATION AND DIVISION OF SIGNED NUMBERS

I. If the signs are the same the product/quotient will be positive.
$$+\times+=+, \quad -\times-=+, \quad +\div+=+, \quad -\div-=+$$

II. If the signs are different the product/quotient will be negative.
$$+\times-=-, \quad -\times+=-, \quad +\div-=-, \quad -\div+=-$$

RULES FOR COMBINING SIGNED NUMBERS

I. To combine numbers with the same sign simply add the numbers and keep the common sign.
Examples: $5 + (+2) = 7$ and $-4 + (-1) = -5$

II. To combine numbers with different signs, find the difference between the absolute values and give the answer the sign of the number that has the largest absolute value.
Example 1: $7 + (-5)$; $|7| - |5| = 2$. Since the sign of 7 was positive and +7 has the larger absolute value, the result will be +2. $7 + (-5) = +2$
Example 2: $5 + (-7)$; $|5| - |7| = 2$. Since the sign of 7 was negative, and –7 has the larger absolute value, the result will be -2. $5 + (-7) = -2$

III. A number and its additive opposite have a sum of zero.
Example: $+8 + (-8) = 0$

IV. The opposite of an additive opposite is the number itself.
Examples: $-(-5) = +5$ and $-(+5) = -5$.

V. To subtract a number, add the opposite.
Example: $8 - (-5) = 8 + (+5) = 13$

Fill in the following table:

(x_1, y_1)	(x_2, y_2)	$\Delta y = y_2 - y_1$	Δy	$\Delta x = x_2 - x_1$	Δx	$\dfrac{\Delta y}{\Delta x}$	$\text{Slope} = \dfrac{\Delta y}{\Delta x}$
(0,5)	(0,6)		+1	0 – (0)	0	$\dfrac{+1}{0}$	Undefined
(–5,4)	(3,4)	4 – (+4)			+8		0
(–4,2)	(0,–2)	–2 – (+2)			+4	$\dfrac{-4}{+4}$	
(–1, –2)	(1,6)				+2	$\dfrac{+8}{+2}$	4

Yes, You Can Learn Algebra!

PT 2, ANSWERS

Remember:
Any number (except zero) divided by itself is one.
Division by zero is not permitted.
Zero divided by any number (except zero) is zero.

RULES FOR MULTIPLICATION AND DIVISION OF SIGNED NUMBERS

I. If the signs are the same the product/quotient will be positive.
$$+ \times + = +, \quad - \times - = +, \quad + \div + = +, \quad - \div - = +$$

II. If the signs are different the product/quotient will be negative.
$$+ \times - = -, \quad - \times + = -, \quad + \div - = -, \quad - \div + = -$$

RULES FOR COMBINING SIGNED NUMBERS

I. To combine numbers with the same sign simply add the numbers and keep the common sign.
    Examples: $5 + (+2) = 7$ and $-4 + (-1) = -5$
II. To combine numbers with different signs, find the difference between the absolute values and give the answer the sign of the number that has the largest absolute value.
    Example 1: $7 + (-5)$; $|7| - |5| = 2$. Since the sign of 7 was positive and +7 has the larger absolute value, the result will be +2. $7 + (-5) = +2$
    Example 2: $5 + (-7)$; $|5| - |7| = 2$. Since the sign of 7 was negative, and –7 has the larger absolute value, the result will be –2. $5 + (-7) = -2$
III. A number and its additive opposite have a sum of zero.
    Example: $+8 + (-8) = 0$
IV. The opposite of an additive opposite is the number itself.
    Examples: $-(-5) = +5$ and $-(+5) = -5$.
V. To subtract a number, add the opposite.
    Example: $8 - (-5) = 8 + (+5) = 13$

Fill in the following table:

(x_1, y_1)	(x_2, y_2)	$\Delta y = y_2 - y_1$	Δy	$\Delta x = x_2 - x_1$	Δx	$\dfrac{\Delta y}{\Delta x}$	Slope $= \dfrac{\Delta y}{\Delta x}$
(0,5)	(0,6)	6 –(+5)	+1	0 – (0)	0	$\dfrac{1}{0}$	Undefined
(–5,4)	(3,4)	4 – (+4)	0	3 – (–5)	+8	$\dfrac{0}{+8}$	0
(–4,2)	(0,–2)	–2 – (+2)	–4	0 – (–4)	+4	$\dfrac{-4}{+4}$	–1
(–1, –2)	(1,6)	6 – (–2)	+8	1 – (–1)	+2	$\dfrac{+8}{+2}$	4

PT 3, QUESTIONS

Remember:
Any number (except zero) divided by itself is one.
Division by zero is not permitted.
Zero divided by any number (except zero) is zero.

RULES FOR MULTIPLICATION AND DIVISION OF SIGNED NUMBERS

I. If the signs are the same the product/quotient will be positive.
$$+ \times + = +, \quad - \times - = +, \quad + \div + = +, \quad - \div - = +$$

II. If the signs are different the product/quotient will be negative.
$$+ \times - = -, \quad - \times + = -, \quad + \div - = -, \quad - \div + = -$$

RULES FOR COMBINING SIGNED NUMBERS

I. To combine numbers with the same sign simply add the numbers and keep the common sign.
Examples: $5 + (+ 2) = 7$ and $-4 + (-1) = -5$

II. To combine numbers with different signs, find the difference between the absolute values and give the answer the sign of the number that has the largest absolute value.
Example 1: $7 + (-5)$; $|7| - |5| = 2$. Since the sign of 7 was positive and +7 has the larger absolute value, the result will be +2. $7 + (-5) = +2$
Example 2: $5 + (-7)$; $|5| - |7| = 2$. Since the sign of 7 was negative, and –7 has the larger absolute value, the result will be –2. $5 + (-7) = -2$

III. A number and its additive opposite have a sum of zero.
Example: $+8 + (-8) = 0$

IV. The opposite of an additive opposite is the number itself.
Examples: $- (-5) = +5$ and $- (+5) = -5$.

V. To subtract a number, add the opposite.
Example: $8 - (- 5) = 8 + (+5) = 13$

Fill in the following table:

(x_1, y_1)	(x_2, y_2)	$\Delta y = y_2 - y_1$	Δy	$\Delta x = x_2 - x_1$	Δx	$\dfrac{\Delta y}{\Delta x}$	$\text{Slope} = \dfrac{\Delta y}{\Delta x}$
(–1,1)	(0,2)			0 – (–1)	+1	$\dfrac{+1}{+1}$	1
(3,2)	(–3,2)	2 – (+2)	0	–3 – (3)		$\dfrac{0}{-6}$	0
(–2, –4)	(0, –5)	–5 – (–4)		0 – (–2)		$\dfrac{-1}{+2}$	
(–4, –2)	(0, –5)	–5 – (–2)				$\dfrac{-3}{+4}$	$-\dfrac{3}{4}$

PT 3, ANSWERS

Remember:
Any number (except zero) divided by itself is one.
Division by zero is not permitted.
Zero divided by any number (except zero) is zero.

RULES FOR MULTIPLICATION AND DIVISION OF SIGNED NUMBERS

I. If the signs are the same the product/quotient will be positive.
$$+ \times + = +, \quad - \times - = +, \quad + \div + = +, \quad - \div - = +$$

II. If the signs are different the product/quotient will be negative.
$$+ \times - = -, \quad - \times + = -, \quad + \div - = -, \quad - \div + = -$$

RULES FOR COMBINING SIGNED NUMBERS

I. To combine numbers with the same sign simply add the numbers and keep the common sign.
    Examples: $5 + (+2) = 7$ and $-4 + (-1) = -5$
II. To combine numbers with different signs, find the difference between the absolute values and give the answer the sign of the number that has the largest absolute value.
    Example 1: $7 + (-5)$; $|7| - |5| = 2$. Since the sign of 7 was positive and +7 has the larger absolute value, the result will be +2. $7 + (-5) = +2$
    Example 2: $5 + (-7)$; $|5| - |7| = 2$. Since the sign of 7 was negative, and –7 has the larger absolute value, the result will be –2. $5 + (-7) = -2$
III. A number and its additive opposite have a sum of zero.
    Example: $+8 + (-8) = 0$
IV. The opposite of an additive opposite is the number itself.
    Examples: $-(-5) = +5$ and $-(+5) = -5$.
V. To subtract a number, add the opposite.
    Example: $8 - (-5) = 8 + (+5) = 13$

Fill in the following table:

(x_1, y_1)	(x_2, y_2)	$\Delta y = y_2 - y_1$	Δy	$\Delta x = x_2 - x_1$	Δx	$\dfrac{\Delta y}{\Delta x}$	Slope $= \dfrac{\Delta y}{\Delta x}$
(–1,1)	(0,2)	2 – (+1)	+1	0 – (–1)	+1	$\dfrac{+1}{+1}$	1
(3,2)	(–3,2)	2 – (+2)	0	–3 – (3)	–6	$\dfrac{0}{-6}$	0
(–2, –4)	(0, –5)	–5 – (–4)	–1	0 – (–2)	+2	$\dfrac{-1}{+2}$	$-\dfrac{1}{2}$
(–4, –2)	(0, –5)	–5 – (–2)	–3	0 – (–4)	+4	$\dfrac{-3}{+4}$	$-\dfrac{3}{4}$

LET'S TRY SOMETHING DIFFERENT, QUESTIONS
(A Cooperative Learning Exercise?)

Remember:

Any number (except zero) divided by itself is one.

Division by zero is not permitted.

Zero divided by any number (except zero) is zero.

RULES FOR MULTIPLICATION AND DIVISION OF SIGNED NUMBERS

   I. If the signs are the same the product/quotient will be positive.

$$+ \times + = +, \quad - \times - = +, \quad + \div + = +, \quad - \div - = +$$

   II. If the signs are different the product/quotient will be negative.

$$+ \times - = -, \quad - \times + = -, \quad + \div - = -, \quad - \div + = -$$

RULES FOR COMBINING SIGNED NUMBERS

   I. To combine numbers with the same sign simply add the numbers and keep the common sign.

        Examples: $5 + (+2) = 7$ and $-4 + (-1) = -5$

   II. To combine numbers with different signs, find the difference between the absolute values and give the answer the sign of the number that has the largest absolute value.

        Example 1: $7 + (-5)$; $|7| - |5| = 2$. Since the sign of 7 was positive and +7 has the larger absolute value, the result will be +2. $7 + (-5) = +2$

        Example 2: $(-4) + 3$; $|4| - |3| = 1$. Since the sign of 4 was negative, and –4 has a larger absolute value, the result will be –1. $(-4) + 3 = -1$

   III. A number and its additive opposite have a sum of zero.

        Example: $+8 + (-8) = 0$

   IV. The opposite of an additive opposite is the number itself.

        Examples: $-(-5) = +5$ and $-(+5) = -5$.

   V. To subtract a number, add the opposite.

        Example: $8 - (-5) = 8 + (+5) = 13$

Fill in the following table:

(x_1, y_1)	(x_2, y_2)	$\Delta y = y_2 - y_1$	Δy	$\Delta x = x_2 - x_1$	Δx	$\dfrac{\Delta y}{\Delta x}$	Slope $= \dfrac{\Delta y}{\Delta x}$
	$(-2, -4)$	$-4 - (+4)$	-8	$-2 - (+6)$	-8	$\dfrac{-8}{-8}$	1
		$2 - (+2)$	0	$-3 - (+5)$	-8	$\dfrac{0}{-8}$	0
$(-7, -4)$		$-5 - (-4)$	-1	$-3 - (-7)$	$+4$	$\dfrac{-1}{+4}$	$-\dfrac{1}{4}$
		$-5 - (-2)$	-3	$0 - (+4)$	-4	$\dfrac{-3}{-4}$	$\dfrac{3}{4}$

LET'S TRY SOMETHING DIFFERENT, ANSWERS
(A Cooperative Learning Exercise?)

Remember:
Any number (except zero) divided by itself is one.
Division by zero is not permitted.
Zero divided by any number (except zero) is zero.

RULES FOR MULTIPLICATION AND DIVISION OF SIGNED NUMBERS

I. If the signs are the same the product/quotient will be positive.
$$+ \times + = +, \quad - \times - = +, \quad + \div + = +, \quad - \div - = +$$

II. If the signs are different the product/quotient will be negative.
$$+ \times - = -, \quad - \times + = -, \quad + \div - = -, \quad - \div + = -$$

RULES FOR COMBINING SIGNED NUMBERS

I. To combine numbers with the same sign simply add the numbers and keep the common sign.
    Examples: $5 + (+2) = 7$ and $-4 + (-1) = -5$
II. To combine numbers with different signs, find the difference between the absolute values and give the answer the sign of the number that has the largest absolute value.
    Example 1: $7 + (-5)$; $|7| - |5| = 2$. Since the sign of 7 was positive and +7 has the larger absolute value, the result will be +2. $7 + (-5) = +2$
    Example 2: $(-4) + 3$; $|4| - |3| = 1$. Since the sign of 4 was negative, and –4 has a larger absolute value, the result will be –1. $(-4) + 3 = -1$
III. A number and its additive opposite have a sum of zero.
    Example: $+8 + (-8) = 0$
IV. The opposite of an additive opposite is the number itself.
    Examples: $-(-5) = +5$ and $-(+5) = -5$.
V. To subtract a number, add the opposite.
    Example: $8 - (-5) = 8 + (+5) = 13$

Fill in the following table:

(x_1, y_1)	(x_2, y_2)	$\Delta y = y_2 - y_1$	Δy	$\Delta x = x_2 - x_1$	Δx	$\dfrac{\Delta y}{\Delta x}$	Slope $= \dfrac{\Delta y}{\Delta x}$
(6,+4)	(−2, −4)	−4 − (+4)	−8	−2 − (+6)	−8	$\dfrac{-8}{-8}$	1
(5,2)	(−3,2)	2 − (+2)	0	−3 − (+5)	−8	$\dfrac{0}{-8}$	0
(−7, −4)	(−3, −5)	−5 − (−4)	−1	−3 − (−7)	+4	$\dfrac{-1}{+4}$	$-\dfrac{1}{4}$
(4, −2)	(0, −5)	−5 − (−2)	−3	0 − (+4)	−4	$\dfrac{-3}{-4}$	$\dfrac{3}{4}$

CHAPTER 13

COMMUTATION AND DISTRIBUTION

abc = bca = cab = acb = bac = cba

6 + 3 = 3 + 6

X (W + 2) = X W + X 2

Overview: Some rules have been established about how we write expressions and the symbols we use. It is important that we agree on what the symbols mean and how we define the operations, so that we can all use the symbols the same way. This lesson has the student practice with these definitions and considers them as part of the properties of real numbers, without any formal proof.

Mathematical
Learning Objective: The student will:

Use the rules of commutation and distribution as arbitrary definitions.

NCTM Standard: Algebra

Understand patterns, relations, and functions.

Definitions:

Rule	An established regulation or guide for conduct, procedure or usage.
Law	The rules of conduct established by an authority; a sequence of natural events occurring with unvarying uniformity; the statement of such a sequence.
Prove	To establish by experience or trial to be true.
Simplify	To make simpler or less complex.
Commute	To change or exchange; to interchange.
Distribute	To spread out.
Property	A characteristic or attribute.
Inductive reasoning	Reasoning based on experimental evidence. Often referred to as empirical induction.
Empirical	Based on experiment or evidence.
Deductive reasoning	Reasoning that uses logic based on rules and definitions to establish principles.
Simplistic	Simplified; usually implying that it is simplified too much.
Imply	To indicate more than the words plainly say; to involve inference; not a direct statement.
Infer	To derive a conclusion from facts or premises.
Suppose	Right there in the dictionary between suppository and supporter-athletic.

Associative Law of Addition: Changing the grouping of numbers to be added does not change the sum. a + (b + c) = (a + b) + c

Example: 7 + (3 + 1) = 7 + 4 = 11
(7 + 3) +1 = 10 + 1 = 11

Associative Law of Multiplication: Changing the grouping of numbers to be multiplied does not change the product. a × (b × c) = (a × b) × c

Example: 2 × (3 × 4) = 2 × 12 = 24
(2 × 3) × 4 = 6 × 4 = 24

Commutative Property of Addition: Changing the order of addition does not change the sum. a + b = b + a

Example: 2 + 4 = 4 + 2 = 6

Commutative Property of Multiplication: Changing the order of multiplication does not change the product. abc = bca = cab = acb = bac = cba

Example: 2×3×4 = 3×4×2 = 4×3×2 = 2×4×3 = 3×2×4 = 4×3×2 = 24

Distributive Property of Multiplication: Multiplication spreads out over addition and subtraction. a(x + y) = ax + ay

Example: 2(3 + 4) = 2(3) + 2(4) = 6 + 8 = 14 and 2(3 + 4) = 2(7) = 14
Example: 2(7 - 5) = 2(7) - 2(5) = 14 - 10 = 4 and 2(7 - 5) = 2(2) = 4

Let us assume these propositions are true and include them in our properties of real numbers (PRN).

PRECISION TEACHING (PT) SAMPLE ANSWERS

Fill in the following table:

Expression	Simplified	Justification
C(x + y)	Cx + Cy	Multiplication spreads out over addition.
6 + 3 = 3 + 6	9	Changing the order of addition does not change the sum.
5(3 +1) =5(3) + 5(1) = 15 + 5	20	Multiplication spreads out over addition.
2×3×5 = 5×2×3	30	Changing the order of multiplication does not change the product.

Scene: Lunchroom - Hamburgers with Rice Pudding for Desert

Sunny: The pudding looks so good I am going to eat it first.

Bunny: My mother says that if you eat the desert first, it spoils your appetite.

Sunny: Like anything is going to spoil my appetite!

Bunny: Well, that's what my mother says.

Sunny: Well, that makes about as much sense as all those rules and properties and laws in math.

Bunny: They have all been shown to work the way the system is defined.

Sunny: And what in the world do they mean by "simplify"? Almost never does something called simplified look simpler.

Bunny: Well, you are right there.

Sunny: I want a new system.

Bunny: What would your system be like?

Sunny: The rules would be easy to remember, you could always use the Calculator, never have to deal with fractions, and **MY** answers would always be right. Yes, I would create a system where everything went **MY** way. I would never ever hear anyone say I was wrong.

Bunny: You would still hear yourself?

SEE PAGE 328 FOR <u>COMMUTATION AND DISTRIBUTION</u>: PRECISION TEACHING (PT) SCORES, FREQUENCY TABLE.

I suggest that students correct their papers, calculate the frequencies and graph their results. Graphing the results on special graph paper (Standard Celeration Chart) can provide visual reinforcement for the students and information about how they are learning. The frequency tables are provided to facilitate this process.

PT 1, QUESTIONS

RULES FOR COMMUTATION AND DISTRIBUTION

I.   Changing the grouping of numbers to be added does not change the sum.

II. Changing the grouping of numbers to be multiplied does not change the product.

III. Changing the order of addition does not change the sum.

IV. Changing the order of multiplication does not change the product.

V.   Multiplication spreads out over addition and subtraction.

Fill in the following table:

Expression	Simplified	Justification
$3 \times 6 = 6 \times 3$		Changing the order of multiplication does not change the product.
$x(q - r)$		Multiplication spreads out over addition and subtraction.
$5(5 + 2) = 5 \times 5 + 5 \times 2$	35	
$4 \times 5 \times 6 = 6 \times 5 \times 4$	120	
$3 \times 4 = 4 \times 3$	12	
$W(x - y)$		Multiplication spreads out over addition and subtraction.
$6 + 4 = 4 + 6$		Changing the order of addition does not change the sum.
$5(3 + 2) = 5 \times 3 + 5 \times 2$	25	
$2 \times 3 \times 5 = 3 \times 5 \times 2$	30	
$6 \times 7 = 7 \times 6$		Changing the order of multiplication does not change the product.
$4(y - z)$		Multiplication spreads out over addition and subtraction.
$5 \times 6 = 6 \times 5$	30	

PT 1, ANSWERS

RULES FOR COMMUTATION AND DISTRIBUTION

I.   Changing the grouping of numbers to be added does not change the sum.

II. Changing the grouping of numbers to be multiplied does not change the product.

III. Changing the order of addition does not change the sum.

IV. Changing the order of multiplication does not change the product.

V.   Multiplication spreads out over addition and subtraction.

Fill in the following table:

Expression	Simplified	Justification
$3 \times 6 = 6 \times 3$	**18**	Changing the order of multiplication does not change the product.
$x(q - r)$	**xq – xr**	Multiplication spreads out over addition and subtraction.
$5(5+2) = 5 \times 5 + 5 \times 2$	35	**Multiplication spreads out over addition and subtraction.**
$4 \times 5 \times 6 = 6 \times 5 \times 4$	120	**Changing the order of multiplication does not change the product.**
$3 \times 4 = 4 \times 3$	12	**Changing the order of multiplication does not change the product.**
$W(x - y)$	**Wx – Wy**	Multiplication spreads out over addition and subtraction.
$6 + 4 = 4 + 6$	**10**	Changing the order of addition does not change the sum.
$5(3 + 2) = 5 \times 3 + 5 \times 2$	25	**Multiplication spreads out over addition and subtraction.**
$2 \times 3 \times 5 = 3 \times 5 \times 2$	30	**Changing the order of multiplication does not change the product.**
$6 \times 7 = 7 \times 6$	**42**	Changing the order of multiplication does not change the product.
$4(y - z)$	**4y – 4z**	Multiplication spreads out over addition and subtraction.
$5 \times 6 = 6 \times 5$	30	**Changing the order of multiplication does not change the product.**

PT 2, QUESTIONS

RULES FOR COMMUTATION AND DISTRIBUTION

I.   Changing the grouping of numbers to be added does not change the sum.

II. Changing the grouping of numbers to be multiplied does not change the product.

III. Changing the order of addition does not change the sum.

IV. Changing the order of multiplication does not change the product.

V.   Multiplication spreads out over addition and subtraction.

Fill in the following table:

Expression	Simplified	Justification
$3\times7 = 7\times3$	21	
$x(m + n)$	$xm + xn$	
$5(4 +2) = 5\times4 +5\times2$		Multiplication spreads out over addition and subtraction.
$2\times5\times6 =6\times5\times2$		Changing the order of multiplication does not change the product.
$7\times8 = 8\times7$	56	
$W(x + y)$	$Wx + Wy$	
$6 + 5 = 5 + 6$		
$5(3 +1) = 5\times3 + 5\times1$		
$2\times3\times7 = 3\times7\times2$	42	
$6\times9 = 9\times6$	54	
$3(y + z)$		Multiplication spreads out over addition and subtraction.
$5\times9 = 9\times5$		Changing the order of multiplication does not change the product.

PT 2, ANSWERS

RULES FOR COMMUTATION AND DISTRIBUTION

I.   Changing the grouping of numbers to be added does not change the sum.

II. Changing the grouping of numbers to be multiplied does not change the product.

III. Changing the order of addition does not change the sum.

IV. Changing the order of multiplication does not change the product.

V.   Multiplication spreads out over addition and subtraction.

Fill in the following table:

Expression	Simplified	Justification
$3 \times 7 = 7 \times 3$	21	**Changing the order of multiplication does not change the product.**
$x(m + n)$	xm + xn	**Multiplication spreads out over addition and subtraction.**
$5(4 + 2) = 5 \times 4 + 5 \times 2$	**30**	Multiplication spreads out over addition and subtraction.
$2 \times 5 \times 6 = 6 \times 5 \times 2$	**60**	Changing the order of multiplication does not change the product.
$7 \times 8 = 8 \times 7$	56	**Changing the order of multiplication does not change the product.**
$W(x + y)$	Wx + Wy	**Multiplication spreads out over addition and subtraction.**
$6 + 5 = 5 + 6$	**11**	**Changing the order of addition does not change the sum.**
$5(3 + 1) = 5 \times 3 + 5 \times 1$	**20**	**Multiplication spreads out over addition and subtraction.**
$2 \times 3 \times 7 = 3 \times 7 \times 2$	42	**Changing the order of multiplication does not change the product.**
$6 \times 9 = 9 \times 6$	54	**Changing the order of multiplication does not change the product.**
$3(y + z)$	**3y + 3z**	Multiplication spreads out over addition and subtraction.
$5 \times 9 = 9 \times 5$	**45**	Changing the order of multiplication does not change the product.

PT 3, QUESTIONS

RULES FOR COMMUTATION AND DISTRIBUTION

I.   Changing the grouping of numbers to be added does not change the sum.

II. Changing the grouping of numbers to be multiplied does not change the product.

III. Changing the order of addition does not change the sum.

IV. Changing the order of multiplication does not change the product.

V.   Multiplication spreads out over addition and subtraction.

Fill in the following table:

Expression	Simplified	Justification
$4 \times 2 = 2 \times 4$		Changing the order of multiplication does not change the product.
$x(d + p)$	$xd + xp$	
$5(7 - 4) = 5 \times 7 - 5 \times 4$		Multiplication spreads out over addition and subtraction.
$7 \times 3 \times 2 = 3 \times 2 \times 7$	$42 = 42$	
$3 \times 6 = 6 \times 3$		
$C(x - y)$	$Cx - Cy$	
$6 + 3 = 3 + 6$	9	
$5(3 + 1) = 5 \times 3 + 5 \times 1$		Multiplication spreads out over addition and subtraction.
$2 \times 3 \times 5 = 5 \times 2 \times 3$	30	
$8 \times 9 = 9 \times 8$		
$2(y + z)$		Multiplication spreads out over addition and subtraction.
$5 \times 6 \times 7 = 7 \times 6 \times 5$	210	

PT 3, ANSWERS

RULES FOR COMMUTATION AND DISTRIBUTION

I.   Changing the grouping of numbers to be added does not change the sum.

II. Changing the grouping of numbers to be multiplied does not change the product.

III. Changing the order of addition does not change the sum.

IV. Changing the order of multiplication does not change the product.

V.   Multiplication spreads out over addition and subtraction.

Fill in the following table:

Expression	Simplified	Justification
$4 \times 2 = 2 \times 4$	8	Changing the order of multiplication does not change the product.
$x(d + p)$	$xd + xp$	**Multiplication spreads out over addition and subtraction.**
$5(7 - 4) = 5 \times 7 - 5 \times 4$	15	Multiplication spreads out over addition and subtraction.
$7 \times 3 \times 2 = 3 \times 2 \times 7$	42	**Changing the order of multiplication does not change the product.**
$3 \times 6 = 6 \times 3$	18	**Changing the order of multiplication does not change the product.**
$C(x - y)$	$Cx - Cy$	**Multiplication spreads out over addition and subtraction.**
$6 + 3 = 3 + 6$	9	**Changing the order of addition does not change the sum.**
$5(3 + 1) = 5 \times 3 + 5 \times 1$	20	Multiplication spreads out over addition and subtraction.
$2 \times 3 \times 5 = 5 \times 2 \times 3$	30	**Changing the order of multiplication does not change the product.**
$8 \times 9 = 9 \times 8$	72	**Changing the order of multiplication does not change the product.**
$2(y + z)$	$2y + 2z$	Multiplication spreads out over addition and subtraction.
$5 \times 6 \times 7 = 7 \times 6 \times 5$	210	**Changing the order of multiplication does not change the product.**

CHAPTER 14

ORDER OF OPERATIONS

$$8 + 3 \times 2 - (8 - 6)^2$$

$$8 + 3 \times 2 - (2)^2$$

$$8 + 3 \times 2 - 4$$

$$8 + 6 - 4$$

$$10$$

Overview: The concept of a system that is arbitrarily agreed upon that leads to universally accepted procedure and yields consistent results will be explored. The Order of Operations will be practiced and its practicality examined in class discussions.

Mathematical	
Learning Objective:	The student will:
	Simplify mathematical expressions.
	Use the conventional Order of Operations.
	Propose an alternate system.

NCTM Standards:	Algebra
	Understand patterns, relations, and functions.

Definitions:

Notation	The use of signs and symbols to represent words.
Arbitrary	Based on one's preference or whim.
Whim	A sudden fancy.
Fancy	Imagination when light, playful, etc.
Pragmatic	Practical; testing the validity of all concepts by their practical results.
Order	A definite plan; system.
Exponent	A superscript after a number (base) that indicates how many times the number (base) is taken as a factor. Example: in y^3 the three is an exponent and y is a base. $y^3 = y \cdot y \cdot y$

To perform algebraic operations, the following order defines the symbols used. Often this order is written as "Parenthesis, Exponents, Multiplication and Division, Addition and Subtraction". Acronym PEMDAS. Mnemonic: Please Excuse My Dear Aunt Sally.

Class Exercise: (Groups of four in a cooperative learning mode might work well for this.)

1. Make up your own system for Order of Operations.

2. Try to convince other students that your system works better.
    (Example: Your system gives an acronym that yields a better Mnemonic.)

3. Assume your system is better, and describe how you would change all the books that say another way is better.

To perform algebraic operations, the following orders define the symbols used:

1. Parenthesis – Perform the operations in a parenthesis from left to right first.

2. Exponents – Raise numbers to exponents after operations in parenthesis.

3. Multiplication and Division – Perform multiplication and division from left to right after exponents.

4. Addition and Subtraction – Perform addition and subtraction from left to right last.

Often this order is written as "Parenthesis, Exponents, Multiplication and Division, Addition and Subtraction". Acronym: PEMDAS. Mnemonic: Please Excuse My Dear Aunt Sally.

PRECISION TEACHING (PT) SAMPLE ANSWERS

Fill in the following table:

Expression	Operation	Result	Justification	Word from mnemonic
$(5 + 3)\,2$	Parenthesis	$(8)2$	Perform the operations in a parenthesis from left to right first.	Please
$(8)2$	Multiplication	16	Perform multiplication and division from left to right after exponents.	My

Fill in the following table:

Expression	Operation	Result	Justification	Word from mnemonic
3×4^2	Exponent	3×16	Raise numbers to exponents after operations in parenthesis.	Excuse
3×16	Multiplication	48	Perform multiplication and division from left to right after exponents.	My

Fill in the following table:

Expression	Operation	Result	Justification	Word from mnemonic
$5 + 3\times 2$	Multiplication	$5 + 6$	Perform multiplication and division from left to right after exponents.	My
$5 + 6$	Addition	11	Perform addition and subtraction from left to right last.	Aunt

Scene: Lunchroom - Shepherds Pie for Lunch

Bunny (bubbly): What words can you think of to match to the Order of Operations to help us remember?

Sunny (sourly):   Like I care.

Bunny: If you don't do the operations in the right order, you'll get the wrong answer.

Sunny (sourly):   Like I care.

Bunny: Let's see, P E M D A S.

Sunny: This stuff we got for lunch reminds me of a word we can use for the "S".

Bunny: Please Enroll My Debonair Airedale Sam.

Sunny: That's stupid. What is an Airedale?

Bunny: These memory tricks are supposed to be stupid, the more stupid, the easier to remember. Let's see, Please Enroll My Debonair Aunt Sally.

Sunny: Well, you made it more stupid.

Bunny: Let's see, Please Excuse My Dear Aunt Sally.

Sunny (rolling his eyes and pretending to gag): That's perfect!

SEE PAGE 329 FOR <u>ORDER OF OPERATIONS</u>: PRECISION TEACHING (PT) SCORES, FREQUENCY TABLE.

I suggest that students correct their papers, calculate the frequencies and graph their results. Graphing the results on special graph paper (Standard Celeration Chart) can provide visual reinforcement for the students and information about how they are learning. The frequency tables are provided to facilitate this process.

PT 1, QUESTIONS

To perform algebraic operations, the following orders define the symbols used:

1. Parenthesis – Perform the operations in a parenthesis from left to right first.

2. Exponents – Raise numbers to exponents after operations in parenthesis.

3. Multiplication and Division – Perform multiplication and division from left to right after exponents.

4. Addition and Subtraction – Perform addition and subtraction from left to right last.

Often this order is written as "Parenthesis, Exponents, Multiplication and Division, Addition and Subtraction". Acronym: PEMDAS. Mnemonic: Please Excuse My Dear Aunt Sally.

Fill in the following table:

Expression	Operation	Result	Justification	Word from mnemonic
(11 – 2)3	Parenthesis		Perform the operations in a parenthesis from left to right first.	
(9)3	Multiplication	27		

Fill in the following table:

Expression	Operation	Result	Justification	Word from mnemonic
11 – 2×3	Multiplication	11 – 6		
11 – 6	Subtraction			Sally

Fill in the following table:

Expression	Operation	Result	Justification	Word from mnemonic
$4 + 5 \times 2 - \dfrac{6}{3}$	Multiplication and division		Perform multiplication and division from left to right after exponents.	
$4 + 10 - 2$	Addition and subtraction			Aunt Sally

PT 1, ANSWERS

To perform algebraic operations, the following orders define the symbols used:

1. Parenthesis – Perform the operations in a parenthesis from left to right first.

2. Exponents – Raise numbers to exponents after operations in parenthesis.

3. Multiplication and Division – Perform multiplication and division from left to right after exponents.

4. Addition and Subtraction – Perform addition and subtraction from left to right last.

Often this order is written as "Parenthesis, Exponents, Multiplication and Division, Addition and Subtraction". Acronym: PEMDAS. Mnemonic: Please Excuse My Dear Aunt Sally.

Fill in the following table:

Expression	Operation	Result	Justification	Word from mnemonic
$(11-2)3$	Parenthesis	**(9)3**	Perform the operations in a parenthesis from left to right first.	**Please**
(9)3	Multiplication	27	**Perform multiplication and division from left to right after exponents.**	**My**

Fill in the following table:

Expression	Operation	Result	Justification	Word from mnemonic
$11-2\times3$	Multiplication	$11-6$	**Perform multiplication and division from left to right after exponents.**	**My**
$11-6$	Subtraction	**5**	**Perform addition and subtraction from left to right last.**	Sally

Fill in the following table:

Expression	Operation	Result	Justification	Word from mnemonic
$4+5\times2-\dfrac{6}{3}$	Multiplication and division	**4 + 10 - 2**	Perform multiplication and division from left to right after exponents.	**My Dear**
$4+10-2$	Addition and subtraction	**12**	**Perform addition and subtraction from left to right last.**	Aunt Sally

PT 2, QUESTIONS

To perform algebraic operations, the following orders define the symbols used:

1. Parenthesis – Perform the operations in a parenthesis from left to right first.

2. Exponents – Raise numbers to exponents after operations in parenthesis.

3. Multiplication and Division – Perform multiplication and division from left to right after exponents.

4. Addition and Subtraction – Perform addition and subtraction from left to right last.

Often this order is written as "Parenthesis, Exponents, Multiplication and Division, Addition and Subtraction". Acronym: PEMDAS. Mnemonic: Please Excuse My Dear Aunt Sally.

Fill in the following table:

Expression	Operation	Result	Justification	Word from mnemonic
$(9 - 2)\,2$	Parenthesis		Perform the operations in a parenthesis from left to right first.	
$(7)2$	Multiplication			

Fill in the following table:

Expression	Operation	Result	Justification	Word from mnemonic
$9 - 2 \times 2$	Multiplication			My
$9 - 4$			Perform addition and subtraction from left to right last.	

Fill in the following table:

Expression	Operation	Result	Justification	Word from mnemonic
$8 + 5 \times 2 - (7 - 4)^2$			Perform the operations in a parenthesis from left to right first.	Please
$8 + 5 \times 2 - (3)^2$	Exponent			Excuse
$8 + 5 \times 2 - 9$	Multiplication	$8 + 10 - 9$		
$8 + 10 - 9$	Addition and subtraction		Perform addition and subtraction from left to right last.	

PT 2, ANSWERS

To perform algebraic operations, the following orders define the symbols used:

1. Parenthesis – Perform the operations in a parenthesis from left to right first.

2. Exponents – Raise numbers to exponents after operations in parenthesis.

3. Multiplication and Division – Perform multiplication and division from left to right after exponents.

4. Addition and Subtraction – Perform addition and subtraction from left to right last.

Often this order is written as "Parenthesis, Exponents, Multiplication and Division, Addition and Subtraction". Acronym: PEMDAS. Mnemonic: Please Excuse My Dear Aunt Sally.

Fill in the following table:

Expression	Operation	Result	Justification	Word from mnemonic
$(9-2)\,2$	Parenthesis	$(7)2$	Perform the operations in a parenthesis first.	Please
$(7)2$	Multiplication	14	**Perform multiplication and division from left to right after exponents.**	My

Fill in the following table:

Expression	Operation	Result	Justification	Word from mnemonic
$9-2\times2$	Multiplication	$9-4$	**Perform multiplication and division from left to right after exponents.**	My
$9-4$	**Subtraction**	5	Perform addition and subtraction from left to right last.	**Sally**

Fill in the following table:

Expression	Operation	Result	Justification	Word from mnemonic
$8+5\times2-(7-4)^2$	**Parenthesis**	$8+5\times2-(3)^2$	Perform the operations in a parenthesis from left to right first.	Please
$8+5\times2-(3)^2$	Exponent	$8+5\times2-9$	**Raise numbers to exponents after operations in parenthesis.**	**Excuse**
$8+5\times2-9$	Multiplication	$8+10-9$	**Perform multiplication and division from left to right after exponents.**	**My**
$8+10-9$	Addition and subtraction	9	**Perform addition and subtraction from left to right last.**	**Aunt Sally**

PT 3, QUESTIONS

To perform algebraic operations, the following orders define the symbols used:

1. Parenthesis – Perform the operations in a parenthesis from left to right first.

2. Exponents – Raise numbers to exponents after operations in parenthesis.

3. Multiplication and Division – Perform multiplication and division from left to right after exponents.

4. Addition and Subtraction – Perform addition and subtraction from left to right last.

Often this order is written as "Parenthesis, Exponents, Multiplication and Division, Addition and Subtraction". Acronym: PEMDAS. Mnemonic: Please Excuse My Dear Aunt Sally.

Fill in the following tables:

Expression	Operation	Result	Justification	Word from mnemonic
$(15-6)/3$		9/3		Please
9/3	Division		Perform multiplication and division from left to right after exponents.	

Fill in the following table:

Expression	Operation	Result	Justification	Word from mnemonic
$15-6/3$	Division		Perform multiplication and division from left to right after exponents.	
$15-2$	Subtraction	13		Sally

Fill in the following table:

Expression	Operation	Result	Justification	Word from mnemonic
$8+5\times4-(3+2)^2$	Parenthesis			Please
$8+5\times4-(5)^2$		$8+5\times4-25$		Excuse
$8+5\times4-25$	Multiplication		Perform multiplication and division from left to right after exponents.	
$8+20-25$		3		Aunt Sally

PT 3, ANSWERS

To perform algebraic operations, the following orders define the symbols used:

1. Parenthesis – Perform the operations in a parenthesis from left to right first.

2. Exponents – Raise numbers to exponents after operations in parenthesis.

3. Multiplication and Division – Perform multiplication and division from left to right after exponents.

4. Addition and Subtraction – Perform addition and subtraction from left to right last.

Often this order is written as "Parenthesis, Exponents, Multiplication and Division, Addition and Subtraction". Acronym: PEMDAS. Mnemonic: Please Excuse My Dear Aunt Sally.

Fill in the following tables:

Expression	Operation	Result	Justification	Word from mnemonic
$(15-6)/3$	**Parenthesis**	9/3	**Perform the operations in a parenthesis from left to right first**	Please
9/3	Division	**3**	Perform multiplication and division from left to right after exponents.	**Dear**

Fill in the following table:

Expression	Operation	Result	Justification	Word from mnemonic
$15-6/3$	Division	$15-2$	Perform multiplication and division from left to right after exponents.	**Dear**
$15-2$	Subtraction	**13**	**Perform addition and subtraction from left to right last.**	Sally

Fill in the following table:

Expression	Operation	Result	Justification	Word from mnemonic
$8+5\times4-(3+2)^2$	Parenthesis	$8+5\times4-(5)^2$	**Perform the operations in a parenthesis from left to right first**	Please
$8+5\times4-(5)^2$	**Exponent**	$8+5\times4-25$	**Raise numbers to exponents after operations in parenthesis.**	Excuse
$8+5\times4-25$	Multiplication	$8+20-25$	Perform multiplication and division from left to right after exponents.	**My**
$8+20-25$	**Addition and subtraction**	3	**Perform addition and subtraction from left to right last.**	Aunt Sally

CHAPTER 15

SYMBOLS

+

x

·

=

()

÷

Overview: A review of definitions and symbols involved in the algebraic process is the purpose of this section. The definitions are presented in a table and a series of multiple choice questions are presented for the timed precision teaching exercise. Notice that this format of a reading exercise (table) followed by multiple-choice questions is consistent with assessments like the ACT.

Mathematical Learning Objective:	The Student will: Address the relationships between such words as variable coefficient and solution using a series of multiple choice questions in an ACT format.
NCTM Standards:	Number and Operations Understand meanings of operations and how they relate to one another.

Definitions of symbols used:

Term	Definition	Symbol/Comment
Addition	Used to indicate combining things or numbers.	$+$
Subtraction	Finding the difference between things or numbers; sometimes thinking "take away" is useful.	$-$
Multiplication	The process of finding the quantity, obtained by adding a specified quantity to itself a specified number of times. It is often easier than addition, if groups of things are counted, $3(5) = 5+5+5 =15$.	$X, (\,), \times, \cdot, |$
Division	The process of dividing. The inverse of multiplication. Separating a number into separate equal parts. Finding a number, quotient, which multiplied times a divisor, size of the parts, yields a dividend, what is being divided. In the equation $12/4 = 3$, 12 is a dividend, 4 is a divisor, and 3 is a quotient	$/, -, \div, \overline{)}$ Note: $$a/b = \frac{a}{b} = a \div b = b\overline{)a}$$ In the equation $a/b = c$, a is a dividend, b is a divisor, and c is a quotient
Exponent	A superscript after a number (base) indicates how many times the number (base) is taken as a factor. Example: $x^3 = x \cdot x \cdot x$	In x^3, the three is an exponent.
Solution	Makes an equation a true statement. If an equation contains a variable, a value of the variable that makes the equation true is called a solution.	
Coefficient	A multiplier of a variable or unknown quantity; a number written in front of a variable, as 6 in 6x.	
Equation	Mathematical expression that contains an = sign.	
Variable	A letter or symbol that stands for a number that can be changed.	Sometimes x, y and z are used.

PRECISION TEACHING (PT) SAMPLE ANSWERS

Select the best answer:

1. In the sentence: 2y =10, 5 is:
   A. A factor
   B. A variable
   C. An exponent
   D. A solution

2. In the sentence: $x^3 = 8$, 3 is:
   F. A coefficient
   G. A variable
   H. An exponent
   J. A solution

3. In the sentence: 4x = 32, 4 is:
   A. A coefficient
   B. A variable
   C. An exponent
   D. A solution

4. In the sentence: $4x^3 = 32$, x is:
   F. A coefficient
   G. A variable
   H. A solution
   J. All of the above

Scene: Lunchroom - Hamburgers for Lunch

Sunny: Why are they doing this stuff to me?

Bunny: It is helpful if we have an ordered system to use to work with numbers.

Sunny: Who wants to work with numbers?

Bunny: You can do it.

Sunny: Well, maybe I'll try if you will help me. Do you really think I can learn this stuff?

Bunny: I'll be happy to help you.

Sunny: Why are you willing to help me?

Bunny: I like you.

Sunny (incredulously): Really?

Bunny: You think I would put up with your whining if I didn't?

PT 1, QUESTIONS

Select the best answer:

1. In the sentence: $4y = 8$, 2 is:
   A. A coefficient
   B. A variable
   C. An exponent
   D. A solution

2. In the sentence: $4y = 8$, 4 is:
   F. A coefficient
   G. A variable
   H. An exponent
   J. A solution

3. In the sentence: $4y = 8$, y is:
   A. An equation
   B. A variable
   C. An exponent
   D. A solution

4. In the sentence: $4x^2 = 36$, 2 is:
   F. A coefficient
   G. A variable
   H. An exponent
   J. A solution

5. In the sentence: $4x^2 = 36$, 3 is:
   A. A factor
   B. A variable
   C. An exponent
   D. A solution

6. In the sentence: $4x^2 = 36$, x is:
   F. A coefficient
   G. A variable
   H. A solution
   J. All of the above

7. In the sentence: $7x - 21$, x is:
   A. An equation
   B. A variable
   C. An exponent
   D. A solution

8. In the sentence: $7x = 21$, 3 is:
   F. A coefficient
   G. A variable
   H. An exponent
   J. A solution

PT 2, QUESTIONS

Select the best answer:

1. In the sentence: 2y = 8, 4 is:
   A. A coefficient
   B. A variable
   C. An exponent
   D. A solution

2. In the sentence: 2y = 8, 2 is:
   F. A coefficient
   G. A variable
   H. An exponent
   J. A solution

3. In the sentence: 2y = 8, y is:
   A. An equation
   B. A variable
   C. An exponent
   D. A solution

4. In the sentence: $4x^3 = y$, 3 is:
   F. A factor
   G. A variable
   H. An exponent
   J. A solution

5. In the sentence: $4x^3 = y$, 4 is:
   A. A coefficient
   B. A variable
   C. An exponent
   D. A solution

6. In the sentence: $4x^3 = 32y$, x and y are:
   F. Variables
   G. Variables
   H. Variables
   J. All of the above

7. The sentence: 2y = 8 is:
   A. An equation
   B. A variable
   C. An exponent
   D. A solution

8. In the sentence: $x^3 = 8$, 2 is:
   F. An equation
   G. A variable
   H. An exponent
   J. A solution

PT 3, QUESTIONS

Select the best answer:

1. In the expression 2^3, 3 is an exponent because:
    A. It makes the sentence a true statement.
    B. It indicates how many times 2 is to be multiplied times itself.
    C. It is a number written in front of a variable.
    D. It stands for a number.

2. In the expression $3x^2$, 3 is a coefficient because:
    F. It makes the sentence a true statement.
    G. It indicates how many times 2 is to be multiplied times itself.
    H. It is a number written in front of a variable.
    J. It stands for a number.

3. In the expression $3x^2$, x is a variable because:
    A. It makes the sentence a true statement.
    B. It indicates how many times 2 is to be multiplied times itself.
    C. It is a number written in front of a variable.
    D. It stands for a number.

4. In the expression $3x^2$, 2 is an exponent because:
    F. It makes the sentence a true statement.
    G. It indicates how many times x is to be multiplied times itself.
    H. It is a number written in front of a variable.
    J. It stands for a number.

5. The sentence 4x = 8, is an equation because:
    A. It makes the sentence a true statement.
    B. It contains an equal sign.
    C. It is a number written in front of a variable.
    D. It stands for a number.

6. In the sentence 4x = 8, 4 is a coefficient because:
    F. It makes the sentence a true statement.
    G. It indicates how many times 2 is to be multiplied times itself.
    H. It is a number written in front of a variable.
    J. It stands for a number.

7. In the sentence 4x = 8, x is a variable because:
    A. It makes the sentence a true statement.
    B. It stands for a number.
    C. It is a number written in front of a variable.
    D. All of the above.

PT 1, 2, 3 ANSWERS

PT, 1	PT, 2	PT, 3
1. D	1. D	1. B
2. F	2. F	2. H
3. B	3. B	3. D
4. H	4. H	4. G
5. D	5. A	5. B
6.G	6. F	6. H
7. B	7. A	7. B
8. J	8. J	

SEE PAGE 329 FOR <u>SYMBOLS</u>: PRECISION TEACHING SCORES (PT), FREQUENCY TABLE.

I suggest that students correct their papers, calculate the frequencies and graph their results. Graphing the results on special graph paper (Standard Celeration Chart) can provide visual reinforcement for the students and information about how they are learning. The frequency tables are provided to facilitate this process.

How Do We Know?

CHAPTER 16

FACTORING AND GREATEST COMMON FACTOR

$$5x + 5 = 5(x + 1)$$

$$\frac{5x^4}{15x^2} = \frac{5xxxx}{3 \cdot 5xx}$$

$$\frac{20}{30} = \frac{2 \cdot 2 \cdot 5}{2 \cdot 3 \cdot 5}$$

Overview: Prime factorization and multiplicative identity will be utilized to justify the concept of "canceling" numbers in rational expressions.

Mathematical
Learning Objective: The student will:

> Practice factoring numbers and recognizing the greatest common factor in numbers and expressions and simplify rational expressions using the multiplicative identity.

NCTM Standards: Number and Operations

> Understand numbers, ways of representing numbers, relationships among numbers, and number systems.

> Algebra
> Understand patterns, relations, and functions.

Definitions of symbols used:

Term	Definition/comment	Symbol
Subtraction	Finding the difference between things, numbers; sometimes thinking "take away" is useful.	–
Multiplication	It is often easier than addition, if groups of things are counted, 3(5) = 5+5+5 =15.	$\mathbf{X}$, ( ), $\times$, $\bullet$, and the vertical line" $\vert$ "
Factor	Any of the quantities which, when multiplied together, form a product. In the sentence 3(5) = 15, the 3 and the 5 are factors of 15.	
Greatest Common Factor (GCF)	The largest number or expression that is a common factor of two or more numbers or expressions. Example: 3 is the GCF of 6 and 9; and x^2 is the GCF of $3x^2$ and x^2y.	
Product	The result obtained by multiplying two or more quantities together.	
Division	The inverse of multiplication.	$/, -, \div, \overline{)}$, $a\!\!/\!\!b = \dfrac{a}{b} = a \div b = b\overline{)a}$
Exponent	A superscript after a number (base) indicates how many times the number (base) is taken as a factor. Example: in x^3 the three is an exponent.	x^3
Raising to an exponent	Writing a number with a superscript indicates how many times the number is multiplied times itself. Example: $x^3 = x \cdot x \cdot x$, 3 is an exponent.	x^3
Prime numbers	A whole number that can be evenly divided by no other whole number than itself and 1. Examples of prime numbers: 2, 3, 5, 7, 11, 13.	
Prime factors	Factors of a whole number that are prime numbers. The prime factors of 6 are 2 and 3.	
Relatively Prime	Two whole numbers are relatively prime when their only common factor is 1.	5 and 4 are relatively prime.
Coefficient	A number written in front of a variable.	As 6 in 6x
Variable	A letter or symbol that stands for a number that can be changed or varied.	Often a lower case x or y is used.

PRECISION TEACHING (PT) SAMPLE ANSWERS:

Select the best answer:
1. The greatest common factor of 18 and 9 is:
    A. 18
    B. 3
    C. 6
    D. 9 Note: 9(2) = 18 and 9(1) = 9

2. The greatest common factor of 9x and $3x^4$:
    F. $3x^2$
    G. 3x Note: 3x (3) = 9x and $3x(x^3) = 3x^4$
    H. 6x
    J. x

Perform the indicated operations:

Expression	Operation	Result	Justification
x^3	Factor expression	xxx	Definition of exponent.
5x + 5	Factor expression	5(x + 1)	Distributive property of multiplication.
$5x^2 + x$	Factor expression	x(5x + 1)	Distributive property of multiplication.
$\dfrac{5x^4}{15x^2}$	Factor expression	$\dfrac{5xxxx}{3 \cdot 5xx}$	Definition of factor.
$\dfrac{5xxxx}{3 \cdot 5xx}$	Simplify expression, cancel $\dfrac{xx}{xx}; \dfrac{xx}{xx} = 1$	$\dfrac{5x^2}{3 \cdot 5}$	Any quantity (except zero) divided by itself is 1, and 1 times any number does not change the value of a number.
$\dfrac{5x^2}{3 \cdot 5}$	Simplify expression. Cancel $\dfrac{5}{5}$ because $\dfrac{5}{5} = 1$	$\dfrac{x^2}{3}$	Any quantity (except zero) divided by itself is 1, and 1 times any number does not change the value of a number.
18	Factor expression	$2 \cdot 3 \cdot 3$	2 and 3 are prime numbers and are factors of 18.
24	Factor expression	$2 \cdot 2 \cdot 2 \cdot 3$	2 and 3 are prime numbers and are factors of 24.
15	Factor expression	$3 \cdot 5$	3 and 5 are prime numbers and are factors of 15.

Scene: Lunchroom - Banana Pudding for Desert

Sunny: Boy, did that algebra class go slow today.

Bunny (sarcastically): Time flies when you are having fun.

Sunny: Groucho Marks says, "Time flies like an arrow, fruit flies like a banana".

Bunny: I heard the frog say, "Time sure is fun when you are having flies."

Sunny: Why didn't you meet me this morning before class, I needed to copy the homework?

Bunny: I was in the library.

Sunny: I assumed you would be in front of the gym since it wasn't raining?

Bunny: See what you get when you assume.

SEE PAGE 329 FOR <u>FACTORING AND GREATEST COMMON FACTOR</u>: PRECISION TEACHING (PT) SCORES, FREQUENCY TABLE.

I suggest that students correct their papers, calculate the frequencies and graph their results. Graphing the results on special graph paper (Standard Celeration Chart) can provide visual reinforcement for the students and information about how they are learning. The frequency tables are provided to facilitate this process.

PT 1, QUESTIONS

Select the best answer:

1. The greatest common factor of 12 and 24 is:
   A. 12
   B. 3
   C. 6
   D. 9

2. The greatest common factor of $12x^2$ and 6x is:
   F. $3x^2$
   G. 3x
   H. 6x
   J. x

3. The greatest common factor of 14 and 21 is:
   A. 7
   B. 3
   C. 6
   D. 2

Perform the indicated operations:

Expression	Operation	Result	Justification
20	Factor expression		2 and 5 are prime numbers and are factors of 20.
30	Factor expression	$3 \times 2 \times 5$	
$\dfrac{20}{30}$	Factor expression		Definition of factor.
$\dfrac{2 \times 2 \times 5}{3 \times 2 \times 5}$	Simplify expression. Cancel $\dfrac{2 \times 5}{2 \times 5}$ because $\dfrac{2 \times 5}{2 \times 5} = 1$		Any quantity (except zero) divided by itself is 1, and 1 times any number does not change the value of a number.
$3x^3 + 5x^2 y$	Factor expression		Distributive property of multiplication.

PT 1, ANSWERS

Select the best answer:

1. The greatest common factor of 12 and 24 is:
   A. 12 Note: 12(1) = 12 and 12(2) = 24
   B. 3
   C. 6
   D. 9

2. The greatest common factor of $12 x^2$ and $6x$ is:
   F. $3 x^2$
   G. $3x$
   H. 6x Note: 6x(2x) = $12 x^2$ and 6x(1) = 6x
   J. x

3. The greatest common factor of 14 and 21 is:
   A. 7 Note: 7(2) = 14 and 7(3) = 21
   B. 3
   C. 6
   D. 2

Perform the indicated operations:

Expression	Operation	Result	Justification
20	Factor expression	$2 \times 2 \times 5$	2 and 5 are prime numbers and are factors of 20.
30	Factor expression	$3 \times 2 \times 5$	**2, 5 and 3 are prime numbers and are factors of 30.**
$\dfrac{20}{30}$	Factor expression	$\dfrac{2 \times 2 \times 5}{2 \times 3 \times 5}$	Definition of factor.
$\dfrac{2 \times 2 \times 5}{3 \times 2 \times 5}$	Simplify expression. Cancel $\dfrac{2 \times 5}{2 \times 5}$ because $\dfrac{2 \times 5}{2 \times 5} = 1$	$\dfrac{2}{3}$	Any quantity (except zero) divided by itself is 1, and 1 times any number does not change the value of a number.
$3 x^3 + 5 x^2 y$	Factor expression	$x^2 (3x + 5y)$	Distributive property of multiplication.

PT 2, QUESTIONS

Select the best answer:

1. The greatest common factor of 12 and 18 is:
    A. 12
    B. 3
    C. 6
    D. 9

2. The greatest common factor of $12x^2$ and $6x^3$ is:
    F. $6x^2$
    G. $3x$
    H. $6x$
    J. x

3. The greatest common factor of 6 and 21 is:
    A. 7
    B. 3
    C. 6
    D. 2

Perform the indicated operations:

Expression	Operation	Result	Justification
$5x^2 + x$	Factor expression		Distributive property of multiplication.
$\dfrac{5y^3}{10y^2}$	Factor expression	$\dfrac{5yyy}{2(5)yy}$	
18	Factor expression		2 and 3 are prime numbers and are factors of 18.
24	Factor expression		2 and 3 are prime numbers and are factors of 24.
$\dfrac{18}{24}$	Factor expression		Definition of factor.
$\dfrac{2\times3\times3}{2\times2\times2\times3}$	Simplify expression. Cancel $\dfrac{2\times3}{2\times3}$; $\dfrac{2\times3}{2\times3}=1$	$\dfrac{3}{2\times2}=\dfrac{3}{4}$	

PT 2, ANSWERS

Select the best answer:

1. The greatest common factor of 12 and 18 is:
    A. 12
    B. 3
    C. 6 Note: 6(2) = 12 and 6(3) = 18
    D. 9

2. The greatest common factor of $12x^2$ and $6x^3$ is:
    F. $6x^2$ Note: $6x^2(2) = 12x^2$ and $6x^2(x) = 6x^3$
    G. 3x
    H. 6x
    J. x

3. The greatest common factor of 6 and 21 is:
    A. 7
    B. 3 Note: 3(2) = 6 and 3(7) = 21
    C. 6
    D. 2

Perform the indicated operations:

Expression	Operation	Result	Justification
$5x^2 + x$	Factor expression	**x(5x + 1)**	Distributive property of multiplication.
$\dfrac{5y^3}{10y^2}$	Factor expression	$\dfrac{5yyy}{2(5)yy}$	**Definition of factor.**
18	Factor expression	**2·3·3**	2 and 3 are prime numbers and are factors of 18.
24	Factor expression	**2·2·2·3**	2 and 3 are prime numbers and are factors of 24.
$\dfrac{18}{24}$	Factor expression	$\dfrac{2 \times 3 \times 3}{2 \times 2 \times 2 \times 3}$	Definition of factor.
$\dfrac{2 \times 3 \times 3}{2 \times 2 \times 2 \times 3}$	Simplify expression. Cancel $\dfrac{2 \times 3}{2 \times 3}; \dfrac{2 \times 3}{2 \times 3} = 1$	$\dfrac{3}{2 \times 2} = \dfrac{3}{4}$	**Any quantity (except zero) divided by itself is 1, and 1 times any number does not change the value of a number.**

How Do We Know?

PT 3, QUESTIONS

Select the best answer:

1. The greatest common factor of 18 and 9 is:
    A. 18
    B. 3
    C. 6
    D. 9

2. The greatest common factor of $3x^2$ and 6x is:
    F. $3x^2$
    G. 3x
    H. 6x
    J. x

3. The greatest common factor of 18 and 24 is:
    A. 18
    B. 3
    C. 6
    D. 9

Perform the indicated operations:

Expression	Operation	Result	Justification
x^3y^2	Factor expression		Definition of exponent.
12	Factor expression	2×2×3	
36	Factor expression		2 and 3 are prime numbers and are factors of 36.
$\dfrac{12}{36}$	Factor expression		
$\dfrac{2\times2\times3}{2\times2\times3\times3}$	Simplify expression. Cancel $\dfrac{2\times2\times3}{2\times2\times3}$ because $\dfrac{2\times2\times3}{2\times2\times3}=1$		Any quantity (except zero) divided by itself is 1, and 1 times any number does not change the value of a number.

PT 3, ANSWERS

Select the best answer:

1. The greatest common factor of 18 and 9 is:
    A. 18
    B. 3
    C. 6
    D. 9 Note: 9(2) = 18 and 9(1) = 9

2. The greatest common factor of $3x^2$ and $6x$ is:
    F. $3x^2$
    G. 3x Note: 3x(x) = $3x^2$ and 3x(2) = 6x
    H. 6x
    J. x

3. The greatest common factor of 18 and 24 is:
    A. 18
    B. 3
    C. 6 Note: 6(3) = 18, 6(4) = 24
    D. 9

Perform the indicated operations:

Expression	Operation	Result	Justification
x^3y^2	Factor expression	**xxxyy**	Definition of exponent.
12	Factor expression	$2 \times 2 \times 3$	**2 and 3 are prime numbers and are factors of 12.**
36	Factor expression	$2 \times 2 \times 3 \times 3$	2 and 3 are prime numbers and are factors of 36.
$\dfrac{12}{36}$	Factor expression	$\dfrac{2 \times 2 \times 3}{2 \times 2 \times 3 \times 3}$	**Definition of factor.**
$\dfrac{2 \times 2 \times 3}{2 \times 2 \times 3 \times 3}$	Simplify expression. Cancel $\dfrac{2 \times 2 \times 3}{2 \times 2 \times 3}$ because $\dfrac{2 \times 2 \times 3}{2 \times 2 \times 3} = 1$	$\dfrac{1}{3}$	Any quantity (except zero) divided by itself is 1, and 1 times any number does not change the value of a number.

CHAPTER 17

LIKE + TERMS + SMRET + EKIL =

2EIKL + 2EMRST

Overview: To solve equations or simplify expressions, often it is necessary to combine like terms. Most of the time the expression does get simplified so let us find out what like terms are.

Mathematical Learning Objective:

The student will:
> Learn to recognize like terms and practice combining them by using the rules for combining signed numbers.

NCTM Standards:

Algebra
> Understand patterns, relations and functions.

Definitions:

Like	Having the same characteristics; equal.
Like terms	Terms where the variable portions of the expression are alike.
Terms	Each quantity in an algebraic expression.
Coefficient	A multiplier of a variable or unknown quantity; a number written in front of a variable, as 6 in 6x. The numerical portion of an expression.
Equal	Of the same quantity, size, or value.
Variable	A letter or symbol that stands for a number that can be changed; often x, y and z are used to denote a variable, as x in 6x.
Commutative Property of Multiplication	The order of multiplication does not change the product. Example: a(b) =b(a)
Associative Property of Multiplication	In multiplication the way the factors are grouped does not change the product. Example: a(bc) = ab(c)

Often terms that are not alike and cannot be combined can be factored. See Chapter 16, Factoring and Greatest Common Factor.

Questions:

1. Is there a difference between a variable and an unknown quantity?

2. Can you think of a way to determine if complicated terms are actually "like terms"?

3. What assumptions allow us to combine the coefficients of like terms?

RULE FOR COMBINING LIKE TERMS

If the variable portions of the terms are the same, the numerical portions may be added and subtracted, the variable portion stays the same.
> Example: $2x + 3x = 5x$

PRECISION TEACHING (PT) SAMPLE ANSWERS

Remember:

Because of the Commutative and Associative Properties of Multiplication, xyz = zyx = yxz = xzy = yzx = zxy, so in a multiplication the order of the terms does not matter so xyz = zyx = yxz = xzy = yzx = zxy, AND all are like terms. Usually multiple variables are listed in alphabetical order.

Example: bxay = abxy

The definition of an exponent tells us that x^2 means x(x) which is very different from 2x which means
x + x.

Example: If x = 5 evaluate x^2 and 2x
$x^2 = 5^2 = 5(5) = 25$ and 2x = 2(5) = 10

RULE FOR COMBINING LIKE TERMS

If the variable portions of the terms are the same, the numerical portions may be added and subtracted, the variable portion stays the same.

Example: 2x + 3x = 5x

Fill in the following table:

Terms	Like or unlike?	Justification
6qz, 7qz	like	The variable portions of the expression are the same.
$3x^2$, $5x^2$	like	The variable portions of the expression are the same.
3abc, 4ba	unlike	The variable portions of the expression are not the same.
$5zx^2$, $7zx^2$	like	The variable portions of the expression are the same.
$3n^4$, $4n^6$	unlike	The variable portions of the expression are not the same.

Fill in the following table:

Expression	Combined	Justification
6az + 7az	13az	If the variable portions of an expression are the same the numerical terms can be added or subtracted as indicated.
$3x^2 - 2x^2$	x^2	If the variable portions of an expression are the same the numerical terms can be added or subtracted as indicated.
$3ab + 4a^2b$	Cannot be combined	The variable terms are not the same.
$2x^2 + 4x + 5x^2 - 5x$	$7x^2 - x$	If the variable portions of an expression are the same the numerical terms can be added or subtracted as indicated.
3axy + 5axy – 7ax	8axy – 7ax	If the variable portions of an expression are the same the numerical terms can be added or subtracted as indicated.
$15z^3x + 3z^3x$	$18z^3x$	If the variable portions of an expression are the same the numerical terms can be added or subtracted as indicated.

LESSON NOTES

SEE PAGE 329 FOR <u>LIKE TERMS</u>: PRECISION TEACHING (PT) SCORES, FREQUENCY TABLE.

I suggest that students correct their papers, calculate the frequencies and graph their results. Graphing the results on special graph paper (Standard Celeration Chart) can provide visual reinforcement for the students and information about how they are learning. The frequency tables are provided to facilitate this process.

PT 1, QUESTIONS

Remember:

Because of the Commutative and Associative Properties of Multiplication, xyz = zyx = yxz = xzy = yzx = zxy, so in a multiplication the order of the terms does not matter so xyz = zyx = yxz = xzy = yzx = zxy, AND all are like terms. Usually multiple variables are listed in alphabetical order.

The definition of an exponent tells us that x^2 means $x(x)$ which is very different from $2x$ which means $x + x$.

> Example: If $x = 5$ evaluate x^2 and $2x$
> $x^2 = 5^2 = 5(5) = 25$ and $2x = 2(5) = 10$

RULE FOR COMBINING LIKE TERMS

If the variable portions of the terms are the same, the numerical portions may be added and subtracted, the variable portion stays the same.

> Example: $2x + 3x = 5x$

Fill in the following table:

Terms	Like or unlike?	Justification
6rqz, 7qzr		The variable portions of the expression are the same.
$3x^2$, $5x^4$	unlike	
3abc, 4ac		
$5zx^2$, zx^2	like	
$3n^2$, $4x^2$		

Fill in the following table:

Expression	Combined	Justification
6az + 7xz		The variable terms are not the same.
$7n^2 + 8n^2$	$15n^2$	
ab + 4ab		If the variable portions of an expression are the same the numerical terms can be added or subtracted as indicated.
$4x^2 + 4x - 3x^2 - x$	$x^2 + 3x$	
3ay + 5axy – 7ax		The variable terms are not the same.
$15z^2x^3 - 3z^2x^3$	$12z^2x^3$	

PT 1, ANSWERS

Remember:
Because of the Commutative and Associative Properties of Multiplication, xyz = zyx = yxz = xzy = yzx = zxy, so in a multiplication the order of the terms does not matter so xyz = zyx = yxz = xzy = yzx = zxy, AND all are like terms. Usually multiple variables are listed in alphabetical order.

The definition of an exponent tells us that x^2 means $x(x)$ which is very different from $2x$ which means $x + x$.

Example: If $x = 5$ evaluate x^2 and $2x$
$$x^2 = 5^2 = 5(5) = 25 \text{ and } 2x = 2(5) = 10$$

RULE FOR COMBINING LIKE TERMS

If the variable portions of the terms are the same, the numerical portions may be added and subtracted, the variable portion stays the same.

Example: $2x + 3x = 5x$

Fill in the following table:

Terms	Like or unlike?	Justification
$6rqz, 7qzr$	like	The variable portions of the expression are the same.
$3x^2, 5x^4$	unlike	**The variable portions of the expression are not the same.**
$3abc, 4ac$	**unlike**	**The variable portions of the expression are not the same.**
$5zx^2, zx^2$	like	**The variable portions of the expression are the same.**
$3n^2, 4x^2$	**unlike**	**The variable portions of the expression are not the same.**

Fill in the following table:

Expression	Combined	Justification
$6az + 7xz$	**Cannot be combined**	The variable terms are not the same.
$7n^2 + 8n^2$	$15n^2$	**If the variable portions of an expression are the same the numerical terms can be added or subtracted as indicated.**
$ab + 4ab$	**5ab**	If the variable portions of an expression are the same the numerical terms can be added or subtracted as indicated.
$4x^2 + 4x - 3x^2 - x$	$x^2 + 3x$	**If the variable portions of an expression are the same the numerical terms can be added or subtracted as indicated.**
$3ay + 5axy - 7ax$	**Cannot be combined**	The variable terms are not the same.
$15z^2x^3 - 3z^2x^3$	$12z^2x^3$	**If the variable portions of an expression are the same the numerical terms can be added or subtracted as indicated.**

PT 2, QUESTIONS

Remember:

Because of the Commutative and Associative Properties of Multiplication, xyz = zyx = yxz = xzy = yzx = zxy, so in a multiplication the order of the terms does not matter so xyz = zyx = yxz = xzy = yzx = zxy, AND all are like terms. Usually multiple variables are listed in alphabetical order.

The definition of an exponent tells us that x^2 means $x(x)$ which is very different from $2x$ which means $x + x$.

Example: If $x = 5$ evaluate x^2 and $2x$

$x^2 = 5^2 = 5(5) = 25$ and $2x = 2(5) = 10$

RULE FOR COMBINING LIKE TERMS

If the variable portions of the terms are the same, the numerical portions may be added and subtracted, the variable portion stays the same.

Example: $2x + 3x = 5x$

Fill in the following table:

Terms	Like or unlike?	Justification
6az, 7az		The variable portions of the expression are the same.
x^2, x^2		The variable portions of the expression are the same.
3ab, 4ba	like	
$5zx^2$, $5z\,x^6$	unlike	
$3n^4$, $4n^4$		

Fill in the following table:

Expression	Combined	Justification
6azx + 9xaz		If the variable portions of an expression are the same the numerical terms can be added or subtracted as indicated.
$x^2 + x^2$		If the variable portions of an expression are the same the numerical terms can be added or subtracted as indicated.
3ab + 4ba	7ab	
$8x^2 + 11x$		
3axy + 5aqr − 7axy		If the variable portions of an expression are the same the numerical terms can be added or subtracted as indicated.
$15yxz^3 + 3yz^3x$		

PT 2, ANSWERS

Remember:

Because of the Commutative and Associative Properties of Multiplication, xyz = zyx = yxz = xzy = yzx = zxy, so in a multiplication the order of the terms does not matter so xyz = zyx = yxz = xzy = yzx = zxy, AND all are like terms. Usually multiple variables are listed in alphabetical order.

The definition of an exponent tells us that x^2 means x(x) which is very different from 2x which means x + x.

Example: If x = 5 evaluate x^2 and 2x

$x^2 = 5^2 = 5(5) = 25$ and 2x = 2(5) = 10

RULE FOR COMBINING LIKE TERMS

If the variable portions of the terms are the same, the numerical portions may be added and subtracted, the variable portion stays the same.

Example: 2x + 3x = 5x

Fill in the following table:

Terms	Like or unlike?	Justification
6az, 7az	like	The variable portions of the expression are the same.
x^2, x^2	like	The variable portions of the expression are the same.
3ab, 4ba	like	The variable portions of the expression are the same.
$5zx^2$, $5zx^6$	unlike	The variable portions of the expression are not the same.
$3n^4$, $4n^4$	like	The variable portions of the expression are the same.

Fill in the following table:

Expression	Combined	Justification
6azx + 9xaz	15axz	If the variable portions of an expression are the same the numerical terms can be added or subtracted as indicated.
$x^2 + x^2$	$2x^2$	If the variable portions of an expression are the same the numerical terms can be added or subtracted as indicated.
3ab + 4ba	7ab	If the variable portions of an expression are the same the numerical terms can be added or subtracted as indicated.
$8x^2 + 11x$	Cannot be combined	The variable terms are not the same.
3axy + 5aqr – 7axy	5aqr – 4axy	If the variable portions of an expression are the same the numerical terms can be added or subtracted as indicated.
$15yxz^3 + 3yz^3x$	$18xyz^3$	If the variable portions of an expression are the same the numerical terms can be added or subtracted as indicated.

PT 3, QUESTIONS

Remember:

Because of the Commutative and Associative Properties of Multiplication, xyz = zyx = yxz = xzy = yzx = zxy, so in a multiplication the order of the terms does not matter so xyz = zyx = yxz = xzy = yzx = zxy, AND all are like terms. Usually multiple variables are listed in alphabetical order.

The definition of an exponent tells us that x^2 means x(x) which is very different from 2x which means x + x.

     Example: If x = 5 evaluate x^2 and 2x

        $x^2 = 5^2 = 5(5) = 25$ and $2x = 2(5) = 10$

RULE FOR COMBINING LIKE TERMS

If the variable portions of the terms are the same, the numerical portions may be added and subtracted, the variable portion stays the same.

     Example: 2x + 3x = 5x

Fill in the following table:

Terms	Like or unlike?	Justification
6qz, 7qz	like	
$3x^2$, $5x^2$	like	
$3ax^2$, $4x^7$		The variable portions of the expression are not the same.
$5zx^2$, $5z^4x^2$		The variable portions of the expression are not the same.
$3x^2$, $4x^2y^2$		

Fill in the following table:

Expression	Combined	Justification
6azbw + 7bzwa	13abzw	
$3x^2 - 2x^2$	x^2	
3b + 4b		If the variable portions of an expression are the same, the numerical terms can be added or subtracted as indicated.
$7x^2 + 10x + 8x^2 + 5x$		If the variable portions of an expression are the same, the numerical terms can be added or subtracted as indicated.
$3x^2 + 5x^2$		
$3x^2 + 4x^2y^2$		

PT 3, ANSWERS

Remember:
Because of the Commutative and Associative Properties of Multiplication, xyz = zyx = yxz = xzy = yzx = zxy, so in a multiplication the order of the terms does not matter so xyz = zyx = yxz = xzy = yzx = zxy, AND all are like terms. Usually multiple variables are listed in alphabetical order.

The definition of an exponent tells us that x^2 means x(x) which is very different from 2x which means x + x.

Example: If x = 5 evaluate x^2 and 2x
$x^2 = 5^2 = 5(5) = 25$ and $2x = 2(5) = 10$

RULE FOR COMBINING LIKE TERMS

If the variable portions of the terms are the same, the numerical portions may be added and subtracted, the variable portion stays the same.

Example: 2x + 3x = 5x

Fill in the following table:

Terms	Like or unlike?	Justification
6qz, 7qz	like	**The variable portions of the expression are the same.**
$3x^2$, $5x^2$	like	**The variable portions of the expression are the same.**
$3ax^2$, $4x^7$	unlike	The variable portions of the expression are not the same.
$5zx^2$, $5z^4x^2$	unlike	The variable portions of the expression are not the same.
$3x^2$, $4x^2y^2$	unlike	**The variable portions of the expression are not the same.**

Fill in the following table:

Expression	Combined	Justification
6azbw + 7bzwa	13abzw	**If the variable portions of an expression are the same the numerical terms can be added or subtracted as indicated.**
$3x^2 - 2x^2$	x^2	**If the variable portions of an expression are the same, the numerical terms can be added or subtracted as indicated.**
3b + 4b	**7b**	If the variable portions of an expression are the same, the numerical terms can be added or subtracted as indicated.
$7x^2 + 10x + 8x^2 + 5x$	**$15x^2 + 15x$**	If the variable portions of an expression are the same, the numerical terms can be added or subtracted as indicated.
$3x^2 + 5x^2$	$8x^2$	**If the variable portions of an expression are the same, the numerical terms can be added or subtracted as indicated.**
$3x^2 + 4x^2y^2$	Cannot be combined	**The variable terms are not the same.**

CHAPTER 18

SOLVING EQUATIONS

If a = b, then a + c = b + c

If a = b, then a – c = b – c

If a = b, then ac = bc

If a = b and (c ≠ 0), then $\dfrac{a}{c} = \dfrac{b}{c}$

Overview: Often students find the equation solving process a very mysterious magical process. A system is presented where each step in the process of finding a solution is justified. A solution is a value for the variable that makes the equation a true statement.

Mathematical Learning Objective:

The student will:

> Solve simple mathematical equations utilizing a process that stresses the importance of performing the same operation on both sides of the equation.

NCTM Standards

Algebra

> Represent and analyze mathematical situations and structures using algebraic symbols.

Definitions:

Term	Definition	Symbol/comment
Equation	A mathematical sentence stating the equality between two quantities, the sentence may be true or false; contains an = sign.	Contains an =
Expression	Mathematical symbol or symbols that show meaning.	
Solution	Makes an equation a true statement. If an equation contains a variable, a value of the variable that makes the equation true is called a solution.	In the sentence $3x = 6$, $x = 2$ is a solution, it makes the sentence a true statement.
Form of a solution	A mathematical equation is considered solved when the variable is by itself on one side of the equation with a coefficient of +1, and the numbers or symbols that make the equation true on the other.	$+1x =$ solution $x =$ solution Often the +1 is not written.
Variable	A letter or symbol that stands for a number that can be changed or varied.	Sometimes a lower case x or y is used.
Evaluate	To find the value or amount.	
Substitution	Using a number for a variable or using a variable for a number.	
Substitute	To put in place of another.	
Substitution Assumption	We will assume that if quantities are defined as equal, the number system allows us to substitute the symbols and the numbers for the quantities interchangeably.	
Transitive Property of Equality	Things equal to the same thing are equal to each other. If $a = b$ and $b = c$, then $a = c$.	

For now let us call these rules assumptions.

RULES FOR SOLVING EQUATIONS

I. The same quantity can be added to both sides of an equation without changing the truth of the equality.

> Example: If a = b, then a + c = b + c

II. The same quantity can be subtracted from both sides of an equation without changing the truth of the equality.

> Example: If a = b, then a – c = b – c

III. Both sides of an equation can be multiplied by the same quantity without changing the truth of the equality.

> Example: If a = b, then ac = bc

IV. Both sides of an equation can be divided by the same quantity (except zero) without changing the truth of the equality.

> Example: If a = b, and (c ≠ 0), then $\dfrac{a}{c} = \dfrac{b}{c}$

V. (Generalization) The same mathematical operation can be performed on both sides of an equation without changing the truth of the equation.

> Example: Exponential property of equality: Both sides of an equation can be raised to the same power.

> Example: If b = c, then $b^2 = c^2$

Scene: Lunchroom - Lasagna for Lunch

Sunny: This don't look like anything I ever ate before.

Bunny: It does look kind of weird doesn't it?

Sunny: Almost as weird as all these rules they keep making up. Why should we believe any of that stuff?

Bunny: In the experiment, we added and subtracted things on the balance to show the equality.

Sunny: I slept.

Bunny: Our instincts tell us these things are true.

Sunny: My end stinks too, but it doesn't tell me very much. Ha! Ha!

Bunny: You are awful.

Sunny: How do we know these rules are always true?

Bunny: The system is defined that way.

Sunny: They're just making up things and calling them "good"

Bunny: These rules work.

Sunny: That is not enough!!!!

SEE PAGE 330 FOR <u>SOLVING EQUATIONS</u>: PRECISION TEACHING (PT) SCORES, FREQUENCY TABLE.

I suggest that students correct their papers, calculate the frequencies and graph their results. Graphing the results on special graph paper (Standard Celeration Chart) can provide visual reinforcement for the students and information about how they are learning. The frequency tables are provided to facilitate this process.

PRECISION TEACHING (PT) SAMPLE ANSWERS:

Given the equation $\frac{x}{3} = 4$, solve for x

Fill in the following table:

Expression	Operation	Result	Justification
$\frac{x}{3} = 4$			Given
$\frac{x}{3} = 4$	Multiply both sides of the equation by 3.	$\frac{3x}{3} = 3(4)$	Multiplying both sides of an equation by the same quantity does not change the truth of the equation.
$\frac{3x}{3} = 3(4)$	Cancel the $\frac{3}{3}$ because $\frac{3}{3} = 1$	$1x = 3(4)$	Any number (except zero) divided by itself is one.
$1x = 3(4)$	Remove the 1	$x = 3(4)$	Multiplying 1 times a number does not change its value.
$x = 3(4)$	$3(4) = 12$	$x = 12$	Solution for x, variable written by itself on one side of an equation with a coefficient of +1.
$12/3 = 4$	Check solution	$4 = 4$	The value for the variable in original equation gives a true statement.

Given the equation $x - 7 = 11$, solve for x.

Fill in the following table:

Expression	Operation	Result	Justification
$x - 7 = 11$			Given
$x - 7 = 11$	Add +7 to both sides.	$x-7+(+7) = 11+(+7)$	The same quantity can be added to both sides of an equation.
$x - 7 +(+7) = 11+(+7)$	Remove a $-7 +7$ because $-7 +7 = 0$.	$x + 0 = 11 +(+7)$	The sum of a number and it opposite is zero.
$x + 0 = 11 +(+7)$	Remove a zero.	$x = 11 +(+7)$	Adding or subtracting zero does not change a number.
$x = 11 +(+7)$	Combine 11+(+7). 11+(+7) = 18.	$x = 18$	Solution for x, variable written by itself on one side of an equation with a coefficient of +1.
$18 - 7 = 11$	Check solution.	$11 = 11$	The value for the variable in original equation gives a true statement.

PRECISION TEACHING (PT) SAMPLE ANSWERS:

Given the equation $\dfrac{x}{100} = \dfrac{5}{20}$, solve for x.

Fill in the following table:

Expression	Operation	Result	Justification
$\dfrac{x}{100} = \dfrac{5}{20}$			Given
$\dfrac{x}{100} = \dfrac{5}{20}$	Multiply both sides of the equation by 100.	$\dfrac{100x}{100} = \dfrac{5(100)}{20}$	Both sides of an equation can be multiplied by the same quantity.
$\dfrac{100x}{100} = \dfrac{5(100)}{20}$	Cancel $\dfrac{100}{100}$ because $\dfrac{100}{100} = 1$	$1x = \dfrac{5(100)}{20}$	Any number (except zero) divided by itself is 1.
$1x = \dfrac{5(100)}{20}$	Remove the 1.	$x = \dfrac{5(100)}{20}$	Multiplication by one does not change the value of a number.
$x = \dfrac{5(100)}{20}$	$\dfrac{5(100)}{20} = 25$	$x = 25$	Solution for x, variable written on one side of an equation with a coefficient of 1 (understood).
$\dfrac{25}{100} = \dfrac{5}{20}$	Check solution.	$\dfrac{25}{100} = \dfrac{5}{20} = \dfrac{1}{4}$	Value for variable makes the original equation a true statement.

Given the equation $\dfrac{x}{5\,\text{in.}} = \dfrac{2.54\,\text{cm}}{1\,\text{in.}}$, solve for x.

Fill in the following table:

Expression	Operation	Result	Justification
$\dfrac{x}{5\,\text{in.}} = \dfrac{2.54\,\text{cm}}{1\,\text{in.}}$			Given
$\dfrac{x}{5\,\text{in.}} = \dfrac{2.54\,\text{cm}}{1\,\text{in.}}$	Multiply both sides of the equation by 5 in.	$\dfrac{(5\,\text{in.})x}{5\,\text{in.}} = \dfrac{(5\,\text{in.})2.54\,\text{cm}}{1\,\text{in.}}$	Both sides of an equation can be multiplied by the same quantity.
$\dfrac{(5\,\text{in.})x}{5\,\text{in.}} = \dfrac{(5\,\text{in.})2.54\,\text{cm}}{1\,\text{in.}}$	Cancel $\dfrac{5\,\text{in.}}{5\,\text{in.}}$ because $\dfrac{5\,\text{in.}}{5\,\text{in.}} = 1$	$1x = \dfrac{(5\,\text{in.})2.54\,\text{cm}}{1\,\text{in.}}$	Any number (except zero) divided by itself is 1.
$x = \dfrac{(5\,\text{in.})2.54\,\text{cm}}{1\,\text{in.}}$	$x = \dfrac{(5\,\text{in.})2.54\,\text{cm}}{1\,\text{in.}} = 12.7\text{cm}$	$x = 12.7\,\text{cm}$	Solution for x, variable written on one side of an equation with a coefficient of +1.
$\dfrac{12.7\text{cm}}{5\text{in.}} = \dfrac{2.54\text{cm}}{1\,\text{in.}}$	Check solution	$\dfrac{2.54\text{cm}}{1\,\text{in.}} = \dfrac{2.54\text{cm}}{1\,\text{in.}}$	Value for variable makes the original equation a true statement.

PT 1, QUESTIONS

Given the equation x + 5 = 7, solve for x.

Fill in the following table:

Expression	Operation	Result	Justification
x + 5 = 7			
x + 5 = 7	Subtract 5 from both sides.		The same quantity can be subtracted from both sides of an equation.
x + 5 − 5 = 7–5		x + 0 = 7 − 5	
x + 0 = 7 − 5	Remove the 0.		0 can be added to a number without changing the value.
x = 7 − 5		x = 2	
2 + 5 = 7	Check solution		The value for the variable in original equation gives a true statement.

Given the equation $\dfrac{x}{5} = \dfrac{6}{10}$, solve for x.

Fill in the following table:

Expression	Operation	Result	Justification
$\dfrac{x}{5} = \dfrac{6}{10}$			Given
$\dfrac{x}{5} = \dfrac{6}{10}$	Multiply both sides of the equation by 5.		
$\dfrac{5x}{5} = \dfrac{5(6)}{10}$		$1x = \dfrac{5(6)}{10}$	
$1x = \dfrac{5(6)}{10}$	Remove the 1.		Multiplication by one does not change the value of a number.
$x = \dfrac{5(6)}{10}$		x = 3	
$\dfrac{3}{5} = \dfrac{6}{10}$	Check solution		The value for the variable in original equation gives a true statement.

PT 1, ANSWERS

Given the equation $x + 5 = 7$, solve for x.

Fill in the following table:

Expression	Operation	Result	Justification
$x + 5 = 7$			Given
$x + 5 = 7$	Subtract 5 from both sides.	$x + 5 - 5 = 7 - 5$	The same quantity can be subtracted from both sides of an equation.
$x + 5 - 5 = 7 - 5$	$-5 + 5 = 0$	$x + 0 = 7 - 5$	**The sum of a number and its opposite equals zero.**
$x + 0 = 7 - 5$	Remove the 0.	$x = 7 - 5$	0 can be added to a number without changing the value.
$x = 7 - 5$	$7 - 5 = 2$	$x = 2$	**Solution for x, variable written by itself on one side of an equation with a coefficient of 1.**
$2 + 5 = 7$	Check solution	$7 = 7$	The value for the variable in original equation gives a true statement.

Given the equation $\dfrac{x}{5} = \dfrac{6}{10}$, solve for x.

Fill in the following table:

Expression	Operation	Result	Justification
$\dfrac{x}{5} = \dfrac{6}{10}$			Given
$\dfrac{x}{5} = \dfrac{6}{10}$	Multiply both sides of the equation by 5.	$\dfrac{5x}{5} = \dfrac{5(6)}{10}$	**Both sides of an equation can be multiplied by the same quantity.**
$\dfrac{5x}{5} = \dfrac{5(6)}{10}$	Cancel the $\dfrac{5}{5}$ because $\dfrac{5}{5} = 1$	$1x = \dfrac{5(6)}{10}$	**Any number (except zero) divided by itself is 1.**
$1x = \dfrac{5(6)}{10}$	Remove the 1.	$x = \dfrac{5(6)}{10}$	Multiplication by one does not change the value of a number.
$x = \dfrac{5(6)}{10}$	**Perform the multiplication and division indicated.**	$x = 3$	**Solution for x, variable written by itself on one side of an equation with a coefficient of 1.**
$\dfrac{3}{5} = \dfrac{6}{10}$	Check solution	$\dfrac{3}{5} = \dfrac{3}{5}$	The value for the variable in original equation gives a true statement.

PT 2, QUESTIONS

Given x + 3 = 9, solve for x.

Fill in the following table:

Expression	Operation	Result	Justification
x + 3 = 9	████████		
x + 3 = 9		x + 3 +(−3) = 9 + (−3)	
x + 3 +(−3) = 9 + (−3)	+ 3 +(−3) = 0		The sum of a number and its opposite equals zero.
x + 0 = 9 − 3		x = 9 − 3	
x = 9 − 3	9 +(− 3) = 6		Solution for x, variable written by itself on one side of an equation with a coefficient of 1.
6 + 3 = 9		9 = 9	

Given 4x = 20, solve for x.
Fill in the following table:

Expression	Operation	Result	Justification
4 x = 20	████████		Given
4 x = 20		$\dfrac{4x}{4} = \dfrac{20}{4}$	
$\dfrac{4x}{4} = \dfrac{20}{4}$	Cancel $\dfrac{4}{4}$ because $\dfrac{4}{4} = 1$		Any number (except zero) divided by itself is one.
$1x = \dfrac{20}{4}$		$x = \dfrac{20}{4}$	
$x = \dfrac{20}{4}$	$\dfrac{20}{4} = 5$		Solution for x, variable written on one side of an equation with a coefficient of 1.
4(5) = 20		20 = 20	

PT 2, ANSWERS

Given $x + 3 = 9$, solve for x.

Fill in the following table:

Expression	Operation	Result	Justification
$x + 3 = 9$			Given
$x + 3 = 9$	Add a –3 to both sides of the equation.	$x + 3 +(-3) = 9 + (-3)$	The same quantity can be added to both sides of an equation.
$x + 3 +(-3) = 9 + (-3)$	$+ 3 +(-3) = 0$	$x + 0 = 9 - 3$	The sum of a number and its opposite equals zero.
$x + 0 = 9 - 3$	Remove the 0.	$x = 9 - 3$	0 can be added to a number without changing the value.
$x = 9 - 3$	$9 +(- 3) = 6$	$x = 6$	Solution for x, variable written by itself on one side of an equation with a coefficient of 1.
$6 + 3 = 9$	Check solution	$9 = 9$	Value for variable makes the original equation a true statement.

Given $4x = 20$, solve for x.
Fill in the following table:

Expression	Operation	Result	Justification
$4 x = 20$			Given
$4 x = 20$	Divide both sides of the equation by 4.	$\dfrac{4x}{4} = \dfrac{20}{4}$	Both sides of an equation can be divided by the same quantity without changing the truth of the equality.
$\dfrac{4x}{4} = \dfrac{20}{4}$	Cancel $\dfrac{4}{4}$ because $\dfrac{4}{4} = 1$	$1x = \dfrac{20}{4}$	Any number (except zero) divided by itself is one.
$1x = \dfrac{20}{4}$	Remove the 1. $1x = x$	$x = \dfrac{20}{4}$	Multiplying a number by one does not change the value of a number.
$x = \dfrac{20}{4}$	$\dfrac{20}{4} = 5$	$x = 5$	Solution for x, variable written on one side of an equation with a coefficient of 1.
$4(5) = 20$	Check solution	$20 = 20$	Value for variable makes the original equation a true statement.

PT 3, QUESTIONS

Given the equation $\dfrac{x}{6} = 4$, solve for x.

Fill in the following table:

Expression	Operation	Result	Justification
$\dfrac{x}{6} = 4$			Given
$\dfrac{x}{6} = 4$		$6\left(\dfrac{x}{6}\right) = 6(4)$	
$6\left(\dfrac{x}{6}\right) = 6(4)$	Cancel $\dfrac{6}{6}$ because $\dfrac{6}{6} = 1$		
$1x = 6(4)$		$x = (6)4$	
$x = (6)4$		$x = 24$	
$\dfrac{24}{6} = 4$			Value for variable makes the original equation a true statement.

Given the equation $x - 7 = 3$, solve for x.

Fill in the following table:

Expression	Operation	Result	Justification
$x - 7 = 3$			
$x - 7 = 3$		$x - 7 + (+7) = 3 + (+7)$	
$x - 7 + (+7) = 3 + (+7)$		$x + 0 = 3 + (+7)$	The sum of a number and it opposite is zero.
$x + 0 = 3 + (+7)$	Remove a zero.		
$x = 3 + (+7)$	Combine $3 + (+7)$. $3 + (+7) = 10$		Solution for x, variable written on one side of an equation with a coefficient of 1.
$10 - 7 = 3$		$3 = 3$	

PT 3, ANSWERS

Given the equation $\dfrac{x}{6} = 4$, solve for x.

Fill in the following table:

Expression	Operation	Result	Justification
$\dfrac{x}{6} = 4$			Given
$\dfrac{x}{6} = 4$	Multiply both sides of the equation by 6.	$6\left(\dfrac{x}{6}\right) = 6(4)$	Multiplying both sides of an equation by the same quantity does not change the truth of the equation.
$6\left(\dfrac{x}{6}\right) = 6(4)$	Cancel $\dfrac{6}{6}$ because $\dfrac{6}{6} = 1$	**1x = 6(4)**	Any number (except zero) divided by itself is 1.
1x = 6X4	**Remove the 1.**	x= (6)4	Multiplication by one does not change the value of a number.
x = (6)4	**(6)4 = 24**	x = 24	Solution for x, variable written on one side of an equation with a coefficient of 1.
$\dfrac{24}{6} = 4$	**Check solution**	**4 = 4**	Value for variable makes the equation a true statement.

Given the equation x – 7 = 3, solve for x.
Fill in the following table:

Expression	Operation	Result	Justification
x – 7 = 3			Given
x – 7 = 3	Add 7 to both sides.	x – 7 +(+7) = 3 +(+7)	The same quantity can be added to both sides of an equation without changing the truth of the equality.
x – 7 +(+7) = 3 +(+7)	Remove a –7 + 7 because –7 +7 = 0.	x + 0 = 3 +(+7)	The sum of a number and it opposite is zero.
x + 0 = 3 +(+7)	Remove a zero.	**x = 3 +(+7)**	Adding or subtracting zero does not change a number.
x = 3 +(+7)	Combine 3+(+7). 3+(+7) = 10	**x = 10**	Solution for x, variable written on one side of an equation with a coefficient of 1.
10 – 7 = 3	**Check solution**	3 = 3	Value for variable makes the equation a true statement.

CHAPTER 19

VRAL
AIBE

Overview: The purpose of these exercises is to acknowledge that describing the concept of variable is more complicated than merely stating, "a variable is a letter or symbol which stands for a number".

Mathematical Learning Objective:	The student will: Evaluate mathematical expressions containing variables to develop an understanding of variables.
NCTM Standards:	Algebra Understand relations and functions and select, convert flexibly among, and use various representations for them.

Some of the words that <u>Roget's Thesaurus</u> associates with variable are:
Inconsistency, instability, vacillation, indecision, alternation, changing, kaleidoscopic, erratic, fickle, mercurial, capricious, shake, shuffle, shift, wayward, transient.

All of those words, and no mention of <u>unknown</u>?

Some of the words <u>Redfield's Rhyming Dictionary</u> rhymes with variable are:
Air-castle, astraddle, baffle, bamboozle, bungle, dingle, embezzle, foible, foozle, frazzle, haggle, jungle, meddle, new-fangle, octuple, ogle, oodle, piffle, quintuple, razzle-dazzle, septuple, scuffle, shuffle, startle, stubble, subtle, tipple, toddle, tousle, tussle, trouble, tweeble and not to be forgotten, waffle and waggle.

Student activity: Just for fun, construct a poem using the form*:

POEM

What you are describing
analogy
analogy
analogy
one word

Example:

Variable
Subtle shuffle
Like a fickle new-fangle
Transient trouble
Unknown

*This is patterned along the lines of the Loupe Poem suggested in **The Private Eye - (5X) Looking/ Thinking by Analogy,** The Private Eye Project.

Often an expression is not an equation. If words like "evaluate when" give a value for the variable, substitute the value for the variable, evaluate the expression, add an equal sign and the value for the expression.

Evaluating an expression when a value for the variable is given:
>   Example: Evaluate 3x when x = 2,
$$3(2) = 6$$

RULES FOR SOLVING EQUATIONS

I. The same quantity can be added to both sides of an equation without changing the truth of the equality.
>   Example: If a = b, then a + c = b + c

II. The same quantity can be subtracted from both sides of an equation without changing the truth of the equality.
>   Example: If a = b, then a – c = b – c

III. Both sides of an equation can be multiplied by the same quantity without changing the truth of the equality.
>   Example: If a = b, then ac = bc

IV. Both sides of an equation can be divided by the same quantity (except zero) without changing the truth of the equality.
>   Example: If a = b, and (c ≠ 0), then $\dfrac{a}{c} = \dfrac{b}{c}$

V. (Generalization) The same mathematical operation can be performed on both sides of an equation without changing the truth of the equation.

Substitution assumption: When a number and a variable are defined as equal they may be substituted for each other.

Scene: Sunny and Bunny in Math Class - Working Together on a Cooperative Learning Worksheet

Sunny (slouched in his chair):
>Is this a Variable I see before me,
>The coefficient toward my hand?
>Come, let me clutch thee,

Bunny: You have been reading too much Shakespeare.

Sunny: I have thee not, and yet I see thee still.

Bunny: Variables are easy to understand.

Sunny:
>Art thou not, fatal Variable, sensible
>To feeling as to sight? Or art thou but
>A Variable of the mind, a false creation,
>Proceeding from the heat oppressed brain?

Bunny (hushed):
>Shut up! Here comes the teacher.

Sunny: (Sunny sits up straight)

(Teacher looking over Sunny's shoulder)
Sunny: Why do we need both x's and y's?

Bunny: An expression often states a relationship between x and y. They can each stand for different numbers.

Teacher: Very good Bunny. Here are some new pencils.
(Exit Teacher)

Sunny (slouched back in his chair.):
>And on the paper gouts of bloody x's and y's
>Which was not so before. There is no such thing.

Bunny: You are crazy!

Sunny: 'Tis a tale, told by an idiot, full of sound and fury
>Signifying nothing.

* With apologies to Shakespeare and Macbeth.

Often an expression is not an equation. If words like "evaluate when" give a value for the variable, substitute the value for the variable, evaluate the expression, add an equal sign and the value for the expression.

Evaluating an expression when a value for the variable is given:
        Example: Evaluate 3x when x = 2,
$$3(2) = 6$$

PRECISION TEACHING (PT) SAMPLE ANSWERS
Evaluate 4x + 1 when x = 3.
Fill in the following table:

Expression	Operation	Result	Justification
4x + 1			Given
x = 3			Given
4x + 1	Substitute 3 for x.	4(3) + 1	Substitution assumption.
4(3) + 1	Multiply 4X3.	12 + 1	Multiplication property of real numbers
12 + 1	Add 12 and 1.	13	Addition properties of real numbers.
4x + 1 = 13 when x = 3	Evaluation of 4x + 1 when x = 3.	13	Definition of evaluate.

A solution is a value for a variable that makes the statement true.
If x + 5 = 7, then find a solution for x.
Fill in the following table:

Expression	Operation	Result	Justification
x + 5 = 7			Given
x + 5 = 7	Subtract 5 from both sides of the equation.	x + 5 – 5 = 7 – 5	The same quantity can be added to both sides of an equation.
x + 5 – 5 = 7 – 5	– 5 + 5 = 0	x + 0 = 7 – 5	The sum of a number and its opposite equals zero.
x + 0 = 7 – 5	Remove 0.	x = 7 – 5	0 can be added to or subtracted from a number without changing the value.
x = 7 – 5	7 – 5 = 2	x = 2	Properties of real numbers.
x = 2	Solution for x + 5 = 7	x = 2	Solution for x, variable written by itself on one side of an equation with a coefficient of +1.
x + 5 = 7	Check solution, substitute 2 for x.	2 + 5 = 7	When a number and a variable are defined as equal they may be substituted for each other.
2 + 5 = 7	Add 2 and 5.	7 = 7	The value for the variable makes the equation a true statement.

LESSON NOTES

SEE PAGE 330 FOR <u>VARIABLE</u>: PRECISION TEACHING (PT) SCORES, FREQUENCY TABLE.

I suggest that students correct their papers, calculate the frequencies and graph their results. Graphing the results on special graph paper (Standard Celeration Chart) can provide visual reinforcement for the students and information about how they are learning. The frequency tables are provided to facilitate this process.

PT 1, QUESTIONS

Substitution assumption: When a number and a variable are defined as equal they may be substituted for each other.

Often an expression is not an equation. If words like "evaluate when" give a value for the variable, substitute the value for the variable, evaluate the expression, add an equal sign and the value for the expression.

Evaluate $3x + 1$ when $x = 2$.
Fill in the following table:

Expression	Operation	Result	Justification
$3x + 1$			
$x = 2$			Given
$3x + 1$		$3(2) + 1$	
$3(2) + 1$		$6 + 1$	
$6 + 1$	Add 6 and 1.		Properties of real numbers.
$3(2) + 1 = 7$	Evaluation of $3x + 1$ when $x = 2$.	7	Definition of evaluate.

A solution is a value for a variable that makes an equation a true statement.
If $x - 5 = 7$, then find a solution for x.
Fill in the following table:

Expression	Operation	Result	Justification
$x - 5 = 7$			Given
$x - 5 = 7$		$x - 5 + 5 = 7 + 5$	
$x - 5 + 5 = 7 + 5$	$-5 + 5 = 0$		
$x + 0 = 7 + 5$		$x = 7 + 5$	
$x = 7 + 5$	Add 7 and 5.		Addition property of real numbers.
$x = 12$	Solution for $x = 7 + 5$.	$x = 12$	
$x - 5 = 7$	Check solution, Substitute 12 for x.		A quantity can be substituted for a variable.
$12 - 5 = 7$	Subtract 5 from 12.	$7 = 7$	The value for the variable makes the equation a true statement.

PT 1, ANSWERS

Substitution assumption: When a number and a variable are defined as equal they may be substituted for each other.

Often an expression is not an equation. If words like "evaluate when" give a value for the variable, substitute the value for the variable, evaluate the expression, add an equal sign and the value for the expression.

Evaluate 3x + 1 when x = 2.

Fill in the following table:

Expression	Operation	Result	Justification
3x + 1			Given
x = 2			Given
3x + 1	**Substitute 2 for x.**	3(2) + 1	**A number can be substituted for a variable.**
3(2) + 1	**Multiply 3 times 2.**	6 + 1	**Multiplication property of real numbers.**
6 + 1	Add 6 and 1.	**6 + 1 = 7**	Properties of real numbers.
3(2) + 1 = 7	Evaluation of 3x + 1 when x = 2.	7	Definition of evaluate.

A solution is a value for a variable that makes an equation a true statement.

If x – 5 = 7, then find a solution for x.

Fill in the following table:

Expression	Operation	Result	Justification
x – 5 = 7			Given
x – 5 = 7	**Add 5 to both sides of the equation.**	x – 5 +5 = 7+5	**The same quantity can be added to both sides of an equation.**
x – 5 +5 = 7 + 5	–5 + 5 = 0	**x + 0 = 7 + 5**	**The sum of a number and its opposite equals zero.**
x + 0 = 7 + 5	**Remove 0.**	x = 7 + 5	**0 can be added to or subtracted from a number without changing the value.**
x = 7 + 5	Add 7 and 5.	**x = 12**	Addition property of real numbers.
x = 12	Solution for x = 7 + 5.	x = 12	**Solution for x, variable written by itself on one side of an equation with a coefficient of +1.**
x – 5 = 7	Check solution, substitute 12 for x.	**12 – 5 = 7**	A quantity can be substituted for a variable.
12 – 5 = 7	Subtract 5 from 12.	7 = 7	The value for the variable makes the equation a true statement.

PT 2, QUESTIONS

Substitution assumption: When a number and a variable are defined as equal they may be substituted for each other.

Often an expression is not an equation. If words like "evaluate when" give a value for the variable, substitute the value for the variable, evaluate the expression, add an equal sign and the value for the expression.

Evaluate $4x - 12$ when $x = 2$.
Fill in the following table:

Expression	Operation	Result	Justification
$4x - 12$			Given
$x = 2$			
$4x - 12$	Substitute 2 for x.		When a number and a variable are defined as equal they may be substituted for each other.
$4(2) - 12$		$8 - 12$	
$8 - 12$	Combine 8 and –12.		To combine numbers with different signs, find the difference between the absolute values and give the answer the sign of the number that has the largest absolute value.
$8+(-12) = -4$ when $x = 2$	Evaluation of $4x + 1$ when $x = 2$	$8+(-12) = -4$	Definition of evaluate.

A solution is a value for a variable that makes an equation a true statement.
If $3x = 12$, then find a solution for x.
Fill in the following table:

Expression	Operation	Result	Justification
$3x = 12$			Given
$3x = 12$		$\dfrac{3x}{3} = \dfrac{12}{3}$	Both sides of an equation can be divided by the same quantity and not change the truth of the equality.
$\dfrac{3x}{3} = \dfrac{12}{3}$	Cancel $\dfrac{3}{3}$ because $\dfrac{3}{3} = 1$		
$x = \dfrac{12}{3}$		$x = 4$	
$x = 4$	Solution for $3x = 12$		
$3x = 12$	Check solution, substitute 4 for x.		When a number and a variable are defined as equal they may be substituted for each other.
$3(4) = 12$	Multiply 3X4.	$12 = 12$	

PT 2, ANSWERS

Substitution assumption: When a number and a variable are defined as equal they may be substituted for each other.

Often an expression is not an equation. If words like "evaluate when" give a value for the variable, substitute the value for the variable, evaluate the expression, add an equal sign and the value for the expression.

Evaluate $4x - 12$ when $x = 2$.
Fill in the following table:

Expression	Operation	Result	Justification
$4x - 12$			Given
$x = 2$			**Given**
$4x - 12$	Substitute 2 for x.	**4(2) – 12**	When a number and a variable are defined as equal they may be substituted for each other.
$4(2) -12$	**Multiply 4 times 2.**	$8 - 12$	**Multiplication property of real numbers.**
$8 - 12$	Combine 8 and –12.	**8+(–12) = –4**	To combine numbers with different signs, find the difference between the absolute values and give the answer the sign of the number that has the largest absolute value.
$8+(-12) = -4$ when $x = 2$	Evaluation of $4x + 12$ when $x = 2$.	$8+(-12) = -4$	Definition of evaluate.

A solution is a value for a variable that makes an equation a true statement.
If $3x = 12$, then find a solution for x.
Fill in the following table:

Expression	Operation	Result	Justification
$3x = 12$			Given
$3x = 12$	**Divide both sides of the equation by 3.**	$\frac{3x}{3} = \frac{12}{3}$	Both sides of an equation can be divided by the same quantity and not change the truth of the equality.
$\frac{3x}{3} = \frac{12}{3}$	Cancel $\frac{3}{3}$ because $\frac{3}{3} = 1$.	$1x = \frac{12}{3}$	**Any number (except zero) divided by itself is 1.**
$x = \frac{12}{3}$	**Divide 12 by 3.**	$x = 4$	**Division properties of real numbers.**
$x = 4$	Solution for $3x = 12$	**x = 4**	Solution for x, variable written by itself on one side of an equation with a coefficient of +1.
$3x = 12$	Check solution, substitute 4 for x.	**3(4) = 12**	When a number and a variable are defined as equal they may be substituted for each other.
$3(4) = 12$	Multiply 3X4.	$12 = 12$	**The value for the variable makes the equation a true statement.**

PT 3, QUESTIONS

Substitution assumption: When a number and a variable are defined as equal they may be substituted for each other.

Often an expression is not an equation. If words like "evaluate when" give a value for the variable, substitute the value for the variable, evaluate the expression, add an equal sign and the value for the expression.

Evaluate $7x - 3$ when $x = 2$.
Fill in the following table:

Expression	Operation	Result	Justification
$7x - 3$			Given
$x = 2$			
$7x - 3$		$7(2) - 3$	When a number and a variable are defined as equal they may be substituted for each other.
$7(2) - 3$	Multiply 7 times 2.		Multiplication property of real numbers.
$14 - 3$		11	
$7(2) - 3 = 11$	Evaluation of $3x + 1$ when $x = 2$.	$7(2) - 3 = 11$	Definition of evaluate.

A solution is a value for a variable that makes an equation a true statement.

$$\text{If } \frac{x}{100} = \frac{15}{20} \text{ then find a solution for x.}$$

Fill in the following table:

Expression	Operation	Result	Justification
$\dfrac{x}{100} = \dfrac{15}{20}$			Given
$\dfrac{x}{100} = \dfrac{15}{20}$		$\dfrac{100x}{100} = \dfrac{15(100)}{20}$	Both sides of an equation can be multiplied by the same quantity.
$\dfrac{100x}{100} = \dfrac{15(100)}{20}$	Cancel the $\dfrac{100}{100}$ because $\dfrac{100}{100} = 1$		Any number (except zero) divided by itself is 1.
$1x = \dfrac{15(100)}{20}$		$x = \dfrac{15(100)}{20}$	
$x = \dfrac{15(100)}{20}$	Perform the multiplication and division indicated.		
$\dfrac{75}{100} = \dfrac{15}{20}$	Check solution.	$\dfrac{75}{100} = \dfrac{15}{20} = \dfrac{3}{4}$	Value for variable makes the equation a true statement.

PT 3, ANSWERS

Substitution assumption: When a number and a variable are defined as equal they may be substituted for each other.

Often an expression is not an equation. If words like "evaluate when" give a value for the variable, substitute the value for the variable, evaluate the expression, add an equal sign and the value for the expression.

Evaluate $7x - 3$ when $x = 2$.
Fill in the following table:

Expression	Operation	Result	Justification
$7x - 3$			Given
$x = 2$			**Given**
$7x - 3$	**Substitute 2 for x.**	$7(2) - 3$	When a number and a variable are defined as equal they may be substituted for each other.
$7(2) - 3$	Multiply 7 times 2.	**14 – 3**	Multiplication property of real numbers.
$14 - 3$	**Combine 14 and –3.**	11	**To combine numbers with different signs, find the difference between the absolute values and give the answer the sign of the number that has the largest absolute value.**
$7(2) - 3 = 11$	Evaluation of $3x + 1$ when $x = 2$.	$7(2) - 3 = 11$	Definition of evaluate.

A solution is a value for a variable that makes an equation a true statement.

$$\text{If } \frac{x}{100} = \frac{15}{20} \text{ then find a solution for x.}$$

Fill in the following table:

Expression	Operation	Result	Justification
$\dfrac{x}{100} = \dfrac{15}{20}$			Given
$\dfrac{x}{100} = \dfrac{15}{20}$	**Multiply both sides of the equation by 100.**	$\dfrac{100x}{100} = \dfrac{15(100)}{20}$	Both sides of an equation can be multiplied by the same quantity.
$\dfrac{100x}{100} = \dfrac{15(100)}{20}$	Cancel the $\dfrac{100}{100}$ because $\dfrac{100}{100} = 1$	$1x = \dfrac{\mathbf{15(100)}}{\mathbf{20}}$	Any number (except zero) divided by itself is 1.
$1x = \dfrac{15(100)}{20}$	**Remove the 1.**	$x = \dfrac{15(100)}{20}$	**Multiplication by one does not change the value of a number.**
$x = \dfrac{15(100)}{20}$	Perform the multiplication and division indicated.	$x = 75$	**Multiplication and division properties of real numbers.**
$\dfrac{75}{100} = \dfrac{15}{20}$	Check solution.	$\dfrac{75}{100} = \dfrac{15}{20} = \dfrac{3}{4}$	Value for variable makes the equation a true statement.

CHAPTER 20

RATIONALE FOR SOLVING EQUATIONS

$$(5)\frac{1}{5}=\frac{5}{5}=1 \qquad\qquad \left(\frac{1}{5}\right)5=\frac{5}{5}=1$$

$$(5)\frac{x}{5}=\frac{5x}{5}=x \qquad\qquad \left(\frac{1}{5}\right)5x=\frac{5x}{5}=x$$

$$\sqrt{x^2} = x$$

$$+5-5=0 \qquad\qquad -5+5=0$$

$$x+5-5=x \qquad\qquad x-5+5=x$$

Overview: The form of a solution will be defined as the desired variable written on one side of an equation with a coefficient of + 1 and the number or numbers, or other variables that make the mathematical sentence a true statement on the other side of the equal sign. This definition will be utilized to make numbers or other variables surrounding the desired variable disappear. Coefficients and divisors will be transformed into ones and numbers added to or subtracted from the variable in question will be made to disappear by creating zeroes.

**Mathematical
Learning Objective:**   The student will:

Solve simple linear equations by using inverse operations and verify their solutions by substituting their answers in the original equation.

NCTM Standards: Algebra

Represent and analyze mathematical situations and structures using algebraic symbols.

Definitions:

Word	Meaning	Example
Inverse	To turn upside down; to reverse the order. This inverse is often thought of as a reciprocal.	The multiplicative inverse of x is $\frac{1}{x}$.
Reciprocal	The quantity resulting from the division of 1 by the given quantity; multiplicative inverse.	The reciprocal of 7 is $\frac{1}{7}$.
Multiplicative inverse	The number that gives a product of one when multiplied times another number.	$\frac{1}{xy}(xy) = 1,$
Inverse of multiplication	Division; a process of undoing multiplication.	$5x(\frac{1}{5}) = x$
Inverse of division	Multiplication; a process of undoing division.	$5(\frac{x}{5}) = x$
Inverse of addition	Subtraction; often used to remove numbers when solving equations.	$+5 - 5 = 0$
Inverse of subtraction	Addition; often used to remove numbers when solving equations.	$-5 + 5 = 0$
Inverse of exponentiation	Taking a root.	$\sqrt{x^2} = x$
Solution	If a mathematical equation contains a variable, a value for the variable that makes the sentence true is called a solution. Sometimes the word root is used for solution. Example: In the equation $3x = 6$, $x = 2$ is a solution, it makes the equation a true statement. $3(2) = 6$	
Form of a solution	An equation is considered solved when the variable is by itself on one side of the equation with a coefficient of +1, and the numbers or symbols that make the equation true on the other.	$+1x$ = solution x = solution Often the +1 is not written.)

How Do We Know?

Our goal in solving equations will be to remove the "stuff" around the variable to obtain the variable on one side of the equation all by itself. In general the solving process is the normal order of operations (PEMDAS) executed in reverse order. Addition and subtraction are cleared first, multiplication or division cleared next and dealing with exponents last. While the generalization that the same mathematical operation can be performed on both sides of an equation is valid, attempting to multiply and divide first can lead to messy fractions, and finding a root before simplification can lead to some very challenging things called radicals.

Remember:
I.   Multiplying a number by 1 does not change the number.
   Example: $1 \cdot 5 = 5$

II. Dividing any number by 1 does not change the number.
   Example: $\dfrac{16}{1} = 16$

III. Any number (except zero) divided by itself is 1.
   Example: $\dfrac{5}{5} = 1$

IV. Any quantity (except zero) divided by itself is 1.
   Example: $\dfrac{1 \text{ second}}{1 \text{ second}} = 1, \quad \dfrac{1 \text{ meter}}{1 \text{ meter}} = 1, \quad \dfrac{1 \text{ yard}}{3 \text{ feet}} = 1$

V.   The product of a number and its reciprocal is one.
   Example: $6 \cdot \dfrac{1}{6} = \dfrac{6}{6} = 1$ and $10 \cdot \dfrac{1}{10} = \dfrac{10}{10} = 1$

VI. Zero added to, or subtracted from a number does not change the number.
   Example: $3 + 0 = 3, \qquad 2 - 0 = 2$

VII. The sum of a number and its additive inverse is zero.
   Example: $5 + (-5) = 0$

And do not forget:
I.   **Substitution assumption:** When a number and a variable are defined as equal they may be substituted for each other.

II. **Additive property of equality:** The same quantity can be added to both sides of an equation.

III. **Subtractive property of equality:** The same quantity can be subtracted from both sides of an equation.

IV. **Multiplicative property of equality:** The same quantity can be multiplied times both sides of an equation.

V.   **Division property of equality:** The same quantity (except zero) can be divided into both sides of an equation.

VI. **Exponential property of equality:** Both sides of an equation can be raised to the same power.

VII. **Transitive property of equality:** Things equal to the same thing are equal to each other.

Inverse of Multiplication:
A solution for an equation is a value for the variable that makes the equation a true statement.
Let us consider the equation: $3x = 12$.

To obtain a solution for x, the multiplication by 3 needs to be undone. We have defined division as the inverse of multiplication, and the division property of equality allows us to divide both sides of the equation by 3.

$$3x = 12$$

$$\frac{3x}{3} = \frac{12}{3}$$

$$x = 4$$

Since the fraction bar means division, $\frac{3}{3} = 1$, we have changed the coefficient of x to +1, and +1 times any number does not change the value of the number. If the statement x = 4 defines a value for x that makes the original equation true, then 4 is a solution or root.

Checking the solution:

$$3x = 12$$

$$3(4) = 12$$

$$12 = 12 \text{ is a true statement}$$

$$x = 4 \text{ is a solution}$$

Inverse of Division:

A solution for an equation is a value for the variable that makes the equation a true statement.

Let us consider the equation:

$$\frac{x}{4} = 5$$

To obtain a solution for x, the division by 4 needs to be undone. We have defined multiplication as the inverse of division, and the multiplication property of equality allows us to multiply both sides of the equation by 4.

$$(4)\frac{x}{4} = (4)5$$

$$x = 20$$

Since the fraction bar means division, $\frac{4}{4} = 1$, we have changed the coefficient of x to +1, and +1 times any number does not change the value of the number. If the statement x = 20 defines a value for x that makes the original equation true, then 20 is a solution or root.

Checking the solution:

$$\frac{x}{4} = 5$$

$$\frac{(20)}{4} = 5$$

$$5 = 5 \text{ is a true statement}$$

$$x = 20 \text{ is a solution}$$

Inverse of Subtraction:

A solution for an equation is a value for the variable that makes the equation a true statement.

Let us consider the equation: $x - 6 = 5$

To obtain a solution for x, the subtraction of 6 needs to be undone. We have defined addition as the inverse of subtraction, so we add 6 to both sides of the equation.

$$x-6=5$$
$$x-6+6=5+6$$
$$x=11$$

Notice that since $-6+6=0$ we can remove it from the left side of the equation. Since $5+6=11$ we can replace $5+6$ with 11. If the statement $x=11$ defines a value for x that makes the original equation true, then 11 is a solution or root.

$$x-6=5$$

Checking the solution:
$$(11)-6=5$$
$$5=5 \text{ is a true statement}$$
$$x=11 \text{ is a solution}$$

Inverse of Addition:

A solution for an equation is a value for the variable that makes the equation a true statement.

Let us consider the equation: $x + 3 = 7$

To obtain a solution for x, the addition of 3 needs to be undone. We have defined subtraction as the inverse of addition, so we subtract 3 from both sides of the equation

$$x+3=7$$
$$x+3-3=7-3$$
$$x=4$$

Notice that since $+3-3=0$ we can remove it from the left side of the equation. Since $7-3=4$ we can replace $7-3$ with 4. If the statement $x=4$ defines a value for x that makes the original equation true, then 4 is a solution or root.

$$x+3=7$$

Checking the solution:
$$(4)+3=7$$
$$7=7 \text{ is a true statement}$$
$$x=4 \text{ is a solution}$$

Hopefully we understand now that a solution is a variable written on one side of the equation all by itself with numbers or variables on the other side. A solution can be obtained by performing inverse operations on the equation. Checking a solution by substituting it back into the original equation is very important.

I find it easier to use a table format to explain the solution process for more complex equations.

Consider a typical linear equation containing both x and y. Remember, a solution for the variable y will be y written on one side of the equation with a coefficient of +1, and everything else on the other side of the equation.

Given the equation $6x - 3y = 18$, solve for y.

Expression	Operation/reason	Result	Justification
$6x - 3y = 18$			Given
$6x - 3y = 18$	Subtract 6x from both sides; performing the inverse of addition to get the y term by itself on one side of the equation.	$+6x - 6x - 3y = -6x + 18$	The same quantity can be subtracted from both sides of an equation without changing the truth of the equality.
$+6x - 6x - 3y = -6x + 18$	Perform indicated addition and subtraction, and $+6x - 6x = 0$	$-3y = -6x + 18$	Properties of real numbers.
$-3y = -6x + 18$	Divide both sides by -3, perform the inverse of multiplication.	$\dfrac{-3y}{-3} = \dfrac{-6x}{-3} + \dfrac{18}{-3}$	Both sides of an equation can be divided by the same quantity (except zero) without changing the truth of the equality.
$\dfrac{-3y}{-3} = \dfrac{-6x}{-3} + \dfrac{18}{-3}$	$\dfrac{-3y}{-3} = y, \dfrac{-6x}{-3} = 2x, \dfrac{18}{-3} = -6$ (Perform indicated operations)	$y = 2x - 6$	Properties of real numbers. This is a solution for y, the variable is written by itself on one side of an equation with a coefficient of +1.

The above verifies the more general approach of removing the "stuff" around the variable to obtain the variable on one side of the equation all by itself. In general, the normal order of operations (PEMDAS) is performed in reverse order during the solving process. Addition and subtraction are cleared first, multiplication or division second and dealing with exponents last. While the generalization that the same mathematical operation can be performed on both sides of an equation is valid, attempting to multiply and divide first can lead to messy fractions, and finding a root before simplification can lead to some very challenging things called radicals.

LESSON NOTES

SEE PAGE 330 FOR <u>RATIONALE FOR SOLVING EQUATIONS</u>: PRECISION TEACHING (PT) SCORES, FREQUENCY TABLE.

I suggest that students correct their papers, calculate the frequencies and graph their results. Graphing the results on special graph paper (Standard Celeration Chart) can provide visual reinforcement for the students and information about how they are learning. The frequency tables are provided to facilitate this process.

PRECISION TEACHING (PT) SAMPLE ANSWERS

Given the equation $3x = 12$, solve for x.
Fill in the following table:

Expression	Operation/reason	Result	Justification
$3x = 12$	■■■■■■■		Given
$3x = 12$	Divide both sides by 3, performing the inverse of multiplication.	$\dfrac{3x}{3} = \dfrac{12}{3}$	Both sides of an equation can be divided by the same quantity (except zero) without changing the truth of the equality.
$\dfrac{3x}{3} = \dfrac{12}{3}$	Cancel the $\dfrac{3}{3}$ because $\dfrac{3}{3} = 1$	$1x = \dfrac{12}{3}$	Any number divided by itself is one.
$1x = \dfrac{12}{3}$	Remove the 1.	$x = \dfrac{12}{3}$	Multiplying 1 times a number does not change its value.
$x = \dfrac{12}{3}$	Perform the indicated division.	$x = 4$	Solution for x, variable written by itself on one side of an equation with a coefficient of +1.
$3(4) = 12$	Check solution.	$12 = 12$	The value for the variable gives a true statement.

Given the equation $x - 2y = 12$, solve for y.
Fill in the following table:

Expression	Operation/reason	Result	Justification
$x - 2y = 12$	■■■■■■■		Given
$x - 2y = 12$	Subtract x from both sides of the equation, performing the inverse of addition to get the y term by itself on one side of the equation.	$-x + x - 2y = -x + 12$	The same quantity can be subtracted from both sides of an equation without changing the truth of the equality.
$-x + x - 2y = -x + 12$	Combine $-x$ and $+x$. $-x + x = 0$.	$0 - 2y = -x + 12$	The sum of a number and its opposite is zero.
$-2y = -x + 12$	Divide both sides of the equation by -2, performing the inverse of multiplication.	$\dfrac{-2y}{-2} = \dfrac{-x}{-2} + \dfrac{12}{-2}$	Both sides of an equation can be divided by the same quantity and not change the truth of the equality.
$\dfrac{-2y}{-2} = \dfrac{-x}{-2} + \dfrac{12}{-2}$	$\dfrac{-2}{-2} = 1$, $\dfrac{-x}{-2} = \dfrac{1}{2}x$, $\dfrac{12}{-2} = -6$ (Perform indicated operations)	$y = 1/2x - 6$	Properties of real numbers. Solution for y; variable written by itself on one side of an equation with a coefficient of +1.

PT 1, QUESTIONS

Given the equation $v = \dfrac{d}{t}$, solve for d.

Fill in the following table:

Equation	Operation/reason	Result	Justification
$v = \dfrac{d}{t}$	███████████████	███████████████	
$v = \dfrac{d}{t}$	Multiply both sides by t, performing the inverse of division.		Both sides of an equation can be multiplied by the same quantity without changing the truth of the equality.
$tv = \dfrac{td}{t}$	Cancel the $\dfrac{t}{t}$ because $\dfrac{t}{t} = 1$.		
$tv = d$	Solve $v = \dfrac{d}{t}$ for d.	Solution for d. $tv = d$	Desired variable written on one side of the equation of coefficient of +1.

Given the equation $2x + 5 = 11$, solve for x.
Fill in the following table:

Expression	Operation/reason	Result	Justification
$2x + 5 = 11$	███████████████	███████████████	
$2x + 5 = 11$		$2x + 5 - 5 = 11 - 5$	The same quantity can be subtracted from both sides of an equation without changing the truth of the equality.
$2x + 5 - 5 = 11 - 5$	Simplify, substitute 0 for +5 −5, because +5 −5 = 0		Properties of real numbers.
$2x = 6$	Divide both sides by 2, perform the inverse of multiplication.	$\dfrac{2x}{2} = \dfrac{6}{2}$	
$\dfrac{2x}{2} = \dfrac{6}{2}$		$x = \dfrac{6}{2}$	Any number dived by itself is one, and multiplication by one does not change a number.
$x = \dfrac{6}{2}$	Perform the indicated division.		Properties of real numbers.
$x = 3$	Solution of $2x + 5 = 11$ for x.	$x = 3$, solution for x.	
$2(3) + 5 = 11$		$6 + 5 = 11$ $11 = 11$	The value for the variable makes the original equation a true statement.

PT 1, ANSWERS

Given the equation $v = \dfrac{d}{t}$, solve for d.

Fill in the following table:

Equation	Operation/reason	Result	Justification
$v = \dfrac{d}{t}$			**Given**
$v = \dfrac{d}{t}$	Multiply both sides by t, performing the inverse of division.	$tv = \dfrac{td}{t}$	Both sides of an equation can be multiplied by the same quantity without changing the truth of the equality.
$tv = \dfrac{td}{t}$	Cancel the $\dfrac{t}{t}$ because $\dfrac{t}{t} = 1$.	$tv = d$	**Any quantity (except zero) divided by itself is one.**
$tv = d$	Solve $v = \dfrac{d}{t}$ for d.	Solution for d. $tv = d$	Desired variable written on one side of the equation of coefficient of +1.

Given the equation $2x + 5 = 11$, solve for x.

Fill in the following table:

Expression	Operation/reason	Result	Justification
$2x + 5 = 11$			Given
$2x + 5 = 11$	**Subtract 5 from both sides of the equation, performing the inverse of addition.**	$2x + 5 - 5 = 11 - 5$	The same quantity can be subtracted from both sides of an equation without changing the truth of the equality.
$2x + 5 - 5 = 11 - 5$	Simplify, substitute 0 for +5 −5, because +5 −5 = 0	$2x + 0 = 6$	Properties of real numbers.
$2x = 6$	Divide both sides by 2, perform the inverse of multiplication.	$\dfrac{2x}{2} = \dfrac{6}{2}$	**Both sides of an equation can be divided by the same quantity (except zero) without changing the truth of the equality.**
$\dfrac{2x}{2} = \dfrac{6}{2}$	**Cancel the $\dfrac{2}{2}$ because $\dfrac{2}{2} = 1$.**	$x = \dfrac{6}{2}$	Any number dived by itself is one, and multiplication by one does not change a number.
$x = \dfrac{6}{2}$	Perform the indicated division.	$x = 3$	Properties of real numbers.
$x = 3$	Solution of $2x + 5 = 11$ for x.	$x = 3$, solution for x.	**Variable written alone on one side of the equation with a coefficient of +1.**
$2(3) + 5 = 11$	**Check solution.**	$6 + 5 = 11$ $11 = 11$	The value for the variable makes the original equation a true statement.

PT 2, QUESTIONS

Given the equation $I = \dfrac{V}{R}$, solve for V.

Fill in the following table:

Expression	Operation/reason	Result	Justification
$I = \dfrac{V}{R}$			
$I = \dfrac{V}{R}$	Multiply both sides of the equation by R to perform the inverse of division.		Both sides of an equation can be multiplied by the same quantity without changing the truth of the equality.
$RI = \dfrac{VR}{R}$		Solution for V. $RI = V$	

Given the equation, $\dfrac{1}{3}x + 6 = 10$, solve for x.

Fill in the following table:

Equation	Operation/reason	Result	Justification
$\dfrac{1}{3}x + 6 = 10$			Given
$\dfrac{1}{3}x + 6 = 10$		$\dfrac{1}{3}x + 6 - 6 = 10 - 6$	The same quantity can subtracted from both sides of an equation without changing the truth of the equality.
$\dfrac{1}{3}x + 6 - 6 = 10 - 6$		$\dfrac{1}{3}x + 0 = 10 - 6$	Properties of real numbers.
$\dfrac{1}{3}x = 4$	Multiply both sides by 3 to perform the inverse of division.		
$3\left(\dfrac{1}{3}\right)x = 3(4)$	Perform the indicated multiplication and division.		Variable written on one side of the equation with a coefficient of +1.
$\dfrac{1}{3}(12) + 6 = 10$		$4 + 6 = 10$ $10 = 10$	The value for the variable makes the original equation a true statement.

PT 2, ANSWERS

Given the equation $I = \dfrac{V}{R}$, solve for V.

Fill in the following table:

Expression	Operation/reason	Result	Justification
$I = \dfrac{V}{R}$			**Given**
$I = \dfrac{V}{R}$	Multiply both sides of the equation by R to remove the R from the denominator (bottom of a fraction}.	$RI = \dfrac{VR}{R}$	Both sides of an equation can be multiplied by the same quantity without changing the truth of the equality.
$RI = \dfrac{VR}{R}$	**Cancel $\dfrac{R}{R}$ because $\dfrac{R}{R}=1$.**	Solution for V. $RI = V$	**Unknown variable written on one side of the equation with a coefficient of +1.**

Given the equation $\dfrac{1}{3}x + 6 = 10$, solve for x.

Fill in the following table:

Equation	Operation/reason	Result	Justification
$\dfrac{1}{3}x + 6 = 10$	**Add a -6 to both sides of an equation, performing the inverse of addition.**	$\dfrac{1}{3}x + 6 + (-6) = 10 + (-6)$	The same quantity can be added to both sides of an equation without changing the truth of the equality.
$\dfrac{1}{3}x + 6 + (-6) = 10 + (-6)$	**Perform indicated addition and subtraction.**	$\dfrac{1}{3}x = 4$	Properties of real numbers.
$\dfrac{1}{3}x = 4$	Multiply both sides by 3, perform the inverse of division.	$3\left(\dfrac{1}{3}\right)x = 3(4)$	**Both sides of an equation can be multiplied by the same quantity without changing the truth of the equality.**
$3\left(\dfrac{1}{3}\right)x = 3(4)$	Perform the indicated multiplication and division.	**Solution for x** **x = 12**	Unknown variable written on one side of the equation with a coefficient of +1.
$\dfrac{1}{3}(12) + 6 = 10$	**Check solution.**	$4 + 6 = 10$ $10 = 10$	The value for the variable makes the original equation a true statement.

PT 3, QUESTIONS

Given the equation 5x + 10y =20, solve for y.
Fill in the following table:

Expression	Operation/reason	Result	Justification
–5x + 10y = 20			Given
–5x + 10y = 20	Add 5x to both sides of the equation, performing the inverse of addition to get the y term by itself on one side of the equation.	+5x – 5x + 10y = +5x + 20	
+5x - 5x + 10y = +5x + 20	Simplify, substitute 0 for +5x – 5x, because +5x – 5x = 0		The sum of any number and its additive opposite is 0.
10y = +5x + 20	Divide both sides of the equation by 10, perform the inverse of multiplication to solve the equation for +y.		Both sides of an equation can be divided by the same quantity (except zero) without changing the truth of the equality.
$\dfrac{10y}{10} = \dfrac{5x}{10} + \dfrac{20}{10}$			Properties of real numbers. Desired variable written alone on one side of the equation with a coefficient of +1.

Given the equation 14x – 7y = 21, solve for y.
Fill in the following table:

Expression	Operation/reason	Result	Justification
14x –7y = 21			
14x –7y = 21	Subtract 14x from both sides of the equation, performing the inverse of addition to get the y term by itself on one side of the equation.		The same quantity can be subtracted from both sides of an equation without changing the truth of the equality.
14x –14x – 7y = –14x + 21		0 – 7y = –14x + 21	The sum of any number and its additive opposite is 0.
–7y = –14x + 21			Both sides of an equation can be divided by the same quantity (except zero) without changing the truth of the equality.
$\dfrac{-7y}{-7} = \dfrac{-14x}{-7} + \dfrac{21}{-7}$	Perform the indicated division		Properties of real numbers. Desired variable written alone on one side of the equation with a coefficient of +1.

PT 3, ANSWERS

Given the equation 5x + 10y =20, solve for y.
Fill in the following table:

Expression	Operation/reason	Result	Justification
–5x + 10y = 20			Given
–5x + 10y = 20	Add 5x to both sides of the equation, performing the inverse of addition to get the y term by itself on one side of the equation.	+5x – 5x + 10y = +5x + 20	**The same quantity can be added to both sides of an equation can be divided by without changing the truth of the equality.**
+5x – 5x + 10y = +5x + 20	Simplify, substitute 0 for +5x - 5x, because +5x - 5x = 0	**0 + 10y = +5x + 20**	The sum of any number and its additive opposite is 0.
10y = +5x + 20	Divide both sides of the equation by 10, perform the inverse of multiplication to solve the equation for +y.	$\frac{10y}{10} = \frac{5x}{10} + \frac{20}{10}$	Both sides of an equation can be divided by the same quantity (except zero) without changing the truth of the equality.
$\frac{10y}{10} = \frac{5x}{10} + \frac{20}{10}$	**Perform indicated division.**	$y = 1/2x + 2$	Properties of real numbers. Desired variable written alone on one side of the equation with a coefficient of +1.

Given the equation 14x – 7y = 21, solve for y.
Fill in the following table:

Expression	Operation/reason	Result	Justification
14x – 7y = 21			**Given**
14x – 7y = 21	Subtract 14x from both sides of the equation, performing the inverse of addition to get the y term by itself on one side of the equation.	**–14x +14x –7y = –14x + 21**	The same quantity can be subtracted from both sides of an equation without changing the truth of the equality.
14x –14x – 7y = –14x + 21	**Simplify, substitute 0 for 14x –14x because 14x – 14x = 0**	0 – 7y = –14x + 21	The sum of any number and its additive opposite is 0.
–7y = –14x + 21	**Divide both sides by –7, perform the inverse of multiplication to solve the equation for +y**	$\frac{-7y}{-7} = \frac{-14x}{-7} + \frac{21}{-7}$	Both sides of an equation can be divided by the same quantity (except zero) without changing the truth of the equality.
$\frac{-7y}{-7} = \frac{-14x}{-7} + \frac{21}{-7}$	Perform the indicated division	**y = 2x – 3**	Properties of real numbers. Desired variable written alone on one side of the equation with a coefficient of +1.

CHAPTER 21

STRAIGHT LINES

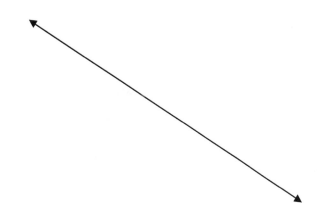

Overview: The slope intercept form of the Straight Line is the basis for innumerable questions on Standardized Tests. So let us review.

Academic Learning Objective:	The student will: Fluently switch between graphs and equations of the slope intercept form of an equation.
NCTM Standards:	Algebra Understand patterns, relations, and functions.

Definitions:

Word	Meaning	Symbol
Straight	Having the same direction throughout its length; not crooked or bent.	
Axis	A central line around which things are evenly arranged.	
x–axis	The horizontal line on a graph, usually indicating an independent variable; the line $y = 0$.	
y–axis	The vertical line on a graph, usually indicating a dependent variable; the line $x = 0$.	
Length	Distance between two points. Often measured in centimeters (cm).	
Rise	Change in the vertical direction (Δy).	$\Delta y = y_2 - y_1$
Run	Change in the horizontal direction (Δx).	$\Delta x = x_2 - x_1$
Line	A thin threadlike mark; a row of things, as of number points across a page.	
Intersect	To meet or cross.	
Intercept	To cut off, or mark off, or mark off between two points.	
y–intercept	The point where a line crosses the y–axis; the value of the expression when $x = 0$.	
Slope intercept form of an equation	When a linear equation is solved for y, it is in the form $y = mx + b$; m, the coefficient of x, is the slope and b is the y–intercept (where the line crosses the y–axis).	$y = mx + b$
Ratio	A comparison of two numbers by division.	
Proportion	An equation stating the equality of two ratios.	
Variable	A letter or symbol that stands for a number that can be changed.	Sometimes x or y
Slope	$m = \text{rise/run}, \dfrac{\text{change in } y}{\text{change in } x} = \dfrac{\Delta y}{\Delta x} = \dfrac{y_2 - y_1}{x_2 - x_1}$, where (x_1, y_1) and (x_2, y_2) represent an ordered pair of coordinates indicating points in the plane.	m
Slope of any line parallel to the y–axis	Undefined because $\Delta x = x_2 - x_1 = 0$ and division by 0 is not permitted.	
Let	To assign (arbitrary assumption).	
Arbitrary	Based on one's preference or whim.	

PRECISION TEACHING (PT) SAMPLE ANSWERS
SLOPE INTERCEPT

Fill in the following table and match the equation with the graph at the bottom:

Graph	Equation	Solved for y	Slope	y intercept	Justification
A	$2y = 6x + 4$	$y = 3x + 2$	3	$(0, +2)$	When a linear equation is solved for y, it is in the form, $y = mx + b$; the coefficient of x is the slope and b is the y–intercept.
B	$x = 2y + 4$	$y = 1/2x – 2$	1/2	$(0, –2)$	When a linear equation is solved for y, it is in the form, $y = mx + b$; the coefficient of x is the slope and b is the y–intercept.
D	$7y = 14x + 21$	$y = 2x + 3$	2	$(0, 3)$	When a linear equation is solved for y, it is in the form, $y = mx + b$; the coefficient of x is the slope and b is the y–intercept.
C	$5y = 0$	$y = 0$ (x–axis)	0	$(0, 0)$	When a linear equation is solved for y, it is in the form, $y = mx + b$; the coefficient of x is the slope and b is the y–intercept.

A
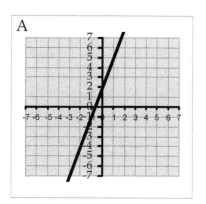

B
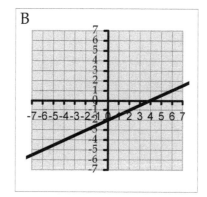

C
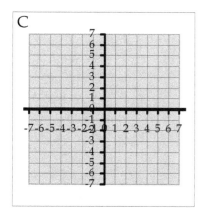

D
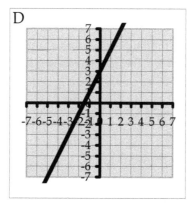

LESSON NOTES

SEE PAGE 330 FOR <u>STRAIGHT LINES</u>: PRECISION TEACHING (PT) SCORES, FREQUENCY TABLE.

I suggest that students correct their papers, calculate the frequencies and graph their results. Graphing the results on special graph paper (Standard Celeration Chart) can provide visual reinforcement for the students and information about how they are learning. The frequency tables are provided to facilitate this process.

SLOPE INTERCEPT ~ PT 1, QUESTIONS

Fill in the following table and match the equation with the graph on the bottom.

Graph	Equation	Solved for y	Slope	y intercept	Justification
A	$3y = 12x + 12$	$y = 4x + 4$		(0,4)	When a linear equation is solved for y, it is in the form, $y = mx + b$; the coefficient of x is the slope and b is the y–intercept.
	$6x = 3y - 9$	$y = 2x + 3$			When a linear equation is solved for y, it is in the form, $y = mx + b$; the coefficient of x is the slope and b is the y–intercept.
	$2y = 4x$		2		When a linear equation is solved for y, it is in the form, $y = mx + b$; the coefficient of x is the slope and b is the y–intercept.
	$x = 2$	$y =$ undefined	Undefined (parallel to the y-axis).	Does not intersect the y-axis.	When a linear equation is solved for y, it is in the form, $y = mx + b$; the coefficient of x is the slope and b is the y–intercept.

A
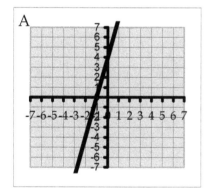

B
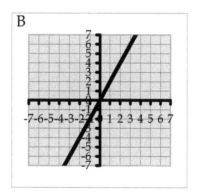

C
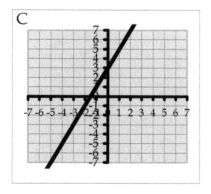

D
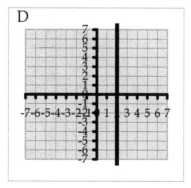

SLOPE INTERCEPT ~ PT 1, ANSWERS

Fill in the following table and match the equation with the graph at the bottom:

Graph	Equation	Solved for y	Slope	y intercept	Justification
A	$3y = 12x + 12$	$y = 4x + 4$	**4**	(0,4)	When a linear equation is solved for y, it is in the form, $y = mx + b$; the coefficient of x is the slope and b is the y–intercept.
C	$6x = 3y - 9$	$y = 2x + 3$	**2**	**(0,3)**	When a linear equation is solved for y, it is in the form, $y = mx + b$; the coefficient of x is the slope and b is the y–intercept.
B	$2y = 4x$	**y = 2x**	2	(0,0)	When a linear equation is solved for y, it is in the form, $y = mx + b$; the coefficient of x is the slope and b is the y–intercept.
D	$x = 2$	$y = $ undefined	Undefined (parallel to the y–axis).	Does not intersect the y–axis.	When a linear equation is solved for y, it is in the form, $y = mx + b$; the coefficient of x is the slope and b is the y–intercept.

A
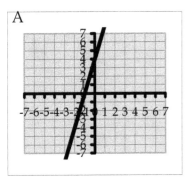

B
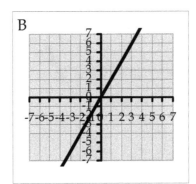

C
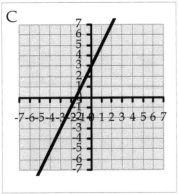

D
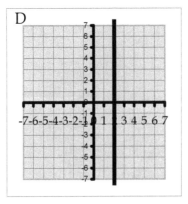

How Do We Know?

SLOPE INTERCEPT ~ PT 2, QUESTIONS

Fill in the following table and match the equation with the graph at the bottom.

Graph	Equation	Solved for y	Slope	y-intercept	Justification
	4x = 6y + 30	y = 2/3x – 5		(0,–5)	
B	20x + 5y = 10	y = –4x + 2			When a linear equation is solved for y, it is in the form, y = mx + b; the coefficient of x is the slope and b is the y–intercept.
	8y = –x + 32	y = –1/8x +4	–1/8		When a linear equation is solved for y, it is in the form, y = mx + b; the coefficient of x is the slope and b is the y–intercept.
	5y = 20	y = 4	0 (line parallel to the x–axis).	(0,4)	When a linear equation is solved for y, it is in the form, y = mx + b; the coefficient of x is the slope and b is the y–intercept.

A
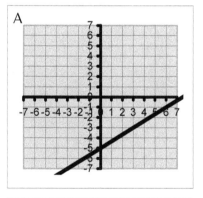

B
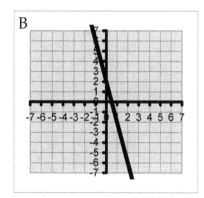

C
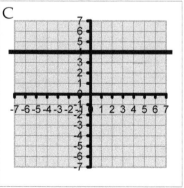

D
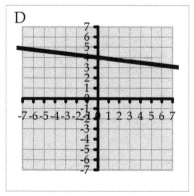

SLOPE INTERCEPT ~ PT 2, ANSWERS

Fill in the following table and match the equation with the graph at the bottom.

Graph	Equation	Solved for y	Slope	y-intercept	Justification
A	$4x = 6y + 30$	$y = 2/3x - 5$	**2/3**	$(0, -5)$	**When a linear equation is solved for y, it is in the form, y = mx + b; the coefficient of x is the slope and b is the y-intercept.**
B	$20x + 5y = 10$	$y = -4x + 2$	**-4**	**(0, 2)**	When a linear equation is solved for y, it is in the form, y = mx + b; the coefficient of x is the slope and b is the y-intercept.
D	$8y = -x + 32$	**$y = -1/8x + 4$**	$-1/8$	**(0,4)**	When a linear equation is solved for y, it is in the form, y = mx + b; the coefficient of x is the slope and b is the y-intercept.
C	$5y = 20$	$y = 4$	0 (line parallel to the x-axis).	$(0,4)$	When a linear equation is solved for y, it is in the form, y = mx + b; the coefficient of x is the slope and b is the y-intercept.

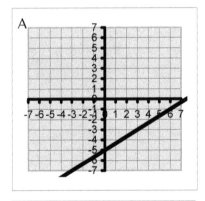

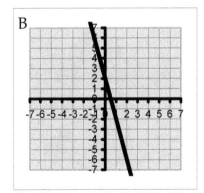

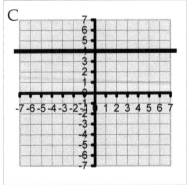

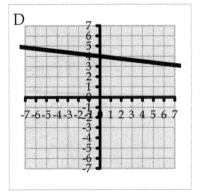

How Do We Know?

SLOPE INTERCEPT ~ PT 3 QUESTIONS

Fill in the following table and match the equation with the graph on the bottom.

Graph	Equation	Solved for y	Slope	y-intercept	Justification
D	$3y = 18x + 6$		6		When a linear equation is solved for y, it is in the form, $y = mx + b$; the coefficient of x is the slope and b is the y-intercept.
	$2y + x = 4$			(0, 2)	When a linear equation is solved for y, it is in the form, $y = mx + b$; the coefficient of x is the slope and b is the y-intercept.
	$7y = 14x + 21$		2		When a linear equation is solved for y, it is in the form, $y = mx + b$; the coefficient of x is the slope and b is the y-intercept.
	$3x + 15y = 0$	$y = -1/5x$			When a linear equation is solved for y, it is in the form, $y = mx + b$; the coefficient of x is the slope and b is the y-intercept.

A
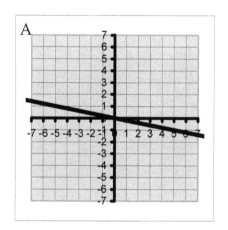

B
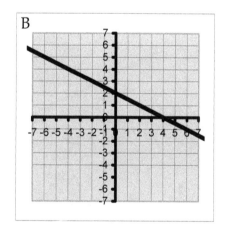

C
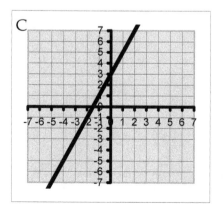

D
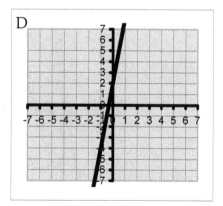

SLOPE INTERCEPT ~ PT 3 ANSWERS

Fill in the following table and match the equation with the graph on the bottom.

Graph	Equation	Solved for y	Slope	y-intercept	Justification
D	$3y = 18x + 6$	$y = 6x + 2$	6	(0, 2)	When a linear equation is solved for y, it is in the form, $y = mx + b$; the coefficient of x is the slope and b is the y-intercept.
B	$2y + x = 4$	$y = -1/2x + 2$	$-1/2$	(0, 2)	When a linear equation is solved for y, it is in the form, $y = mx + b$; the coefficient of x is the slope and b is the y-intercept.
C	$7y = 14x + 21$	$y = 2x + 3$	2	(0, 3)	When a linear equation is solved for y, it is in the form, $y = mx + b$; the coefficient of x is the slope and b is the y-intercept.
A	$3x + 15y = 0$	$y = -1/5x$	$-1/5$	(0, 0)	When a linear equation is solved for y, it is in the form, $y = mx + b$; the coefficient of x is the slope and b is the y-intercept.

A
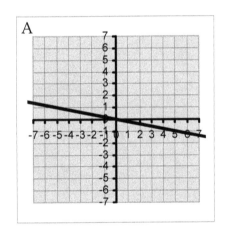

B
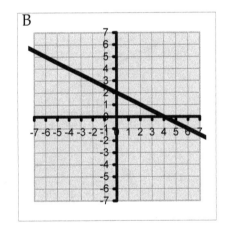

C
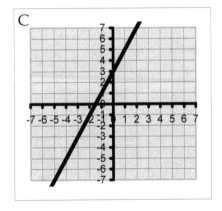

D
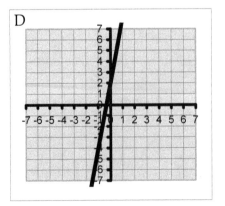

How Do We Know?

STRAIGHT LINES, *x, y* VALUES

It is often easy to graph and describe a straight line using the slope intercept form of the straight line. However, it is important to keep in mind that equations represent relationships between variables. An understanding of how a change in the x value changes the y value in a practical sense is what algebra is about. So let's look at straight lines from the point of view of changing x's and y's.

Remember:

An equation is solved for a variable when the variable is written on one side, all by itself with a coefficient of +1, and a value or other variables on the other side of the equation.

To solve an equation for y, you clear away the "stuff" around the y by performing the same mathematical operation on both sides of the equation, generally performing addition and subtraction first, multiplication and division second, and dealing with exponents last.

If we make up a value for x to substitute into an equation, that made up value is an arbitrary assumption. We could choose any value. If we choose a great big number for x then the solution might be a great big number and the x,y coordinates would be difficult to fit on graph paper. There are some tricks to fit big numbers on graph paper, but we will learn those later.

Easy values to choose for x are 0, –1, and +1. If the coefficient of x is a fraction, the calculation and graphing can be made easier if you choose the bottom number (denominator) as one of the values for x.

To get easy numbers to graph, trial and error and practice will take some time, but what is time to a great thinker like you?

In the exercises on graphing x,y values (PT 4, PT 5, PT 6), you can think about why I selected the values for x or y that I did.

PRECISION TEACHING (PT) SAMPLE ANSWERS
STRAIGHT LINES, *x,y* VALUES

Fill in the following table. Match each equation to the corresponding graph.

Graph	Equation	Equation solved for y	Value for x	Value for y	Justification for x value	Justification for y value
C	x = 2y + 4	y = 1/2x – 2	0	–2	Arbitrary assumption	The value of y when x has a value of 0.
			2	–1	Arbitrary assumption	The value of y when x has a value of 2.
B	2y = 6x + 4	y = 3x + 2	0	2	Arbitrary assumption	The value of y when x has a value of 0.
			1	5	Arbitrary assumption	The value of y when x has a value of 1.
A	3x + 15y = 0	y = –1/5x	0	0	Arbitrary assumption	The value of y when x has a value of 0.
			5	–1	Arbitrary assumption	The value of y when x has a value of 5.

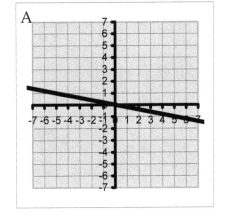

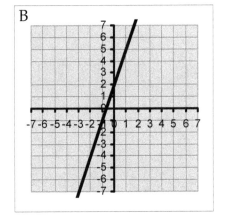

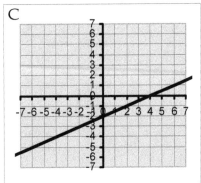

How Do We Know?

STRAIGHT LINES, *x,y* VALUES ~ PT 4, QUESTIONS

Fill in the following table. Match each equation to the corresponding graph.

Graph	Equation	Equation solved for y	Value for x	Value for y	Justification for x value	Justification for y value
	x + y = 0	y = –x	0		Arbitrary assumption	The value of y when x has a value of 0.
			2		Arbitrary assumption	The value of y when x has a value of 2.
	3y = 15x + 12		0	4	Arbitrary assumption	The value of y when x has a value of 0.
			–1	–1	Arbitrary assumption	The value of y when x has a value of 5.
B	2y = 2x - 8	y = x – 4	0			The value of y when x has a value of 0,
			1			The value of y when x has a value of 1.
	4x = 6y – 12	y = 2/3x + 2	0		Arbitrary assumption	
			3		Arbitrary assumption	

A

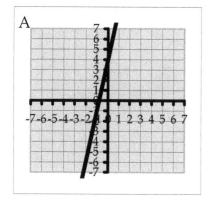

B

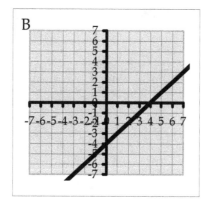

C

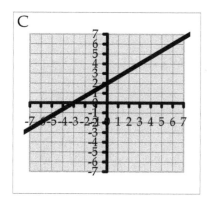

D

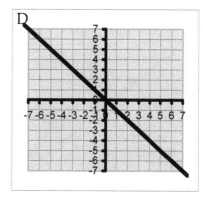

STRAIGHT LINES, *x,y* VALUES~ PT 4, ANSWERS

Fill in the following table. Match each equation to the corresponding graph.

Graph	Equation	Equation solved for y	Value for x	Value for y	Justification for x value	Justification for y value
D	x + y = 0	y = –x	0	**0**	Arbitrary assumption	The value of y when x has a value of 0.
			2	–2	Arbitrary assumption	The value of y when x has a value of 2.
A	3y = 15x + 12	**y = 5x + 4**	0	4	Arbitrary assumption	The value of y when x has a value of 0.
			–1	–1	Arbitrary assumption	The value of y when x has a value of 5.
B	2y = 2x – 8	y = x – 4	0	–4	**Arbitrary assumption**	The value of y when x has a value of 0.
			1	–3	**Arbitrary assumption**	The value of y when x has a value of 1.
C	4x = 6y – 12	y = 2/3x + 2	0	2	Arbitrary assumption	**The value of y when x has a value of 0.**
			3	4	Arbitrary assumption	**The value of y when x has a value of 3.**

A

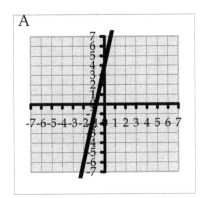

B

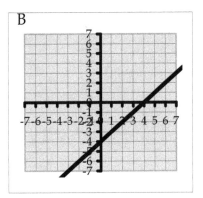

C

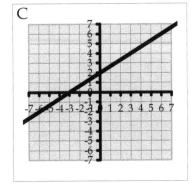

D

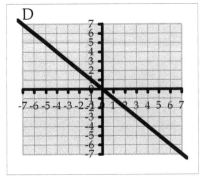

How Do We Know?

STRAIGHT LINES, x,y VALUES ~ PT 5, QUESTIONS

Fill in the following table. Match each equation to the corresponding graph below.

Graph	Equation	Equation solved for y	Value for x	Value for y	Justification for x value	Justification for y value
	3y = 12x + 12		0	4		The value of y when x has a value of 0.
			–1	0	Arbitrary assumption	
	6x = 3y + 9		0		Arbitrary assumption	The value of y when x has a value of 0.
			1		Arbitrary assumption	The value of y when x has a value of 1.
D	x = 2	y = undefined	2	7	The value of x when y has a value of 7.	Arbitrary assumption
				–7		Arbitrary assumption
				0		Arbitrary assumption
	5y = –10x + 20	y = –2x + 4	0		Arbitrary assumption	The value of y when x has a value of 0.
			2		Arbitrary assumption	

A
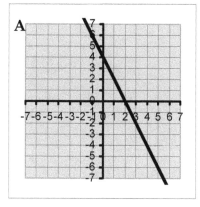

B
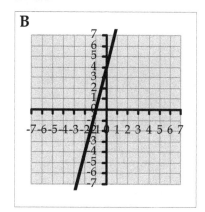

C
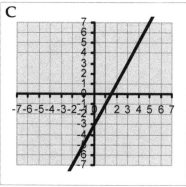

D
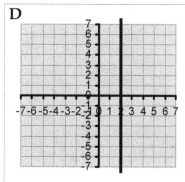

STRAIGHT LINES, *x,y* VALUES ~ PT 5, ANSWERS

Fill in the following table. Match each equation to the corresponding graph below.

Graph	Equation	Equation solved for y	Value for x	Value for y	Justification for x value	Justification for y value
B	3y = 12x + 12	**y = 4x + 4**	0	4	**Arbitrary assumption**	The value of y when x has a value of 0.
			–1	0	Arbitrary assumption	**The value of y when x has a value of –1**
C	6x = 3y + 9	**y = 2x – 3**	0	–3	Arbitrary assumption	The value of y when x has a value of 0.
			1	**–1**	Arbitrary assumption	The value of y when x has a value of 1.
D	x = 2	y = undefined	2	7	The value of x when y has a value of 7.	Arbitrary assumption
			2	–7	**The value of x when y has a value of –7.**	Arbitrary assumption
			2	0	**The value of x when y has a value of 0.**	Arbitrary assumption
A	5y = –10x + 20	y = –2x + 4	0	**4**	Arbitrary assumption	The value of y when x has a value of 0.
			2	**0**	Arbitrary assumption	**The value of y when x has a value of 2.**

A

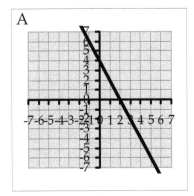

B

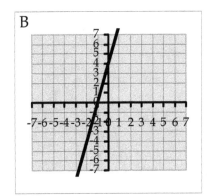

C

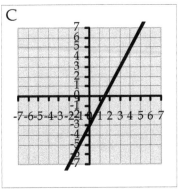

D

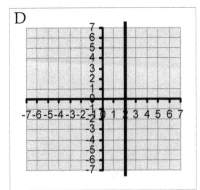

How Do We Know?

STRAIGHT LINES, x,y VALUES ~ PT 6, QUESTIONS

Fill in the following table. Match each equation to the corresponding graph.

Graph	Equation	Equation solved for y	Value for x	Value for y	Justification for x value	Justification for y value
	$x - y = 0$		0		Arbitrary assumption	The value of y when x has a value of 0.
			1		Arbitrary assumption	The value of y when x has a value of 1.
	$6y = 6$		0		Arbitrary assumption	The value of y when x has a value of 0.
			1		Arbitrary assumption	The value of y when x has a value of 1.
	$3y = -9x + 21$		0		Arbitrary assumption	The value of y when x has a value of 0,
			1		Arbitrary assumption	The value of y when x has a value of 1.
	$4y = 12x + 4$		0		Arbitrary assumption	The value of y when x has a value of 0.
			-1		Arbitrary assumption	The value of y when x has a value of -1.

A

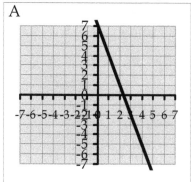

B

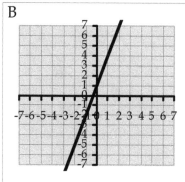

C

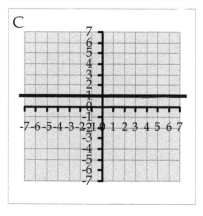

D

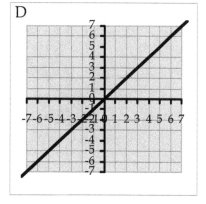

STRAIGHT LINES, *x,y* VALUES ~ PT 6, ANSWERS

Fill in the following table. Match each equation to the corresponding graph.

Graph	Equation	Equation solved for y	Value for x	Value for y	Justification for x value	Justification for y value
D	x – y = 0	**y = x**	0	**0**	Arbitrary assumption	The value of y when x has a value of 0.
			1	**1**	Arbitrary assumption	The value of y when x has a value of 1.
C	6y = 6	**y = 1**	0	**1**	Arbitrary assumption	The value of y when x has a value of 0.
			1	**1**	Arbitrary assumption	The value of y when x has a value of 1.
A	3y = –9x + 21	**y = –3x + 7**	0	**7**	Arbitrary assumption	The value of y when x has a value of 0.
			1	**4**	Arbitrary assumption	The value of y when x has a value of 1.
B	4y = 12x + 4	**y = 3x + 1**	0	**1**	Arbitrary assumption	The value of y when x has a value of 0.
			–1	**–2**	Arbitrary assumption	The value of y when x has a value of –1.

A
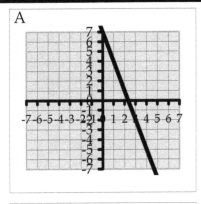

B
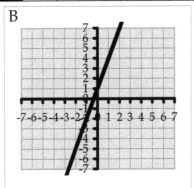

C
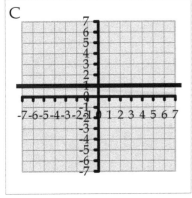

D
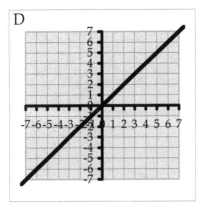

How Do We Know?

ADDENDUM I

HANDS ON ACTIVITIES

LESSON NOTES

How Do We Know?

DEVELOPING EQUATIONS

Overview: Many quantities in the physical world are related, as one thing changes something else changes also. In science, when two quantities are suspected of being related, paired values of the quantities are measured and the results are graphed. From the graph the relationship between the measured quantities can be explored. In this exercise the student will develop the rationale that:

Diameter = 2(radius)

Mathematical Learning Objective:

The student will:

Practice obtaining data by measuring quantities relative to a circle.

Graph data and become familiar with such terms as slope and proportionality constant.

NCTM Standards:

Number and operations
Understand numbers, ways of representing numbers, relationships among numbers, and number systems.

Measurement
Understand measurable attributes of objects and the units, systems, and processes of measurement.

Algebra
Understand patterns, relations, and functions.

How Do We Know?

Definitions:

Word	Definition	Symbol
Area	A measurement of the surface of figure, measured in square units of length.	A
Radius	Any straight line from the center of a circle to the periphery.	r
Diameter	A straight line passing through the center of a circle, from one side to the other.	d
Ratio	A comparison of two numbers by division.	$-, \div, /, :$
Symbol of Proportionality	A symbol indicating a relationship between two variables.	$\propto$ or "= k"
Constant of Proportionality	An unchanging constant that relates the value of two variables.	k
Proportion	An equation stating the equality of two ratios.	
Variable	A letter or symbol that stands for a number that can be changed.	Sometimes x or y
Circumference	The line bounding a circle, the length of that line.	c
Compass	An instrument with two pivoted legs, for drawing circles.	
pi	The symbol designating the ratio of the circumference of a circle to its diameter.	π
Best fit straight line	A line which estimates (guesses at) the best line which characterizes the cohesion of the confluence and correlates the consanguinity and concurrence of the data points. It is not the line that directly connects the points.	
Alliteration	The repetition of initial consonant sounds in two or more neighboring words or syllables.	
Rise	Change in the vertical direction(Δy).	$\Delta y = y_2 - y_1$
Run	Change in the horizontal direction(Δx).	$\Delta x = x_2 - x_1$
Slope (m)	m = rise/run, $\dfrac{\text{change in y}}{\text{change in x}} = \dfrac{\Delta y}{\Delta x} = \dfrac{y_2 - y_1}{x_2 - x_1}$ where (x_1, y_1) and (x_2, y_2) represent an ordered pair of coordinates, indicating points in the plane.	m

DIAMETER FROM RADIUS

PURPOSE: To measure the radius and diameter of circles and develop an equation to relate the two variables.

MATERIALS:
Compass
Centimeter ruler
Graph paper

PROCEDURE:
1. Using ruler, measure the distance to use for the radius of a circle. Enter this value in the column for radius. Measure in centimeters and estimate to the nearest 0.1 cm.

2. Draw a circle with the radius you have determined.

3. Measure the diameter of the circle. The diameter is the length from the outside of the circle, through the center, to the other side. Measure in centimeters and estimate to the nearest 0.1 cm. Enter this value in the column for diameter.

4. Repeat steps 1-3 to measure two more circles.

5. Plot the data for radius on the horizontal axis and diameter on the vertical axis. Use the radius and diameter of each circle as an ordered pair, i.e. a point (x, y) = (radius, diameter), and plot each point on the graph.

6. Draw the "best fit straight line" for the data.

7. Select a convenient pair of points on the "best fit straight line" and use to calculate slope:

$$m = \frac{\text{rise}}{\text{run}} = \frac{\text{change in y}}{\text{change in x}} = \frac{\Delta y}{\Delta x} = \frac{y_2 - y_1}{x_2 - x_1}.$$

Data table:

Circle	Radius(r)	Diameter(d)	Ratio $\dfrac{\text{diameter}}{\text{radius}}$
#1			
#2			
#3			

How Do We Know?

CALCULATION:

We can see that as the radius increases, so does the diameter. An expression that states this relationship is:

$$d \propto r$$

The symbol meaning proportional ($\propto$) can be replaced by: " = k" where k is the constant of proportionality and the equation becomes:

$$d = kr$$

and

$$k = \frac{d}{r}$$

This constant is the ratio $\frac{d}{r}$. If we measured accurately we find the ratio to be 2. It is also the slope of the "best fit straight line" when diameter is graphed against radius. Since the relationship between radius and diameter is linear, the constant of proportionality, k, can be calculated from the measurements of diameter and radius for one circle. A better value for k would be the slope of the "best fit straight line". This slope from the "best fit straight line" is sort of an average. Calculating a linear regression using a graphing calculator can give a very accurate value for a slope from data like this.

The final equation is:

$d = 2r$, or diameter = 2(radius)

While this exercise will seem trivial for some students, the use of the words to describe the process is fundamental to many scientific inquiries and this example should familiarize the student with these words.

Scene: Lunchroom - Pepperoni Pizza for Lunch

Bunny (bubbly): We can measure the radius and using the formula we can know the diameter.

Sunny (sourly): This pizza is a circle. Will that formula tell me how much pizza I am getting?

Bunny: No, not exactly, diameter is a length. How much is in the circle is something else.

Sunny: Then that formula doesn't seem to help me very much.

Bunny: We are kind of just starting. Maybe the next formula we come to will tell us about how much is in the circle.

Sunny: Why do we need this stuff?

Bunny: We are learning that we can measure one thing and calculate something else.

Sunny: Thank God we can use calculators.

Bunny: Sometimes it is easier to remember what we are doing if we work it out with a pencil and paper.

Sunny: Did you hear about the constipated mathematician?

Bunny: No

Sunny: He worked it out with a pencil.

Bunny: Let's hope he didn't forget the paper.

DEVELOPING
EQUATIONS

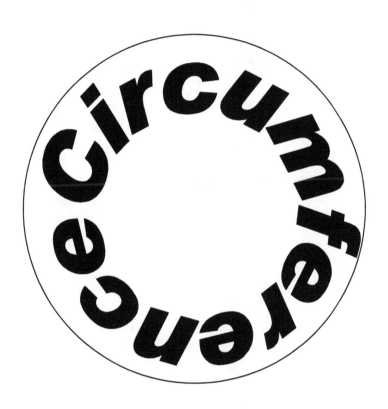

CIRCUMFERENCE FROM DIAMETER

Overview: Many quantities in the physical world are related, as one thing changes something else changes also. In science, when two quantities are suspected of being related, paired values of the quantities are measured and the results are graphed. From the graph the relationship between the measured quantities can be explored. In this exercise the student will develop the rationale that:

circumference = π(diameter)

Mathematical Learning Objective:	The student will:
	Practice obtaining data by measuring quantities relative to a circle.
	Graph data and become familiar with such terms as slope and proportionality constant.
NCTM Standards:	Number and operations
	Understand numbers, ways of representing numbers, relationships among numbers, and number systems.
	Measurement
	Understand measurable attributes of objects and the units, systems, and processes of measurement.
	Algebra
	Understand patterns, relations, and functions.

Definitions:

Word	Definition	Symbol
Area	A measurement of the surface of figure, measured in square units of length.	A
Radius	Any straight line from the center of a circle to the periphery.	r
Diameter	A straight line passing through the center of a circle, from one side to the other.	d
Ratio	A comparison of two numbers by division.	$-, \div, /, :$
Symbol of Proportionality	A symbol indicating a relationship between two variables.	$\propto$ or "= k"
Constant of Proportionality	An unchanging constant that relates the value of two variables.	k
Proportion	An equation stating the equality of two ratios.	
Variable	A letter or symbol that stands for a number that can be changed.	Sometimes x or y
Circumference	The line bounding a circle, the length of that line.	c
Compass	An instrument with two pivoted legs, for drawing circles.	
pi	The symbol designating the ratio of the circumference of a circle to its diameter.	π
Best fit straight line	A line which estimates (guesses at) the best line which characterizes the cohesion of the confluence and correlates the consanguinity and concurrence of the data points. It is not the line that directly connects the points.	
Alliteration	The repetition of initial consonant sounds in two or more neighboring words or syllables.	
Run	Change in the horizontal direction (Δx).	$\Delta x = x_2 - x_1$
Slope	$m = \text{rise/run}, \dfrac{\text{change in y}}{\text{change in x}} = \dfrac{\Delta y}{\Delta x} = \dfrac{y_2 - y_1}{x_2 - x_1}$ where (x_1, y_1) and (x_2, y_2) represent an ordered pair of coordinates, indicating points in the plane.	m
Rise	Change in the vertical direction (Δy).	$\Delta y = y_2 - y_1$

PURPOSE: To measure the circumference and diameter of circles and develop an equation to relate the two variables.

MATERIALS:
Centimeter ruler
Graph paper
Centimeter measuring tape
Three cylinders (cans, PVC pipe, wooden dowels, etc.) with diameter in the range of 5 to 15 centimeters.

PROCEDURE:
1. Select three cylinders of various sizes.

2. Use a ruler to estimate the diameter of the cylinder to the nearest 0.1 centimeter. Measure outside edge to outside edge and record the largest value for diameter of the circle. Enter this value in the column for diameter.

3. Use the measuring tape to measure the distance around the cylinder to the nearest 0.1 centimeter. Enter this value in the column for circumference.

4. Repeat steps 2 and 3 for the remaining cylinders.

5. Plot the data for diameter on the horizontal axis and circumference on the vertical axis. Use the values for the diameter and circumference of each cylinder as an ordered pair, i.e. a point (x, y) = (diameter, circumference), and plot each point on the graph.

6. Draw the best line to fit the data.

7. Select a convenient pair of points on the "best fit straight line" and use to calculate slope:

$$m = \frac{\text{rise}}{\text{run}} = \frac{\text{change in } y}{\text{change in } x} = \frac{\Delta y}{\Delta x} = \frac{y_2 - y_1}{x_2 - x_1}$$

Circle	Diameter (d) (cm)	Circumference (c)	Ratio $\left(\dfrac{c}{d}\right)$
#1			
#2			
#3			

How Do We Know?

CALCULATION:

We can see that as the diameter increases, so does the circumference. An expression that states this relationship is:

$$c \propto d$$

and

$$c = kd$$

and

$$k = \frac{c}{d}$$

The symbol meaning proportional ($\propto$) can be replaced by: " $= k$" where k is the constant of proportionality.

This constant is the ratio $\frac{c}{d}$. If we measured accurately we find the ratio to be about 3.14. It is also the slope of the line when circumference is plotted against radius. In mathematics this ratio has a very special name, it is *pi* (π), and the expression becomes:

$$\pi = \frac{c}{d}$$

and

$$c = \pi d$$

Since the relationship between diameter and circumference is linear and goes through the origin (0, 0), the constant of proportionality can be calculated from one of the paired values of diameter and circumference. A better value would be the slope of the "best fit" straight line. This slope from the "best fit straight line" is sort of an average. Calculating a linear regression using a graphing calculator can give a very accurate value for a slope from data like this.

While this exercise will seem trivial for some students, the words to describe the process are fundamental to many scientific inquiries, and this example should familiarize the student with these words.

Scene: In Math Classroom

Bunny: My mom uses a tape like this when she is sewing.

Sunny: What are we supposed to do with it?

Bunny: Wrap it around the can and measure the circumference of the cylinder.

Sunny: What do we need the ruler for?

Bunny: To measure the diameter.

Sunny: What are we going to do with the numbers?

Bunny: I bet we are going to develop a formula for circumference.

Sunny: I already know the formula. It's pi r square.

Bunny: No, that's not right. That's the formula for area. Area = πr^2

Sunny: No, that's not right. Cake are square, pies are round.

* Bunny: What?

Sunny: What is on second.

Bunny: Who?

Sunny: Who's on first.

Bunny: Who?

Sunny: That's right!

* Taken from Abbot and Costello, "Who Is On First".

DEVELOPING
EQUATIONS

AREA FROM RADIUS

Overview: Many quantities have relationships in the physical world, as one thing changes something else changes. In science, when two quantities are suspected of being related, paired values of the quantities are measured and the results are graphed. From the graph the relationship between the measured quantities can be explored. In this exercise the student will develop the rationale that:

$$\text{Area} = \pi(\text{radius})^2$$

Mathematical Learning Objective:	The student will: Practice obtaining data by measuring quantities relative to a circle. Graph data and become familiar with such terms as slope and proportionality constant.
NCTM Standards:	Number and operations Understand numbers, ways of representing numbers, relationships among numbers, and number systems. Measurement Understand measurable attributes of objects and the units, systems, and processes of measurement. Algebra Understand patterns, relations, and functions.

How Do We Know?

Definitions:

Word	Definition	Symbol
Area	A measurement of the surface of figure, measured in square units of length.	A
Radius	Any straight line from the center of a circle to the periphery.	r
Diameter	A straight line passing through the center of a circle, from one side to the other.	d
Ratio	A comparison of two numbers by division.	$-, \div, /, :$
Symbol of Proportionality	A symbol indicating a relationship between two variables.	$\propto$ or "= k"
Constant of Proportionality	An unchanging constant that relates the value of two variables.	k
Proportion	An equation stating the equality of two ratios.	
Variable	A letter or symbol that stands for a number that can be changed.	Sometimes x or y
Circumference	The line bounding a circle, the length of that line.	c
Compass	An instrument with two pivoted legs, for drawing circles.	
pi	The symbol designating the ratio of the circumference of a circle to its diameter.	π
Best fit straight line	A line which estimates (guesses at) the best line which characterizes the cohesion of the confluence and correlates the consanguinity and concurrence of the data points. It is not the line that directly connects the points.	
Alliteration	The repetition of initial consonant sounds in two or more neighboring words or syllables.	
Run	Change in the horizontal direction(Δx).	$\Delta x = x_2 - x_1$
Rise	Change in the vertical direction(Δy).	$\Delta y = y_2 - y_1$
Slope (m)	m = rise/run, $\dfrac{\text{change in y}}{\text{change in x}} = \dfrac{\Delta y}{\Delta x} = \dfrac{y_2 - y_1}{x_2 - x_1}$ where (x_1, y_1) and (x_2, y_2) represent an ordered pair of coordinates, indicating points in the plane.	m

PURPOSE: To measure the radius and area of circles and develop an equation to relate the two variables.

MATERIALS:
Compass
Centimeter ruler
Graph paper with centimeter graduations
Log graph paper

PROCEDURE:
1. Use the ruler to measure the distance for the radius of a circle. Enter this value in the column for radius. Measure in centimeters and estimate to the nearest 0.1 cm.

2. Draw a circle with the radius you have determined on centimeter graph paper.

3. Count the number of square centimeters inside the circle. Count the ones that have most of the square centimeter inside the circle. Do not count the ones with most of the square centimeter outside the circle.

<u>Remember, this is a measurement and all measurements are approximations.</u>

4. Repeat steps 1-3 to measure two more circles.

5. Plot the data for radius on the horizontal axis and area on the vertical axis of regular graph paper.

6. Draw the line to connect the data points.

7. Plot the data for radius on the horizontal axis, and area on the vertical axis on the log graph paper.

8. Draw the best straight line to fit the data. (A straight line indicates that an exponential function might relate the two variables).

9. Plot the data for radius squared (r^2) on the horizontal axis and area on the vertical axis on regular graph paper.

10. Draw the best straight line to fit the data from the r^2 versus area graph.

11. Select a convenient pair of points on the "best fit straight line" from the area versus r^2 graph and use to calculate slope: $m = \dfrac{rise}{run} = \dfrac{change\ in\ y}{change\ in\ x} = \dfrac{\Delta y}{\Delta x} = \dfrac{y_2 - y_1}{x_2 - x_1}$.

Data table:

Circle	Radius(r)	Area(A)	r²	Ratio A/r²
#1				
#2				
#3				

CALCULATION:

We can see that as the radius increases, so does the area. An expression that states this relationship is:

$$A \propto r$$

On regular graph paper the line is not straight so the symbol meaning proportional ($\propto$) cannot be replaced by: " = k".

When the area is graphed against the radius on the log graph paper the best fit line connecting the points is straight, so it is probable that the area is proportional to some exponential function of the radius.

Since the graph of A versus r² is a straight line, let us use this graph to find our proportionality constant.

$$A \propto r^2$$

And since we have a straight line, the proportionality sign ($\propto$) can be replaced by "= k"

$$A = k\, r^2$$

And

$$k = \frac{A}{r^2}$$

This constant is the ratio A/r². If we measured accurately we find the ratio to be about 3.14. This proportionality constant is very important in math and is given its own symbol (π) and name (*pi*). Since the relationship between Area and radius squared is linear, the constant of proportionality can be calculated from one value, a better value would be the slope of the best fit straight line. This slope from the best fit straight line is sort of an average. Calculating a linear regression using a graphing calculator can give a very accurate value for a slope from data like this.

$$\pi = \frac{A}{r^2}$$

which becomes

$$A = \pi r^2$$

Scene: Math Classroom

Bunny (bubbly): I just love to draw circles.

Sunny (sourly): Why do we have to draw them on this graph paper?

Bunny: So we can count the number of square centimeters inside the circle.

Sunny: But some don't fit inside the circle, they hang out.

Bunny: You get to decide whether it is mostly inside or outside.

Sunny (sarcastically): Choices! Choices! Choices! I can't stand all the pressure.

Bunny: Get over it!

Sunny: I keep losing count of which squares I have counted.

Bunny: Mark the ones you have counted, Silly.

Sunny: Who you callin' Silly? I'm captain of the J. V. football team.

Bunny: You have told me already.

Sunny: I am a big wheel.

Bunny: You know what dogs do to wheels?

TANGENT
THE

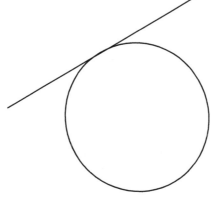

Overview: This activity presents students an opportunity to experience a number of mathematical terms, measure angles, distances, and compare the values from their data to calculator generated values.

Mathematical Learning Objective:

The student will:

Draw tangent lines to a circle and determine the slopes of the lines.

Compare their data to known values.

NCTM Standards:

Geometry

Specify locations and describe spatial relationships using coordinate geometry and other representational systems.

Measurement

Understand measurable attributes of objects and the units, systems, and processes of measurement.

Definitions:

Word	Definition	Symbol
Angle	The space or shape made by the intersection of two straight lines. On coordinate graph paper, usually measured clockwise from the x-axis.	$\angle$. In this activity measured in degrees(°)
Degree	A unit of measure for angles and arcs; 1/360 of a circle.	°
Length	Distance between two points.	In this experiment measured in centimeters(cm)
Rise	Change in the vertical direction(Δy).	$\Delta y = y_2 - y_1$
Run	Change in the horizontal direction(Δx).	$\Delta x = x_2 - x_1$
Tangent	A line touching a curved surface at one point, but not intersecting it.	
Slope (m)	m = rise/run, $\dfrac{\text{change in y}}{\text{change in x}} = \dfrac{\Delta y}{\Delta x} = \dfrac{y_2 - y_1}{x_2 - x_1}$ where (x_1,y_1) and (x_2,y_2) represent an ordered pair of coordinates, indicating points in the plane.	m
Intersect	To meet or cross.	
Vertex	The point of intersection of the two sides of an angle.	
Origin	The source; the intersection of the x-axis and the y-axis; the point (0,0).	(0,0)

Measuring can make numbers real for us. We will make our measurements of length in centimeters. We will measure angles in degrees. Angles will be measured counter clockwise from the horizontal (x-axis).

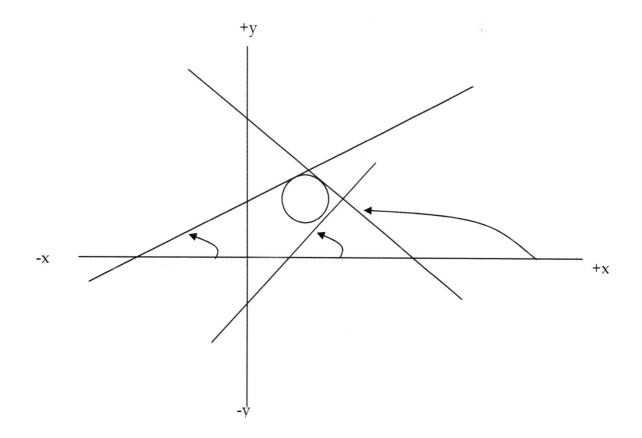

PURPOSE: To measure the slope of a line and relate it to the concept of tangent.

MATERIALS:
Graph paper graduated in cm
Ruler
Protractor
Compass
Scientific calculator or Trigonometry Table

PROCEDURE:

1. Draw a circle on a piece of graph paper. Locate the circle near the origin of a regular x,y graph plot.

2. Draw at least three tangent lines.

3. Draw the tangent lines long enough to cross the x and y axes on the graph paper. Locate two points on the line. The points may be the points where the line crosses the x- and y-axes.

4. Find the slope, rise/run of the lines.

5. Measure the angle formed by the tangent line and the x axis, counterclockwise from the x-axis for all three lines.

6. Fill in the table below.

7. Obtain the tangent of the angle from a calculator or a trigonometry table.

Line	Angle $\angle°$	Point 1 (x_1,y_1)	Point 2 (x_2,y_2)	Rise (y_2-y_1)	Run (x_2-x_1)	Ratio rise/run (fraction)	Ratio rise/run (decimal)	Tangent of the angle
#1								
#2								
#3								
#4								

If your slope is negative, most calculators will give you a negative angle for the tangent, indicating measuring counterclockwise from the x-axis. Is there a relationship between the positive angle you measured and the negative angle given by the calculator? Remember, a straight line contains $180°$ (inner angle).

Scene: Lunchroom - Fish Sticks for Lunch

Sunny: How do we know this stuff is true?

Bunny: Because when we measure the numbers come out right.

Sunny: Where does this tangent stuff come from?

Bunny: People started measuring things thousands of years ago and this is one of the ideas they came up with.

Sunny: How do we know it is true?

Bunny: Because this stuff has been done and found to be true for thousands of years.

Sunny: They didn't have calculators thousands of years ago.

Bunny: People started this "stuff" to measure things.

Sunny: I still am not sure why it fits together.

Bunny: I feel a sense of satisfaction when I see order and agreement in what I am doing.

Sunny: What has this stuff got to do with the real world?

Bunny: It was invented to measure land, and land is money, and you can't get more "real world" than money.

LESSON NOTES

How Do We Know?

ADDENDUM II

LESSON NOTES

How Do We Know?

Decimals, Muliplication, and Division

DECIMALS

Number	Hundreds	Tens	Ones	Decimal	Tenths $\frac{1}{10}$	Hundredths $\frac{1}{100}$	Thousandths $\frac{1}{1000}$
561.717	5	6	1	.	7	1	7

MULTIPLICATION

Webster's Dictionary says that multiplication is the operation by which any given quantity or number can be increased by being added to itself any number of times.

$$3 \times 12 = (12+12+12) = 36$$

DIVISION

The Encyclopedia Britannica tells us that:

If a and b are whole numbers and a<b, there exists two numbers c and r such that a = bc + r.

Which would lead to: a/b = c + r/b = __c + r/b__ ; 3/2 = __1 ½__

b) a   2) 3

Overview: Seems to me, that although they are useful, calculators introduce an abstraction into learning mathematics that obscures the practicality of numbers. A review of multiplication, division, and decimals will refresh the student's knowledge.

Mathematical Learning Objective:	The student will:
	Express number value in terms of the decimal system.
	Solve multiplication and long division problems with numbers containing decimals.

NCTM Standards:	Number and operations:
	Understand numbers, ways of representing numbers, relationships among numbers, and number systems.

Definitions:

Term	Definition/comment	Symbol/Example
Multiplication	It is often easier than addition, if groups of things are counted, 3(5) = 5+5+5 = 15.	$X, (), \times, \bullet$
Factor	One of the numbers that when multiplied times a number or other numbers yields a product.	In the sentence bc = a, "b" and "c" are factors of the product "a".
Product	The number obtained by multiplying two or more numbers together.	In the sentence $2 \times 3 = 6$, "2" and "3" are factors of the product "6".
Division	The inverse of multiplication. The process of finding one of the factors (quotient) that when multiplied by another factor (divisor) yields an answer (dividend).	$/, -, \div, \overline{)}$ Note: $\frac{a}{b} = \frac{a}{b} = a \div b = b\overline{)a}$
Dividend	The quantity divided in a division problem. The top number of a fraction (numerator). The product of a divisor and a quotient.	In the sentence a/b = c, which yields a = bc, the dividend is "a"
Divisor	The bottom part of a fraction (denominator). One of the factors which when multiplied times a quotient yields a dividend.	In the sentence a/b = c, the divisor is "b".
Quotient	The answer to a division problem. One of the factors which when multiplied times a divisor yields a dividend.	In the sentence a/b = c, the quotient is "c".
Decimal	A proper fraction in which the bottom number (denominator) is a power of ten which is signified in the decimal as a point placed to the left of the decimal number.	$\frac{35}{100} = 0.35$
Place value	The value of an integer in a number is indicated by the place in the number relative to a decimal point.	
Remainder	The undivided part in a division problem; what is left over. It is less than or of lower degree than the divisor.	

To the Student: It seems to me that many students forget their multiplication tables and forget the process of long division, and then dealing with fractions becomes a real nightmare and math is not fun any more. I hope that you will relearn your multiplication tables and that this review will clarify what dividing numbers is about. If you give it a try you might even begin to like math again.

Our counting system is based on counting units of ten

Number	Hundreds	Tens	Ones	Decimal	Tenths $\frac{1}{10}$	Hundredths $\frac{1}{100}$	Thousandths $\frac{1}{1000}$
561.717	5	6	1	.	7	1	7
0.001			0	.	0	0	1
0.214			0	.	2	1	4
-833	-8	-3	-3	.			

Adding a zero to a number after the decimal point does not change the value of a number:
Examples: 1 = 1.0 = 1.00 = 1.000, and 3.62 = 3.620 = 3.6200

We will need to add on these zeroes for some division problems. This adding on of zeros is sometimes called annexing zeroes. These zeroes we add help us keep the decimal places lined up and remind us there is no number other than zero in that space.

If we are talking about measurements, there is an implied meaning that zeroes after a decimal point in a number represent values that have been measured and found to be zero. Calculations with measurements bring new meanings to numbers. Numbers can be meaningful but not significant. How can that be? A paradox? You will learn more about that in your physical science classes.

SOME NOTES ON ADDITION AND SUBTRACTION
Let's think about counting. When we get to 9 and add 1 (9 + 1 = 10) it is as if the next number,10, pulls the numbers 1 through 9 into the tens column leaving what's left, zero, in the ones column and giving a 1 to the tens column. When we add 2 (9 + 2 = 11) it only takes 1 to push a 1 into the tens column and leaves a 1 in the ones column. The table below shows what happens when we add 2 to forty nine (49 +2 = 51) and 2 to 99 (99 + 2 = 101).

Hundreds	Tens	Ones		Hundreds	Tens	Ones		Hundreds	Tens	Ones
0	0	9 + 1	=	0	0	10	=	0	1	0
0	0	9 + 2	=	0	0	11	=	0	0	10+ 1
0	0	10+1	=	0	1	1				
0	4	9 + 2	=	0	4	11	=	0	4	10 + 1
0	4	10+1	=	0	5	1				
0	9	9 + 2	=	0	9	11	=	0	9	10 + 1
0	9	10 + 1	=	0	9 +1	1	=	0	10	1
0	10	1	=	1	0	1				

When we reach ten in the ones column, a one spills over into the tens column, and we put a zero in the ones column and a one in the tens column. When we reach ten tens, a one spills over into the hundreds column. This process of moving a number representing groups of ten of something to a higher place value is often called "carry over". In an addition problem, it looks something like:

ADDITION

Add: 63 and 49

	Operation			Operation	
Carry over		1			
63 + 49	Add 3 and 9, get 12, Place the 2 in the ones column under the nine, carry over the 1.	63 + 49 2	Add 1 and 6 and 4, get 11. Place a 1 in the tens column and put a 1 in the hundreds column.	63 + 49 112

SUBTRACTION

The process of subtraction in the decimal system often requires a group of ten of something to be brought back into the lower place value column. This decreases the number in the higher place value column by 1 and increases the number in the lower place column by 10. This process is often referred to as "borrowing".

Hundreds	Tens	Ones		Hundreds	Tens	Ones		Hundreds	Tens	Ones
7	5	3	=	6	10 + 5	3	=	6	15	3
	3	5	=		2	10 + 5	=		2	15

In a subtraction problem this "borrowing" looks something like this:

Subtract: 29 from 73

	Operation			Operation		
Borrowed		1				
73 - 29	To subtract 9 from 3 we must get ten from the tens column, add it to 3 and get 13; and the 7 in the tens column is decreased to 6.	6 (10+3) - 2 9 4	In the tens column, subtract 2 from 6 and get 4.	6 (13) - 2 9 4 4	73 - 29 44

You can see that when we borrow a ten from the tens column we add ten to the three in the ones column. The tens column is decreased to 6.

Terms like "carry over" and "borrow" and "bring down" are not usually defined in precise mathematically correct terms. These terms are sort of folksy usages. This kind of term is often referred to as colloquial. Your mathematics teacher will be smart enough to define them for you using terms like "regrouping".

MULTIPLICATION

A review of multiplication tables will be helpful. The "×" means multiplication in the following exercises.

Multiply: 3 times 56

Carry over number		1
Factor	56	56
Factor	X3	X3
		168

Carry over number				Carry over number				Carry over number		1	1
Factor	6	6		Factor	50	50		Factor	56	56	56
Factor	X3	X3		Factor	X3	X3		Factor	X3	X3	X3
Product		18		Product		150		Partial	18	8	
								Products	150	15	
								Product	168	168	168

Notice that the last representation of the multiplication is the way it is normally written. In the last multiplication of 3 times 50, the zero in the ones column is not written and the carry over number is added to the 15 for the final product. Take special notice that the 5 in fifteen is placed in the tens column. Most people would have you multiply 3 times 6 and write the 8 in the ones column. Multiply 3 times 5 and then perform addition of the carry over number to the fifteen in your head. You can do that, can you not? With a little practice it won't be so mysterious.

Multiply 4.3 X 7.6

Carry over number		1		Carry over number				Carry over number		
Factor	7.6	7.6		Factor	7.6	7.6		Factor	7.6	7.6
Factor	X.3	X.3		Factor	X4.0	X4.0		Factor	X4.3	X4.3
Product		2.28		Partial product		30.40		Partial products		2.28
										+30.4
								Product		32.68

Notice:

!. The carry over number is added after the multiplication.

2. In the last multiplication the zero in the product of 4.3 times 7.6 is not shown, but a space is left so that the place value of the addition is correct.

3. In each case the number of numbers after the decimal place is the same as the total number of decimal places in the factors. You count the decimal places in the factors and mark off from the end (right side) of the product. In the above example there are a total of two decimal places in the products and the answer has two decimal places.

DIVISION

Eight little pigs are in a straw house when four wolves blow it down. How many pigs does each wolf get?

As a ratio this is: $\dfrac{8\,pigs}{4\,wolves}$. Notice that this ratio has units of pigs/wolves.

From the definitions above: divisor × quotient = dividend and: $\dfrac{dividend}{divisor}$ = quotient, and the quotient will have units of pigs/wolf.

So, the number of wolves, four, is the divisor, and the number of pigs, eight, is the dividend. The number of pigs each wolf gets is the quotient. As a division problem this looks like:

Division Problem	Divisor		Dividend		Quotient	
	Number	Justification	Number	Justification	Number	Justification
$4\overline{)8}$	4	Bottom number in a ratio.	8	Top number in a ratio.	To be determined.	The number that times the divisor (4) equals the dividend (8).

Solution process:

Division Problem	Operation	Result	Operation	Result	Operation	Result
$4\overline{)8}$	We estimate the quotient. What times four gives a number close to, but less than or equal to eight? We try 2.	$4\overline{)8}$ with 2 above	Multiply the divisor times the quotient and write it under the dividend. We want to check so we subtract.	$\begin{array}{r} 2 \\ 4\overline{)8} \\ -8 \\ \hline 0 \end{array}$	The estimated quotient works and there are no pigs left over.	$\begin{array}{r} 2\,r\,0 \\ 4\overline{)8} \\ -8 \\ \hline 0 \end{array}$

Notice we lined up the 2 over the eight and were careful to lineup the - 8 under the dividend and each wolf gets exactly 2 pigs, and everybody is happy, except maybe the pigs. Sometimes there are numbers (pigs) left over and they are called remainders (r).

This quotient represents how many pigs 1 wolf gets.

As a ratio this is: $\dfrac{2\,pigs}{1\,wolf}$

The whole problem can be expressed as a proportion; this is: $\dfrac{8\,pigs}{4\,wolves} = \dfrac{2\,pigs}{1\,wolf}$

Moving right along with the story, these four wolves come to a wooden house where there is only one pig. They blow the house down and are puzzled about how to share the pig.

As a ratio this is: $\dfrac{1\,pig}{4\,wolves}$. Notice that this ratio has units of pig/wolves.

Now polite, civilized wolves would probably let the pig go. However, most wolves are not polite and civilized, so the story has to get messy and we will get messy and introduce decimals to division. How do you do!

Division Problem	Divisor		Dividend		Quotient	
	Number	Justification	Number	Justification	Number	Justification
4) 1̄	4	Bottom number in a ratio.	1	Top number in a ratio.	To be determined.	The number that times the divisor (4) equals the dividend (1).

Remember above we gave ourselves permission to add zeros at the end of a number. Adding a zero at the end of a number, after the decimal point does not change the value of a number: 1 = 1.0 = 1.00 = 1.000, and 3.62 = 3.620 = 3.6200

Some zeroes will need to be added to the dividend (the number being divided) after the decimal point. The decimal points lineup all the way from the final remainder to the quotient (answer).

Division Problem	Operation	Result	Operation	Result
4) 1̄	Four will not go into 1 a whole number of times so we put a 0 over the one. We need to add a zero after the decimal point because 4 will go into 1.0 a decimal fraction number of times.	0 4) 1.0	We estimate the quotient. What number times four gives a number close to but less than or equal to 1.0? We try 0.2, do the multiplication and subtract and get a remainder of 0.2 (highlighted).	0.2 4) 1.0 - 0.8 0.2
0.2 4) 1.0 - 0.8 0.2	We need to add another zero because 4 will not go into 0.2 (which has become a new dividend) a whole number of times, but will go into 0.20 a decimal fraction number of times.	0.2 4) 1.00 - 0.80 0.20	We estimate the quotient. What number times four gives a number close to but less than or equal to 0.20 (highlighted)? We try 0.05, we the multiply 0.05 times 4 and get 0.20, we subtract and get a remainder of 0.00.	0.25 4) 1.00 - 0.80 0.20 - 0.20 0.00

Of course the wolves will have to kill the pig to divide him up and will probably eat their ¼ of the pig on the spot. But what did you think they were going to do with the pigs anyway? Fatten them up to show at the County Fair?

Sometimes in the little pigs stories, the pigs escape and end up in a house made of bricks built by a wise pig. The wolf cannot blow down the brick house and so the story ends. For this story, let's let the eight little pigs from the straw house escape to the wise pig's house. After all there were eight pigs running every which of way, squealing like pigs and the wolves got confused. Now the 8 pigs get to the wise pig's house and he lets them in just before the wolves get there. We are going toneed smart wolves since wolves cannot blow down a brick house. Well, we have smarter wolves and they bring dynamite and blowup the house. You ask, "how did they get the permit to buy the dynamite?" I don't know, but for the story the wolves need the dynamite. So there are four wolves and nine pigs, how many pigs will each wolf get?

As a ratio this is: $\dfrac{9\,\text{pigs}}{4\,\text{wolves}}$. Notice that this ratio has units of pigs/wolves.

From the definitions above: divisor × quotient = dividend   and: $\dfrac{\text{dividend}}{\text{divisor}}$ = quotient

Now we have 9 pigs and four wolves. How many pigs does each wolf get?

Division Problem	Divisor		Dividend		Quotient	
	Number	Justification	Number	Justification	Number	Justification
4) 9	4	Bottom number in a ratio.	9	Top number in a ratio.	To be determined.	The number that times the divisor (4) equals the dividend (9).

Division process

Division Problem	Operation	Result	Operation	Result
4) 9	We estimate the quotient. What number times four gives a number close to but less than or equal to nine? We try 2. We multiply 2 times 4, get 8, subtract and end up with a remainder of 1.	2 4) 9 - 8 1	We need to add a zero because 4 will not go into 1 a whole number of times, but will go into 1.0 (highlighted) a decimal fraction number of times.	2. 4) 9.0 - 8.0 1.0
2. * 4) 9.0 - 8.0 1.0	We estimate the quotient. What times four gives a number close to but less than or equal to 1.0. We try 0.2. Multiply 0.2 times 4, get 0.8 and subtract. We get a remainder of 0.2.	2.2 4) 9.0 - 8.0 1.0 - 0.8 0.2	We need to add another zero because 4 will not go into 0.2 a whole number of times, but will go into 0.20 (highlighted) a decimal fraction number of times.	2.2 4) 9.00 - 8.00 1.00 - 0.80 0.20
2.2 4) 9.00 - 8.00 1.00 - 0.80 0.20	We estimate the quotient, what times four gives a number close to but less than or equal to 0.20. We try 0.05, multiply 0.05 times 4, get 0.20 and subtract to get a remainder of 0.00.	2.25* 4) 9.00 - 8.00 1.00 - 0.80 0.20 - 0.20 0.00		

*This quotient could be expressed as 2 remainder 1, or 2 ¼, but we have added zeros at the end of the number and continued the division process to obtain 2.25.

PRECISION TEACHING (PT) SAMPLE ANSWERS

Fill in the following table:

Number	Hundreds	Tens	Ones	Decimal .	Tenths $\frac{1}{10}$	Hundredths $\frac{1}{100}$	Thousandths $\frac{1}{1000}$
15.43		1	5	.	4	3	

Divide 13 pieces of candy among 5 children.

Division Problem	Divisor		Dividend		Quotient	
$5)\overline{13}$	**Number**	**Justification**	**Number**	**Justification**	**Number**	**Justification**
	5	Bottom number in a ratio.	13	Top number in a ratio.	To be determined.	The number that times the divisor (6) equals the dividend (12).

Fill in the following table:

Division Problem	Operation	Result	Operation	result
$5)\overline{13}$	Five will not go into 1 a whole number of times so we put a 0 over the 1.	$5)\overline{\overset{0}{13}}$	We estimate the quotient; what times the divisor (5) gives a number close to but less than or equal to 13. We try 2. Multiply 2 times 5 and get 10, subtract to get a remainder of 3 (highlighted).	$5)\overline{\overset{02}{13}}$ $\underline{-10}$ 3
$5)\overline{\overset{02}{13}}$ $\underline{-10}$ 3	We need to add a zero because 5 will not go into 3 (which has become a new dividend) a whole number of times, but will go into 3.0 a decimal fraction number of times.	$5)\overline{\overset{02}{13.0}}$ $\underline{-10}$ 3.0	We estimate the quotient; what times the divisor (5) gives a number close to but less than or equal to 3.0? We try .6. Multiply 5 times .6 and get 3.0, subtract to get a remainder of 0.0.	$5)\overline{\overset{02.6}{13.0}}$ $\underline{-10}$ 3.0 $\underline{-3.0}$ 0.0

(Notice that the some of the numbers described in the "**Operation**" are placed in a box)

Multiply 7 X 23
Fill in the following table:

Carry over number	▇	2
Factor	23	23
Factor	X7	X7
Product	▇	161

LESSON NOTES

SEE PAGE 331 FOR <u>DECIMALS, MULTIPLICATION, AND DIVISION</u>: PRECISION TEACHING (PT) SCORES, FREQUENCY TABLE.

I suggest that students correct their papers, calculate the frequencies and graph their results. Graphing the results on special graph paper (Standard Celeration Chart) can provide visual reinforcement for the students and information about how they are learning. The frequency tables are provided to facilitate this process.

How Do We Know?

PT 1, QUESTIONS

Fill in the following table:

Number	Hundreds	Tens	Ones	Decimal $\cdot$	Tenths $\frac{1}{10}$	Hundredths $\frac{1}{100}$	Thousandths $\frac{1}{1000}$
674.1				$\cdot$			

Divide 22 Easter eggs between 4 children.
Fill in the following table:

Division Problem	Divisor		Dividend		Quotient	
	Number	**Justification**	**Number**	**Justification**	**Number**	**Justification**
4) 22		Bottom number in a ratio.		Top number in a ratio.		The number that times the divisor (4) equals the dividend (22).

Follow the instructions in the "Operation":

Division Problem	Operation	Result	Operation	Result
4) 22	Four will not go into 2 a whole number of times so we put a 0 over the two.	4) 22	We estimate the quotient. What number times the divisor (4) gives a number close to but less than or equal to 22? We try 5, do the multiplication, subtract and get a remainder of 2.	$\frac{0}{4)\,22}$
$\begin{array}{r} 05 \\ 4)\,22 \\ -20 \\ \hline 2 \end{array}$	We need to add another zero because 4 will not go into 2 (which has become a new dividend) a whole number of times, but will go into 2.0 a decimal fraction number of times.	$\begin{array}{r} 05 \\ 4)\,22 \\ -20 \\ \hline 2 \end{array}$	We estimate the quotient. What number times the divisor (4) gives a number close to but less than or equal to 2.0 (highlighted)? We try .5, we the multiply .5 times 4 and get 2.0, we subtract and get a remainder of 0.0.	$\begin{array}{r} 05 \\ 4)\,22.0 \\ -20.0 \\ \hline 2.0 \end{array}$

Multiply 7 X 89
Fill in the following table:

Carry over number		6
Factor	89	89
Factor	X7	X7
Product		

PT 1, ANSWERS

Fill in the following table:

Number	Hundreds	Tens	Ones	Decimal	Tenths $\frac{1}{10}$	Hundredths $\frac{1}{100}$	Thousandths $\frac{1}{1000}$
674.1	6	7	4	.	1		

Divide 22 Easter eggs between 4 children.
Fill in the following table by following the instructions in the "Operation":

Division Problem	Divisor		Dividend		Quotient	
	Number	Justification	Number	Justification	Number	Justification
4) 22	4	Bottom number in a ratio.	22	Top number in a ratio.	To be determined.	The number that times the divisor (4) equals the dividend (22).

Fill in the following table:

Division Problem	Operation	Result	Operation	Result
4) 22	Four will not go into 2 a whole number of times so we put a 0 over the two.	0 4) 22	We estimate the quotient. What number times the divisor (4) gives a number close to but less than or equal to 22? We try 5, do the multiplication, subtract and get a remainder of 2 (highlighted).	05 4) 22 - 20 2
05 4) 22 - 20 2	We need to add another zero because 4 will not go into 2 (which has become a new dividend) a whole number of times, but will go into 2.0 a decimal fraction number of times.	05 4) 22.0 - 20.0 2.0	We estimate the quotient. What number times the divisor (4) gives a number close to but less than or equal to 2.0? We try 0.5, we the multiply 0.5 times 4 and get 2.0, we subtract and get a remainder of 0.0.	05.5 4) 22.0 - 20.0 2.0 - 2.0 0.0

Multiply 7 X 89
Fill in the following table:

Carry over number		6
Factor	89	89
Factor	X7	X7
Product		623

PT 2, QUESTIONS

Fill in the following table:

Number	Hundreds	Tens	Ones	Decimal ·	Tenths $\frac{1}{10}$	Hundredths $\frac{1}{100}$	Thousandths $\frac{1}{1000}$
896.193				.			

Divide 18 by 4; 18 ÷ 4

Division Problem	Divisor		Dividend		Quotient	
	Number	Justification	Number	Justification	Number	Justification
4) 18	4		18		To be determined.	

Divide 18 oranges between four monkeys.
Follow the instructions in the "Operation":

Division Problem	Operation	Result	Operation	Result
4) 18	Four will not go into 1 a whole number of times so we put a 0 over the one.	4) 18	We estimate the quotient. What number times the divisor (4) gives a number close to but less than or equal to 18? We try 4, multiply 4 times 4, get 16, subtract and get a remainder of 2.	0 ‾ 4) 18
04 ‾ 4) 18 16 ‾ 2	We need to add a decimal point and a zero because 4 will not go into 2 (which has become a new dividend) a whole number of times, but will go into 2.0 a decimal fraction number of times.	04 ‾ 4) 18 16 ‾ 2	We estimate the quotient. What number times the divisor (4) gives a number close to but less than or equal to 2.0 (highlighted)? We try .5, we the multiply .5 times 4 and get 2.0. We subtract and get a remainder of 0.	04. ‾ 4) 18.0 - 16 ‾ 2.0

Multiply 3 X 39
Fill in the following table:

Carry over number		2
Factor	39	39
Factor	X 3	X3
Product		

PT 2, ANSWERS

Fill in the following table:

Number	Hundreds	Tens	Ones	Decimal .	Tenths $\frac{1}{10}$	Hundredths $\frac{1}{100}$	Thousandths $\frac{1}{1000}$
896.193	8	9	6	.	1	9	3

Divide 18 by 4; 18 ÷ 4

Division Problem	Divisor		Dividend		Quotient	
	Number	Justification	Number	Justification	Number	Justification
$4\overline{)18}$	4	Bottom number in a ratio.	18	Top number in a ratio.	To be determined.	The number that times the divisor (4) equals the dividend (18).

Divide 18 oranges between four monkeys.
Follow the instructions in the "Operation":

Division Problem	Operation	Result	Operation	Result
$4\overline{)18}$	Four will not go into 1 a whole number of times so we put a 0 over the one.	$\dfrac{0}{4\overline{)18}}$	We estimate the quotient. What number times the divisor (4) gives a number close to but less than or equal to 18? We try 4, multiply 4 times 4, get 16, subtract and get a remainder of 2. (highlighted)	$\begin{array}{r} 04 \\ \hline 4)18 \\ 16 \\ \hline 2 \end{array}$
$\begin{array}{r} 04 \\ \hline 4)18 \\ 16 \\ \hline 2 \end{array}$	We need to add a decimal point and a zero because 4 will not go into 2 (which has become a new dividend) a whole number of times, but will go into 2.0 a decimal fraction number of times.	$\begin{array}{r} 4. \\ \hline 4)18.0 \\ -16 \\ \hline 2.0 \end{array}$	We estimate the quotient. What number times the divisor (4) gives a number close to but less than or equal to 2.0 (highlighted)? We try .5, we the multiply .5 times 4 and get 2.0. We subtract and get a remainder of 0.	$\begin{array}{r} 4.5 \\ \hline 4)18.0 \\ -16 \\ \hline 2.0 \\ -2.0 \\ \hline 0.0 \end{array}$

Multiply 3 X 39
Fill in the following table:

Carry over number	■	2
Factor	39	39
Factor	X 3	X3
Product	■	117

PT 3, QUESTIONS

Fill in the following table:

Number	Hundreds	Tens	Ones	Decimal .	Tenths $\frac{1}{10}$	Hundredths $\frac{1}{100}$	Thousandths $\frac{1}{1000}$
647				.			

Problem: 28/8
Fill in the following table:

Division Problem	Divisor			Dividend			Quotient		
$8\overline{)28}$	Number	Justification		Number	Justification		Number	Justification	
		Bottom number in a ratio.			Top number in a ratio.			The number that times the divisor (8) equals the dividend (28).	

Follow the instructions in the "Operation":

Division Problem	Operation	Result	Operation	Result
$8\overline{)28}$	Eight will not go into 2 a whole number of times so we put a 0 over the 2.	$8\overline{)28}$	We estimate the quotient; what number times the divisor (8) gives a number close to but less than or equal to 28? We try 3, multiply 3 times 8, get 24, subtract and get a remainder of 4.	$\frac{0}{8\overline{)28}}$
$\frac{03}{8\overline{)28}}$ -24 4	We need to add a decimal point and a zero because 8 will not go into 4 (which has become a new dividend) a whole number of times, but will go into 4.0 a decimal fraction number of times.	$\frac{03}{8\overline{)28}}$ -24 4	We estimate the quotient: what number times the divisor (8) gives a number close to but less than or equal to 4.0 (highlighted)? We try .5, we then multiply .5 times 8 and get 4.0. We subtract and get a remainder of 0.0.	$\frac{03}{8\overline{)28.0}}$ -24.0 4.0

Multiply 0.46 X 7
Fill in the following table:

Carry over number		4
Factor	0.46	0.46
Factor	X7	X7
Product		

PT 3, ANSWERS

Fill in the following table:

Number	Hundreds	Tens	Ones	Decimal .	Tenths $\frac{1}{10}$	Hundredths $\frac{1}{100}$	Thousandths $\frac{1}{1000}$
647	6	4	7	.			

Problem: 28/8

Fill in the following table:

Division Problem	Divisor		Dividend		Quotient	
	Number	Justification	Number	Justification	Number	Justification
8) 28	8	Bottom number in a ratio.	28	Top number in a ratio.	To be determined.	The number that times the divisor (8) equals the dividend (28).

Follow the instructions in the "Operation":

Division Problem	Operation	Result	Operation	Result
8) 28	Eight will not go into 2 a whole number of times so we put a 0 over the 2.	0 8) 28	We estimate the quotient; what number times the divisor (8) gives a number close to but less than or equal to 28? We try 3, multiply 3 times 8, get 24. We subtract and get a remainder of 4 (highlighted).	03 8) 28 - 24 4
03 8) 28 - 24 4	We need to add a decimal point and a zero because 8 will not go into 4 (which has become a new dividend) a whole number of times, but will go into 4.0 a decimal fraction number of times.	03 8) 28.0 - 24.0 4.0	We estimate the quotient: what number times the divisor (8) gives a number close to but less than or equal to 4.0 (highlighted)? We try .5, we then multiply .5 times 8 and get 4.0. We subtract and get a remainder of 0.0.	03.5 8) 28.0 - 24.0 4.0 - 4.0 0.0

Multiply 0.46 X 7

Fill in the following table:

Carry over number	■	4
Factor	0.46	0.46
Factor	X7	X7
Product		3.22

How Do We Know?

O

T

N

E

C

R

E

P

O

Overview: In real life, percent numbers give a value for a fraction that with practice, the mind can easily grasp and compare. Fractions are converted to equivalent fractions which have 100 as the denominator. The fraction may be thought of as a ratio of a $\frac{part}{whole}$. The challenge in solving percent problems is reading the problem and identifying what is the "part" and what is the "whole". In most instances, the information is presented in written form; therefore percent problems give us an opportunity to practice getting information from word problems. In this chapter, we are going to practice writing fractions as decimals, percents, and equivalent fractions with 100 as the denominator. Word problems are presented for practice in reading problems to decide what information is given and what information is asked for.

Examples of solved percent problems will be presented; however, the solving procedure for ratio and proportion will be considered fully in the chapters on solving equations.

Mathematical Learning Objective:

The student will:

Practice converting fractions into decimals and percents, and decimals into equivalent fractions with 100 as the denominator.

Read word problems and select the information necessary to solve the problems.

NCTM Standards:

Algebra

Represent and analyze mathematical situations and structures using algebraic symbols.

Number and operations

Understand numbers, ways of representing numbers, relationships among numbers, and number systems.

Definitions:

Word	Definition	Symbol
Ratio	A comparison of two numbers by division.	$-, \div, /, :$
Proportion	An equation stating the equality of two ratios.	
Percent	In, to, or for every hundred.	%
Fraction bar	Indicates division of the top number (numerator) by the bottom number (denominator).	$-$
Substitution assumption	If quantities are defined as equal, they may be substituted for each other.	
Fraction	A quantity less than a whole that has a numerator and a denominator. When describing parts of a whole, each part must be the same size and sometimes there are more parts than in the whole (Improper fractions) therefore the part and whole description is only sometimes a useful picture	$\dfrac{\text{part}}{\text{whole}}$
Analogy	Resemblance in some particulars between things otherwise unlike.	
Percent Number	In the percent ratio, we are going to call the number over 100 the percent number.	$\dfrac{1}{2} = \dfrac{50}{100} = 50\%$. The 50 is the percent number.
Discount	The amount taken away from a listed price.	
Markup	The amount added to a listed price. Often for a store, the listed price is a wholesale price.	

The words part and whole are placed in quotation marks because the exact definition of the words "part" and "whole" will often not describe the situation. Sometimes, in percent increase problems for example, a "part" will be greater than the "whole".

One method of solving percent problems is ratios and proportions. Let us look at what the "part", whole ratio looks like in these proportions.

$$\frac{\text{part}}{\text{whole}} = \frac{\text{percent} \#}{100}$$

Example:
Cut a circular pie into four equal pieces. One piece represents what percent?

$$\frac{\text{part}}{\text{whole}} = \frac{1}{4} = \frac{25}{100} = 25\%$$

Example:
A dress for $60 is on sale at 20% off. What is the discount?
The discount on a sale item is often the "part".

$$\frac{\text{part}}{\text{whole}} = \frac{\text{discount}}{\$60} = 20\% = \frac{20}{100} = 0.2$$

$$\frac{\text{discount}}{\$60} = 0.2$$

Solved for discount: $\qquad$ discount $= \$60 \times 0.2 = \$12$

Notice: The actual calculation is done with the decimal form of the percent number.

In chemistry the amount of an element in a sample is often very important.

Example:
Bauxite is an ore that contains aluminum. In a lab experiment a 50 gram sample of bauxite was examined and found to contain 10 grams of aluminum. What is the percent of aluminum in the sample of bauxite?

$$\% \text{ aluminum} = \frac{\text{part}}{\text{whole}} = \frac{10 \text{ grams}}{50 \text{ grams}} = 0.2 = \frac{20}{100} = 20\%$$

Percents are often used to describe behaviors in groups of people.

Example:
Happytown had a population of 436 people in 1970. In 1980 the population was 1744. Find the percent change. The change is: final – original = 1744 – 436 = 1308

$$\text{Percent increase} = \frac{\text{change}}{\text{original}} = \frac{1308}{436} = 3.00 = \frac{3.00}{1} \times \frac{100}{100} = \frac{300}{100} = 300\%$$

In science a measured value is often compared to a listed or reference value and a percent error is calculated.

Example:
In a lab experiment the density of iron was found to be 8.2 g/cm³. Iron has a density of 7.9 g/cm³. What is the percent error in the experimental density determination?
error = measured value – known value = 8.2 g/cm³ - 7.9 g/cm³ = 0.3 g/cm³.

$$\frac{\text{part}}{\text{whole}} = \frac{\text{error}}{\text{known value}} = \frac{0.3\,\text{g/cm}^3}{7.9\,\text{g/cm}^3} = .038 = \frac{.038}{1} \times \frac{100}{100} = \frac{3.8}{100} = 3.8\%$$

Since: $\dfrac{\text{part}}{\text{whole}} = \dfrac{\text{percent\#}}{100}$, the above process can be simplified to: $\dfrac{\text{part}}{\text{whole}} \times 100 = \text{percent\#}$

Notice the decimal form of the $\dfrac{\text{part}}{\text{whole}}$ is used for calculations.

$$\frac{\text{part}}{\text{whole}} = \frac{\text{percent\#}}{100}$$

$$\text{percent\#} = \frac{\text{part}}{\text{whole}} \times 100$$

$$\frac{\text{part}}{\text{whole}} = \text{decimal}$$

$$\text{part} = \text{decimal} \times \text{whole}$$

$$\text{whole} = \frac{\text{part}}{\text{decimal}}$$

How Do We Know?

The same number can be expressed as a decimal, a fraction, a number over 100, or a percent number. All of these expressions are representations of the same number.

Example: $0.64 = \dfrac{16}{25} = \dfrac{64}{100} = 64 \text{ percent} = 64\%$

The fraction bar means division.

Example: $\dfrac{16}{25} = 16 \div 25 = 0.64$

Dividing a number by 1 does not change the value of the number.

Example: $0.64 = \dfrac{0.64}{1}$

Dividing a number by itself: Any number (except zero) divided by itself is 1.

Example: $\dfrac{100}{100} = 1$

Identity Property: Multiplying a number by one does not change the value.

Example: $\dfrac{0.64}{1} \times 1 = \dfrac{0.64}{1} \times \dfrac{100}{100}$

To turn a percent number into a number over 100, remove the percent word or symbol and write as the number over 100.

Example: $64 \text{ percent} = 64\% = \dfrac{64}{100}$

Precision Teaching (PT) Sample Answers

Fill in the following table:

Expression	Change	Justification for change
$\dfrac{3}{4}$	0.75	Fraction bar means division.
0.75	$\dfrac{0.75}{1}$	A number can be divided by one and not change the value of the number.
$\dfrac{0.75}{1}$	$\dfrac{0.75}{1}\text{X}1$	A number can be multiplied by one and not change the value of the number.
1	$\dfrac{100}{100}=1$	Any number (except 0) divided by itself is 1.
$\dfrac{0.75}{1}\text{X}1$	$\dfrac{0.75}{1}\text{X}\dfrac{100}{100}$	Quantities defined as equal may be substituted for each other.
$\dfrac{0.75}{1}\text{X}\dfrac{100}{100}$	$\dfrac{75}{100}$	To multiply fractions, multiply top numbers for a new top number and multiply bottom numbers for a new bottom number.
$\dfrac{75}{100}$	0.75	Definition of % sign.

Fill in the following table:

Decimal	Ratio	$\dfrac{\text{number}}{100}$	Percent (%)
0.75	$\dfrac{0.75}{1}$ or $\dfrac{75}{100}$ or $\dfrac{3}{4}$	$\dfrac{75}{100}$	75%
0.4	$\dfrac{0.4}{1}$ or $\dfrac{40}{100}$ or $\dfrac{2}{5}$	$\dfrac{40}{100}$	40%
0.5	$\dfrac{0.5}{1}$ or $\dfrac{50}{100}$ or $\dfrac{1}{2}$	$\dfrac{50}{100}$	50%
0.25	$\dfrac{0.25}{1}$ or $\dfrac{25}{100}$ or $\dfrac{1}{4}$	$\dfrac{25}{100}$	25%
0.125	$\dfrac{0.125}{1}$ or $\dfrac{12.5}{100}$ or $\dfrac{1}{8}$	$\dfrac{12.5}{100}$	12.5%
0.9	$\dfrac{0.9}{1}$ or $\dfrac{90}{100}$ or $\dfrac{9}{10}$	$\dfrac{90}{100}$	90%

SEE PAGE 331 FOR <u>PERCENT</u>: PRECISION TEACHING (PT) SCORES, FREQUENCY TABLE.

I suggest that students correct their papers, calculate the frequencies and graph their results. Graphing the results on special graph paper (Standard Celeration Chart) can provide visual reinforcement for the students and information about how they are learning. The frequency tables are provided to facilitate this process.

PT 1, QUESTIONS

Fill in the following table:

Expression	Change	Justification for change
$\dfrac{3}{5}$	0.60	Fraction bar means division.
0.60	$\dfrac{0.60}{1}$	
$\dfrac{0.60}{1}$	$\dfrac{0.60}{1} \times 1$	A number can be multiplied by one and not change the value of the number.
1	$1 = \dfrac{100}{100}$	
$\dfrac{0.60}{1} \times 1$	$\dfrac{0.60}{1} \times \dfrac{100}{100}$	Quantities defined as equal may be substituted for each other.
$\dfrac{0.60}{1} \times \dfrac{100}{100}$	$\dfrac{60}{100}$	
$\dfrac{60}{100}$	60%	

Fill in the following table:

Decimal	Ratio	$\dfrac{\text{number}}{100}$	Percent (%)
0.15		$\dfrac{15}{100}$	
	$\dfrac{0.3}{1}$ or $\dfrac{30}{100}$ or $\dfrac{3}{10}$		30%
1.5		$\dfrac{150}{100}$	
0.75		$\dfrac{75}{100}$	
0.0125	$\dfrac{0.0125}{1}$ or $\dfrac{1.25}{100}$ or $\dfrac{1}{80}$		1.25 %
0.6			60%

PT 1, ANSWERS

Fill in the following table:

Expression	Change	Justification
$\dfrac{3}{5}$	0.60	Fraction bar means division.
0.60	$\dfrac{0.60}{1}$	**A number can be divided by one and not change the value of the number.**
$\dfrac{0.60}{1}$	$\dfrac{0.60}{1} \times 1$	A number can be multiplied by one and not change the value of the number.
1	$1 = \dfrac{100}{100}$	**Any number (except 0) divided by itself is 1.**
$\dfrac{0.60}{1} \times 1$	$\dfrac{0.60}{1} \times \dfrac{100}{100}$	Quantities defined as equal may be substituted for each other.
$\dfrac{0.60}{1} \times \dfrac{100}{100}$	$\dfrac{60}{100}$	**To multiply fractions, multiply top numbers for a new top number and multiply bottom numbers for a new bottom number.**
$\dfrac{60}{100}$	60%	**Definition of % sign.**

Fill in the following table:

Decimal	Ratio			$\dfrac{\text{number}}{100}$	Percent (%)
0.15	$\dfrac{0.15}{1}$ or	$\dfrac{15}{100}$ or	$\dfrac{3}{20}$	$\dfrac{15}{100}$	**15%**
0.3	$\dfrac{0.3}{1}$ or	$\dfrac{30}{100}$ or	$\dfrac{3}{10}$	$\dfrac{\mathbf{30}}{\mathbf{100}}$	30%
1.5	$\dfrac{\mathbf{1.5}}{\mathbf{1}}$ or	$\dfrac{\mathbf{150}}{\mathbf{100}}$ or	$\dfrac{\mathbf{3}}{\mathbf{2}}$	$\dfrac{150}{100}$	**150%**
0.75	$\dfrac{\mathbf{0.75}}{\mathbf{1}}$ or	$\dfrac{\mathbf{75}}{\mathbf{100}}$ or	$\dfrac{\mathbf{3}}{\mathbf{4}}$	$\dfrac{75}{100}$	**75%**
0.0125	$\dfrac{0.0125}{1}$ or	$\dfrac{1.25}{100}$ or	$\dfrac{1}{80}$	$\dfrac{\mathbf{1.25}}{\mathbf{100}}$	1.25 %
0.6	$\dfrac{\mathbf{0.6}}{\mathbf{1}}$ or	$\dfrac{\mathbf{60}}{\mathbf{100}}$ or	$\dfrac{\mathbf{3}}{\mathbf{5}}$	$\dfrac{\mathbf{60}}{\mathbf{100}}$	60%

How Do We Know?

PT 2, QUESTIONS

Fill in the following table:

Expression	Change	Justification for change
$\dfrac{4}{5}$	0.80	
0.80	$\dfrac{0.80}{1}$	A number can be divided by one and not change the value of the number.
$\dfrac{0.80}{1}$	$\dfrac{0.80}{1}\text{X}1$	
1	$1=\dfrac{100}{100}$	Any number (except 0) divided by itself is 1.
$\dfrac{0.80}{1}\text{X}1$	$\dfrac{0.80}{1}\text{X}\dfrac{100}{100}$	
$\dfrac{0.80}{1}\text{X}\dfrac{100}{100}$	$\dfrac{80}{100}$	To multiply fractions, multiply top numbers for a new top number and multiply bottom numbers for a new bottom number.
$\dfrac{80}{100}$	80%	

Fill in the following table:

Decimal	Ratio	$\dfrac{\text{number}}{100}$	Percent (%)
	$\dfrac{0.35}{1}$ or $\dfrac{35}{100}$ or $\dfrac{7}{20}$		35%
0.03		$\dfrac{3}{100}$	
2.5			250%
	$\dfrac{0.05}{1}$ or $\dfrac{5}{100}$ or $\dfrac{1}{20}$	$\dfrac{5}{100}$	
	$\dfrac{1.25}{1}$ or $\dfrac{125}{100}$ or $\dfrac{5}{4}$		
0.7			

PT 2, ANSWERS

Fill in the following table

Expression	Change	Justification
$\dfrac{4}{5}$	0.80	**Fraction bar means division.**
0.80	$\dfrac{0.80}{1}$	A number can be divided by one and not change the value of the number.
$\dfrac{0.80}{1}$	$\dfrac{0.80}{1} \times 1$	**A number can be multiplied by one and not change the value of the number.**
1	$1 = \dfrac{100}{100}$	Any number (except 0) divided by itself is 1.
$\dfrac{0.80}{1} \times 1$	$\dfrac{0.80}{1} \times \dfrac{100}{100}$	**Quantities defined as equal may be substituted for each other.**
$\dfrac{0.80}{1} \times \dfrac{100}{100}$	$\dfrac{80}{100}$	To multiply fractions multiply top numbers for a new top number and multiply bottom numbers for a new bottom number.
$\dfrac{80}{100}$	80%	**Definition of % sign.**

Fill in the following table:

Decimal	Ratio	$\dfrac{number}{100}$	Percent (%)
0.35	$\dfrac{0.35}{1}$ or $\dfrac{35}{100}$ or $\dfrac{7}{20}$	$\dfrac{\mathbf{35}}{\mathbf{100}}$	35 %
0.03	$\dfrac{\mathbf{0.03}}{\mathbf{1}}$ or $\dfrac{\mathbf{3}}{\mathbf{100}}$	$\dfrac{3}{100}$	**3%**
2.5	$\dfrac{\mathbf{2.5}}{\mathbf{1}}$ or $\dfrac{\mathbf{250}}{\mathbf{100}}$	$\dfrac{\mathbf{250}}{\mathbf{100}}$	250%
0.05	$\dfrac{0.05}{1}$ or $\dfrac{5}{100}$ or $\dfrac{1}{20}$	$\dfrac{5}{100}$	**5%**
1.25	$\dfrac{1.25}{1}$ or $\dfrac{125}{100}$ or $\dfrac{5}{4}$	$\dfrac{\mathbf{125}}{\mathbf{100}}$	**125%**
0.7	$\dfrac{\mathbf{0.7}}{\mathbf{1}}$ or $\dfrac{\mathbf{70}}{\mathbf{100}}$ or $\dfrac{\mathbf{7}}{\mathbf{10}}$	$\dfrac{\mathbf{70}}{\mathbf{100}}$	**70%**

PT 3, QUESTIONS

Fill in the following table:

Expression	Change	Justification for change
$\dfrac{1}{25}$	0.04	Fraction bar means division.
0.04	$\dfrac{0.04}{1}$	
$\dfrac{0.04}{1}$	$\dfrac{0.40}{1}\times 1$	
1	$1=\dfrac{100}{100}$	Any number (except 0) divided by itself is 1.
$\dfrac{0.40}{1}\times 1$	$\dfrac{0.40}{1}\times\dfrac{100}{100}$	
$\dfrac{0.40}{1}\times\dfrac{100}{100}$	$\dfrac{4}{100}$	
$\dfrac{4}{100}$	4%	Definition of % sign.

Fill in the following table:

Decimal	Ratio	$\dfrac{\text{number}}{100}$	Percent (%)
	$\dfrac{0.05}{1}$ or $\dfrac{5}{100}$ or $\dfrac{1}{20}$		
		$\dfrac{38}{100}$	
			6.25 %
0.53			
	$\dfrac{0.2}{1}$ or $\dfrac{20}{100}$ or $\dfrac{1}{5}$		
		$\dfrac{170}{100}$	

PT 3, ANSWERS

Fill in the following table

Expression	Change	Justification
$\frac{1}{25}$	0.04	Fraction bar means division.
0.04	$\frac{0.04}{1}$	**A number can be divided by one and not change the value of the number.**
$\frac{0.04}{1}$	$\frac{0.40}{1}\times 1$	**A number can be multiplied by one and not change the value of the number.**
1	$1=\frac{100}{100}$	Any number (except 0) divided by itself is 1.
$\frac{0.40}{1}\times 1$	$\frac{0.40}{1}\times\frac{100}{100}$	**Quantities defined as equal may be substituted for each other.**
$\frac{0.40}{1}\times\frac{100}{100}$	$\frac{4}{100}$	**To multiply fractions multiply top numbers for a new top number and multiply bottom numbers for a new bottom number.**
$\frac{4}{100}$	4%	Definition of % sign.

Fill in the following table:

Decimal	Ratio	$\frac{number}{100}$	Percent (%)
0.05	$\frac{0.05}{1}$ or $\frac{5}{100}$ or $\frac{1}{20}$	$\frac{5}{100}$	5%
0.38	$\frac{0.38}{1}$ or $\frac{38}{100}$ or $\frac{19}{50}$	$\frac{38}{100}$	38%
0.0625	$\frac{0.0625}{1}$ or $\frac{6.25}{100}$ or $\frac{1}{16}$	$\frac{6.25}{100}$	6.25 %
0.53	$\frac{0.53}{1}$ or $\frac{53}{100}$	$\frac{53}{100}$	53%
0.2	$\frac{0.2}{1}$ or $\frac{20}{100}$ or $\frac{1}{5}$	$\frac{20}{100}$	20%
1.7	$\frac{1.7}{1}$ or $\frac{170}{100}$	$\frac{170}{100}$	170%

Scene: Lunchroom - Hotdogs for Lunch

Sunny: That jerk didn't even know the "Upside down Z" Method for solving percent problems.

Bunny: Neither do I.

Sunny: Don't you remember it? Ms. Franklin taught it to us two years ago.

Bunny: I don't remember it.

Sunny: The "Upside down Z" made percent problems so easy.

Bunny: If it was so great, why don't you remember it?

Sunny: I thought I did.

Bunny: Mr. Thomas gave you the chance to explain it to the class.

Sunny: He is the math teacher, he ought to know it.

Bunny: You looked really silly trying to explain it.

Sunny: Well, his system of rules and definitions is what's silly.

Bunny: I like his system. There is an order to it.

Sunny: His system takes too much time.

Bunny: The poet says: "Time will take care of itself, so just leave time alone".

Sunny: That doesn't make any sense. Time is important.

Bunny: What's time to a poet?

PRECISION TEACHING (PT) SAMPLE ANSWERS - WORD PROBLEMS

Fill in the following table with the best answer: Simply list "To be found" for the desired quantity. If your teacher directs, solve the proportion for a desired quantity.

Situation	"part"	"whole"	Ratio $\frac{\text{"part"}}{\text{"whole"}}$	Percent
In a classroom there are 13 boys and 12 girls. What percent are boys?	13 boys	25 students in class	$\dfrac{13 \text{ boys}}{25 \text{ students}}$	To be found
A dress for $60 is on sale at 20% off. What is the discount?	Discount, to be found	$60	$\dfrac{\text{discount}}{\$60}$	20%
A basketball player hit 60% of his free throws. He hit 15 free throws. How many did he attempt?	15 free throws	Number attempted, to be found	$\dfrac{15 \text{ hit}}{\text{number attempted}}$	60%
Sam tossed a coin 10 times. Four times heads came up. What percent heads came up?	4 heads	10 tosses	$\dfrac{4 \text{ heads}}{10 \text{ tosses}}$	To be found

WORD PROBLEMS

PT 4, QUESTIONS

Fill in the following table with the best answer: Simply list "To be found" for the desired quantity. If your teacher directs, solve the proportion for a numerical quantity.

Situation	"part"	"whole"	ratio $\dfrac{\text{"part"}}{\text{"whole"}}$	Percent
If there is one ace in a deck of cards, and the percentage of aces is 2.5%, how many cards are in the deck?		How many cards? To be found.	$\dfrac{1 \text{ ace}}{\text{how many cards}}$	
Sunny ate 75 percent of a pizza. The pizza had been cut into eight equal parts. How many pieces did Sunny eat?	Pieces Sunny ate. To be found.	8 pieces		75%
Bunny's volleyball team won 12 games. They played 20 games. What was their winning percentage?	12 wins		$\dfrac{12 \text{ wins}}{20 \text{ games}}$	To be found
A sample of iron ore was found to contain 5 grams of iron. This represented 20% of the ore. What was size of the ore sample?			$\dfrac{5 \text{ grams iron}}{\text{grams ore}}$	
A restaurant check was $25.00, Sally thought the waiter was cute and wants to leave a 30% tip. How much money does she leave?	Amount of tip. To be found			30%
Sam tossed a coin 50 times. Heads occurred 21 times. What % of the time did heads occur?	21 heads	50 tosses		

WORD PROBLEMS

PT 4, ANSWERS

Fill in the following table with the best answer: Simply list "To be found" for the desired quantity. If your teacher directs, solve the proportion for a desired quantity.

Situation	"part"	"whole"	ratio $\dfrac{\text{"part"}}{\text{"whole"}}$	Percent
If there is one ace in a deck of cards, and the percentage of aces is 2.5%, how many cards are in the deck?	**1 ace**	How many cards. To be found	$\dfrac{1 \text{ ace}}{\text{how many cards}}$	**2.5%**
Sunny ate 75 percent of a pizza. The pizza had been cut into eight equal parts. How many pieces did Sunny eat?	Pieces Sunny ate. To be found.	8 pieces	$\dfrac{\textbf{pieces Sonny ate}}{\textbf{8 pieces}}$	75%
Bunny's volleyball team won 12 games. They played 20 games. What was their winning percentage?	12 wins	**20 games**	$\dfrac{16 \text{ wins}}{20 \text{ games}}$	To be found.
A sample of iron ore was found to contain 5 grams of iron. This represented 20% of the ore. What was size of the ore sample?	**5 grams**	**Sample size. To be found.**	$\dfrac{5 \text{ grams iron}}{\text{grams ore}}$	**20%**
A restaurant check was $25.00, Sally thought the waiter was cute and wants to leaves a 30% tip. How much money does she leave?	Amount of tip. To be found	**$25.00**	$\dfrac{\textbf{tip}}{\textbf{\$25.00}}$	**30%**
Sam tossed a coin 50 times. Heads occurred 21 times. What % of the time did heads occur?	21 heads	50 tosses	$\dfrac{\textbf{21 heads}}{\textbf{50 tosses}}$	**To be found.**

WORD PROBLEMS

PT 5, QUESTONS

Fill in the following table with the best answer: Simply list "To be found" for the desired quantity. If your teacher directs, solve the proportion for a desired quantity.

Situation	"part"	"whole"	ratio $\dfrac{\text{"part"}}{\text{"whole"}}$	Percent
If there are 3 aces left in a deck of 42 cards, what percent of the deck are aces?			$\dfrac{3\,\text{aces}}{42\,\text{cards}}$	To be found.
Sunny ate 37.5 percent of a pizza. The pizza had been cut into eight equal parts. How many pieces did Sunny eat?	Pieces Sunny ate. To be found.			37.5%
Bunny's volleyball team won 16 games. They played 20 games. What was their winning percentage?				
A sample of iron ore was found to contain 20% iron. How many grams would be in a 47 gram sample?	Grams of iron to be found.		$\dfrac{\text{grams iron}}{47\,\text{grams}}$	
A restaurant check was $25.00. Sally thought the waiter was cute and left a $5.00 tip. What percent of the bill did she leave as a tip?	$5.00			
Sam tossed a coin 100 times. Fifty-two percent of the time heads came up. How many times did heads come up?	# heads			52%

WORD PROBLEMS

PT 5, ANSWERS

Fill in the following table with the best answer: Simply list "To be found" for the desired quantity. If your teacher directs, solve the proportion for a desired quantity.

Situation	"Part"	"Whole"	Ratio $\dfrac{\text{"part"}}{\text{"whole"}}$	Percent
If there are 3 aces left in a deck of 42 cards, what is the percentage of aces in the deck?	**3 aces**	**42 cards**	$\dfrac{3\,\text{aces}}{42\,\text{cards}}$	To be found.
Sunny ate 37.5 percent of a pizza. The pizza had been cut into eight equal parts. How many pieces did Sunny eat?	Pieces Sunny ate. To be found.	**8 pieces**	$\dfrac{\mathbf{x\,pieces}}{\mathbf{8\,pieces}}$	37.5%
Bunny's volleyball team won 16 games. They played 20 games. What was their winning percentage?	**16 wins**	**20 games**	$\dfrac{\mathbf{16\,wins}}{\mathbf{20\,games}}$	To be found.
A sample of iron ore was found to contain 20% iron. How many grams of iron would be in a 47 gram sample?	Grams of iron. To be found.	**47 grams**	$\dfrac{\text{grams iron}}{47\,\text{grams}}$	20%
A restaurant check was $25.00. Sally thought the waiter was cute and left a $5.00 tip. What percent of the bill did she leave as a tip?	$5.00	**$25.00**	$\dfrac{\mathbf{\$5.00}}{\mathbf{\$25.00}}$	To be found.
Sam tossed a coin 100 times. Fifty-two percent of the time heads came up. How many times did heads come up?	# heads. To be found.	**100 tosses**	$\dfrac{\mathbf{\#\,heads}}{\mathbf{100\,tosses}}$	52%

WORD PROBLEMS

PT 6, QUESTIONS

Fill in the following table with the best answer: Simply list "To be found" for the desired quantity. If your teacher directs, solve the proportion for a desired quantity.

Situation	"part"	"whole"	ratio $\dfrac{\text{"part"}}{\text{"whole"}}$	Percent
Sunny's football team played 10 games and won all 10. What percent of wins did the team have?				
There were four apples. Sunny ate three. What percent of the apples did Sunny eat?			$\dfrac{3 \text{ apples}}{4 \text{ apples}}$	To be found.
A 3.5 gram sample of copper ore was found to contain 0.5 g copper. What percent of the ore is copper?				
Sunny paid $100 dollars in taxes. This represented 10% if his total income. How much was his total income?				
At a restaurant, Bunny thought the waiter was cute and left a tip of $10. This was 25% of the bill. What was the amount of the bill?	$10.00		$\dfrac{\$10.00}{\text{amount of bill}}$	
Sam bought a shirt for $15 that was marked originally at $25. What was the discount? What percent of the original price was the discount?	Discount, $10	$25		To be found.

WORD PROBLEMS

PT 6, ANSWERS

Fill in the following table with the best answer: Simply list "To be found" for the desired quantity. If your teacher directs, solve the proportion for a desired quantity.

Situation	"part"	"whole"	ratio $\dfrac{\text{"part"}}{\text{"whole"}}$	Percent
Sunny's football team played 10 games and won all 10. What percent of wins did the team have?	10 wins	10 wins	$\dfrac{10\,\text{wins}}{10\,\text{games}}$	To be found.
There were four apples. Sunny ate three. What percent of the apples did Sunny eat?	3 apples Sunny ate.	4 apples	$\dfrac{3\,\text{apples}}{4\,\text{apples}}$	To be found.
A 3.5 gram sample of copper ore was found to contain 0.5 g copper. What percent of the ore is copper?	0.5 grams copper	3.5 gram sample	$\dfrac{0.5\,\text{grams copper}}{3.5\,\text{gram sample}}$	To be found.
Sunny paid $100 dollars in taxes. This represented 10% if his total income. How much was his total income?	$100	Total income. To be found.	$\dfrac{\$100}{\text{total income}}$	10%
At a restaurant, Bunny thought the waiter was cute and left a tip of $10. This was 25 % of the bill. What was the amount of the bill?	$10.00	Amount of the bill. To be found.	$\dfrac{\$10.00}{\text{amount of bill}}$	25%
Sam bought a shirt for $15 that was marked originally at $25. What was the discount? What percent of the original price was the discount?	Discount, $10	$25	$\dfrac{\$10}{\$25}$	To be found.

CONVERSION FACTORS

DIMENSIONAL ANALYSIS

1 km	=	1000 meters
1 kg	=	1000 gram
16 oz	=	1 lb.
4 quarts	=	1 gallon
1 liter	=	1000 mLiter
1 inch	=	2.54 cm
2 pints	=	1 quart
3 feet	=	1 yard
760 mm Hg	=	1 atm
1 atm	=	101.3 kPa
1 ml	=	1 cm^3
1 mile	=	1.6 km
1 meter	=	100 cm
1 meter	=	1000 mm
12 inches	=	1 foot

Overview: This lesson presents a procedure for performing unit conversions using dimensional analysis to decide the conversion factor to use, followed by a ratio and proportion approach. A ratio and proportion approach is presented in Chapter 18.

**Mathematical
Learning Objectives:**   Students will:

Obtain two conversion factors from a defining relationship.

Utilize the properties of one to perform unit conversions using dimensional analysis.

NCTM Standards: Algebra

Represent and analyze mathematical situations and structures using algebraic symbols.

Measurement

Understand measurable attributes of objects and the units, systems, and processes of measurement.

Definitions:

Word	Definition	Symbol
Ratio	A comparison of two numbers by division.	$-, \div, /, :$
Proportion	An equation stating the equality of two ratios.	
Mathematics	The science of quantity, shapes and arrangements of objects.	
Variable	A letter or symbol that stands for a number that can be changed.	Sometimes x or y
Convert	To exchange for something equal in value.	
Factor	Any of the quantities which when multiplied together form a product.	
Conversion Factor (CF)	A ratio with the value of 1 that can be used to change the name of a quantity.	CF
Numerical	Something involving or expressed in numbers.	
Unit of Measure	A quantity that is used as a standard of measurement or exchange	
Dimension	Any measurable extent.	
Extent	The point, degree or limit over which something extends.	
Complex	Composed of two or more parts.	

The two things that are needed to describe a measured quantity are, the number and the name of the quantity measured. Unit conversions change the name of a quantity and this change in name will usually include a change in the number. A defining relationship can yield two ratios, both with a value of 1.

Defining Relationships

1 km = 1000 meters
1 kg = 1000 gram
16 oz = 1 lb.
4 quarts = 1 gallon
1 liter = 1000 mLiter
1 inch = 2.54 cm
2 pints = 1 quart
3 feet = 1 yard
760 mm Hg = 1 atm
1 atm =101.3 kPa
1 ml = 1 cm³
1 mile = 1.6 km
1 meter = 100 cm
1 meter = 1000 mm
12 inches = 1 foot

Symbol/Abbreviation	Meaning
ft	foot
oz	ounces
in	inches
lb	pounds
pt	pint
qt	quart
g	gram
m	meter
atm	Atmosphere of pressure
Pa	Pascal of pressure
kPa	kilopascal of pressure
mm Hg	millimeters of Mercury pressure
yd	yard
L	liter

Symbol/Abbreviation	Meaning	As exponent of 10	Scientific notation (multiplier)
M	Mega (million)	10^6	1×10^6
k	kilo (thousand)	10^3	1×10^3
d	deci (tenth)	10^{-1}	1×10^{-1}
c	centi (hundredth)	10^{-2}	1×10^{-2}
m	milli (thousandth)	10^{-3}	1×10^{-3}
μ	micro (millionth)	10^{-6}	1×10^{-6}
n	nano (billionth)	10^{-9}	1×10^{-9}

These symbols can be used with any base unit, g (grams, mass), m (meters, length), Pa (Pascal, pressure), N (Newton, force), etc. To use, put the prefix on one side and the multiplier on the other. Notice that a lower case "m" is used as an abbreviation for both meter and milli (one thousandth). Sorry about that.

Examples: $1 \, ng = 1 \times 10^{-9} \, g$
$1 \, km = 1 \times 1000 \, m$

Every defining relation ship yields two conversion factors (CF).

Example: 1 dozen = 12 donuts yields $\dfrac{1 \, dozen}{12 \, donuts}$ and $\dfrac{12 \, donuts}{1 \, dozen}$

Note that since equal things are being divided that the conversion factors have a value of 1 because any quantity (except zero) divided by itself equals 1. The ratio of quantity desired to quantity given will also equal one because conversion factors change only the name of a quantity NOT the amount of the quantity.

Since the conversion factor has a value of 1 and the ratio of the quantity (units given) and the quantity (units desired) is also going to be one.

$$\frac{\text{Quantity (units desired)}}{\text{Quantity (units given)}} = CF \left[\frac{\text{units desired}}{\text{units given}} \right]$$

When the Quantity (units given) is multiplied times both sides of the equation

$$\frac{\text{Quantity (units given)} \times \text{Quantity (units desired)}}{\text{Quantity (units given)}} = \text{Quantity (units given)} \times CF \left[\frac{\text{units desired}}{\text{units given}} \right]$$

We get:

$$\text{Quantity (units desired)} = \text{Quantity (units given)} \times CF \left[\frac{\text{units desired}}{\text{units given}} \right]$$

Notice: Units given cancel leaving the units desired for the answer.

STEPS TO PERFORM A UNIT CONVERSION

1. Write the equality for the conversion.
2. Write the quantity to be converted.
3. Choose a conversion factor (CF) that has the units desired **ON THE SAME SIDE OF THE DIVISION BAR** as the units given in the problem, **AND** the units given, **ON THE OPPOSITE SIDE OF THE DIVISION BAR.**

4. Match the numbers with the units from the defining equation:

$$\text{Quantity and units given} \times \text{CF} \left[\frac{\text{units desired}}{\text{units given}} \right] = \text{Quantity and units desired}$$

5. Perform the calculation, remember that the horizontal line means division and often science textbooks will use a vertical line to indicate multiplication in unit conversion problems.

Example: How many dozen are in 42 donuts?

$$\frac{42 \text{ donuts}}{} \times \frac{1 \text{ dozen}}{12 \text{ donuts}} = 3.5 \text{ dozen}$$

Notice: Units given, $\frac{\text{donuts}}{\text{donuts}}$, cancel leaving the units desired, dozen, for the answer.

PRECISION TEACHING (PT) SAMPLE ANSWERS

Write both conversion factors for the relationships listed:

Defining relationship	Conversion Factor	Conversion Factor	Justification for Conversion Factors
3 feet = 1 yd	$\frac{3 \text{ feet}}{1 \text{ yd}}$	$\frac{1 \text{ yd}}{3 \text{ feet}}$	A quantity (except zero) divided by itself equals one.
16 oz = 1 lb.	$\frac{1 \text{ lb.}}{16 \text{ oz}}$	$\frac{16 \text{ oz}}{1 \text{ lb.}}$	A quantity (except zero) divided by itself equals one.

Perform the following conversions:

Conversion	Quantity Given	Conversion factor	Quantity desired	Justification for Conversion
63 feet = ? yd	63 feet	$\frac{1 \text{ yd}}{3 \text{ feet}}$	21 yd	Multiplying by one does not change a number.
64 oz = ? lbs.	64 oz	$\frac{1 \text{ lb.}}{16 \text{ oz}}$	4 lbs.	Multiplying by one does not change a number.

SCENE: LUNCHROOM

Sunny: I just don't get which conversion factor to use.

Bunny: You can decide if you want a larger or smaller number and choose the right ratio, or just let the units tell you if you have chosen correctly. If you choose the correct ratio, the units you want to change will cancel.

Sunny: How do conversion factors get a value of one? They don't look like a one to me.

Bunny: Anything divided by itself is one, and multiplying by one does not change a quantity. Conversion factors let you change the name of a quantity, not the value of the quantity.

Sunny: Change, change, change. Do you know how many psychiatrists it takes to change a light bulb?

Bunny (rolling her eyes, in mock disgust): No, how many?

Sunny: Just one, but the light bulb has to want to change. Ha! Ha!

SEE PAGE 331 FOR <u>CONVERSION FACTORS – DIMENSIONAL ANALYSIS</u>: PRECISION TEACHING SCORES, FREQUENCY TABLE.

I suggest that students correct their papers, calculate the frequencies and graph their results. Graphing the results on special graph paper (Standard Celeration Chart) can provide visual reinforcement for the students and information about how they are learning. The frequency tables are provided to facilitate this process.

How Do We Know?

PT 1, QUESTIONS

Write both conversion factors for the relationships listed:

Defining relationship	Conversion Factor	Conversion Factor	Justification for Conversion Factors
1 inch = 2.54 cm		$\dfrac{2.54 \text{ cm}}{1 \text{ inch}}$	
4 quarts = 1 gallon		$\dfrac{1 \text{ gallon}}{4 \text{ quarts}}$	A quantity (except zero) divided by itself equals one.
16 oz. = 1 lb.	$\dfrac{16 \text{ oz.}}{1 \text{ lb.}}$		
1 km = 1000 m	$\dfrac{1 \text{ km}}{1000 \text{ m}}$		A quantity (except zero) divided by itself equals one.

Perform the following conversions:

Conversion	Quantity given	Conversion factor	Quantity desired	Justification for Conversion
5 inches = ? cm	5 inches		12.7 cm	Multiplying by one does not change a number.
380 km = ? meter	380 km	$\dfrac{1000 \text{ m}}{1 \text{ km}}$		
12 m = ? km	12 m	$\dfrac{1 \text{ km}}{1000 \text{ m}}$		Multiplying by one does not change a number.
3 gallon = ? quarts	3 gallon		12 quarts	
530 m = ? km		$\dfrac{1 \text{ km}}{1000 \text{ m}}$		Multiplying by one does not change a number.

PT 1, ANSWERS

Write both conversion factors for the relationships listed:

Defining relationship	Conversion Factor	Conversion Factor	Justification for Conversion Factors
1 inch = 2.54 cm	**1 inch** / **2.54 cm**	2.54 cm / 1 inch	**A quantity (except zero) divided by itself equals one.**
4 quarts = 1 gallon	**4 quarts** / **1 gallon**	1 gallon / 4 quarts	A quantity (except zero) divided by itself equals one.
16 oz. = 1 lb.	16 oz. / 1 lb.	**1 lb.** / **16 oz.**	**A quantity (except zero) divided by itself equals one.**
1 km = 1000 m	1 km / 1000 m	**1000 m** / **1 km**	A quantity (except zero) divided by itself equals one.

Perform the following conversions:

Conversion	Quantity given	Conversion factor	Quantity desired	Justification for Conversion
5 inches = ? cm	5 inches	**2.54 cm** / **1 inch**	12.7 cm	Multiplying by one does not change a number.
380 km = ? meter	380 km	1000 m / 1 km	**380000 m**	**Multiplying by one does not change a number.**
12 m = ? km	12 m	1 km / 1000 m	**0.012 km**	Multiplying by one does not change a number.
3 gallon = ? quarts	3 gallon	**4 quarts** / **1 gallon**	12 quarts	**Multiplying by one does not change a number.**
530 m = ? km	**530 m**	1 km / 1000 m	0.53 km	Multiplying by one does not change a number.

How Do We Know?

PT 2, QUESTIONS

Write both conversion factors for the relationships listed:

Defining relationship	Conversion Factor	Conversion Factor	Justification for Conversion Factors
760 mmHg = 1 atm		$\dfrac{1\ atm}{760\ mmHg}$	A quantity (except zero) divided by itself equals one.
1 atm = 101.3 kPa	$\dfrac{1\ atm}{101.3\ kPa}$		
1 mL = 1 cm^3		$\dfrac{1\ cm^3}{1\ mL}$	A quantity (except zero) divided by itself equals one.
1 L = 1000 mL	$\dfrac{1\ L}{1000\ mL}$	$\dfrac{1000\ mL}{1\ L}$	

Perform the following conversions:

Conversion	Quantity given	Conversion factor	Quantity desired	Justification for Conversion
2 atm = ? kPa	2 atm		202.6 kPa	Multiplying by one does not change a number.
380 mm Hg = ? atm		$\dfrac{1\ atm}{760\ mmHg}$		Multiplying by one does not change a number.
12 mL = ? cm^3	12 mL		12 cm^3	
3 atm = ? kPa	3 atm	$\dfrac{101.3\ kPa}{1\ atm}$		Multiplying by one does not change a number.
3 atm = ? mm Hg	3 atm		2280 mmHg	

PT 2, ANSWERS

Write both conversion factors for the relationships listed:

Defining relationship	Conversion Factor	Conversion Factor	Justification for Conversion Factors
760 mmHg = 1 atm	**760 mmHg** / **1 atm**	1 atm / 760 mmHg	A quantity (except zero) divided by itself equals one.
1 atm = 101.3 kPa	1 atm / 101.3 kPa	**101.3 kPa** / **1 atm**	**A quantity (except zero) divided by itself equals one.**
1 mL = 1 cm^3	**1 mL** / **1 cm^3**	1 cm^3 / 1 mL	A quantity (except zero) divided by itself equals one.
1 L = 1000 mL	1 L / 1000 mL	1000 mL / 1 L	**A quantity (except zero) divided by itself equals one.**

Perform the following conversions:

Conversion	Quantity given	Conversion factor	Quantity desired	Justification for Conversion
2 atm = ? kPa	2 atm	**101.3 kPa** / **1 atm**	202.6 kPa	Multiplying by one does not change a number.
380 mm Hg = ? atm	**380 mm Hg**	1 atm / 760 mmHg	**0.5 atm**	Multiplying by one does not change a number.
12 mL = ? cm^3	12 mL	**1 cm^3** / **1 mL**	12 cm^3	**Multiplying by one does not change a number.**
3 atm = ? kPa	3 atm	101.3 kPa / 1 atm	**303.9 kPa**	Multiplying by one does not change a number.
3 atm = ? mm Hg	3 atm	**760 mmHg** / **1 atm**	2280 mmHg	**Multiplying by one does not change a number.**

How Do We Know?

PT 3, QUESTIONS

Write both conversion factors for the relationships listed:

Defining relationship	Conversion Factor	Conversion Factor	Justification for Conversion Factors
1 inch = 2.54 cm		$\dfrac{1 \text{ inch}}{2.54 \text{ cm}}$	
1 m = 100 cm	$\dfrac{100 \text{ cm}}{1 \text{ m}}$		A quantity (except zero) divided by itself equals one.
1 m = 1000 mm	$\dfrac{1000 \text{ mm}}{1 \text{ m}}$	$\dfrac{1 \text{ m}}{1000 \text{ mm}}$	
1 mL = 1 cm^3		$\dfrac{1 \text{ mL}}{1 \text{ cm}^3}$	A quantity (except zero) divided by itself equals one.
1 mile = 1.6 km			A quantity (except zero) divided by itself equals one.

Perform the following conversions:

Conversion	Quantity given	Conversion factor	Quantity desired	Justification for Conversion
63 miles = ? km	63 miles		100.8 km	Multiplying by one does not change a number.
12 mL = ? cm^3	12 mL	$\dfrac{1 \text{ cm}^3}{1 \text{ mL}}$		Multiplying by one does not change a number.
100 miles = ? km	100 miles		160 km	
125 m = ? cm	125 m		12500 cm	Multiplying by one does not change a number.
15 cm = ? m	15 cm	$\dfrac{1 \text{ m}}{100 \text{ cm}}$		Multiplying by one does not change a number.
16 miles = ? km	16 miles	$\dfrac{1.6 \text{ km}}{1 \text{ mile}}$		
64 mL = ? cm3	64 mL		64 cm3	Multiplying by one does not change a number.

PT 3, ANSWERS

Write both conversion factors for the relationships listed:

Defining relationship	Conversion Factor	Conversion Factor	Justification for Conversion Factors
1 inch = 2.54 cm	$\dfrac{\textbf{2.54 cm}}{\textbf{1 inch}}$	$\dfrac{1\ inch}{2.54\ cm}$	**A quantity (except zero) divided by itself equals one.**
1 m = 100 cm	$\dfrac{100\ cm}{1\ m}$	$\dfrac{\textbf{1 m}}{\textbf{100 cm}}$	A quantity (except zero) divided by itself equals one.
1 m = 1000 mm	$\dfrac{1000\ mm}{1\ m}$	$\dfrac{1\ m}{1000\ mm}$	**A quantity (except zero) divided by itself equals one.**
1 mL = 1 cm^3	$\dfrac{\textbf{1 cm}^3}{\textbf{1 mL}}$	$\dfrac{1\ mL}{1\ cm^3}$	A quantity (except zero) divided by itself equals one.
1 mile = 1.6 km	$\dfrac{\textbf{1.6 km}}{\textbf{1 mile}}$	$\dfrac{\textbf{1 mile}}{\textbf{1.6 km}}$	A quantity (except zero) divided by itself equals one.

Perform the following conversions:

Conversion	Quantity given	Conversion factor	Quantity desired	Justification for Conversion
63 miles = ? km	63 miles	$\dfrac{\textbf{1.6 km}}{\textbf{1 mile}}$	100.8 km	Multiplying by one does not change a number.
12 mL = ? cm^3	12 mL	$\dfrac{1\ cm^3}{1\ mL}$	**12 cm^3**	Multiplying by one does not change a number.
100 miles = ? km	100 miles	$\dfrac{\textbf{1.6 km}}{\textbf{1 mile}}$	160 km	**Multiplying by one does not change a number.**
125 m = ? cm	125 m	$\dfrac{\textbf{100 cm}}{\textbf{1 m}}$	12500 cm	Multiplying by one does not change a number.
15 cm = ? m	15 cm	$\dfrac{1\ m}{100\ cm}$	**0.15 m**	Multiplying by one does not change a number.
16 miles = ? km	16 miles	$\dfrac{1.6\ km}{1\ mile}$	**25.6 km**	**Multiplying by one does not change a number.**
64 mL = ? cm3	64 mL	$\dfrac{\textbf{1 cm}^3}{\textbf{1 mL}}$	64 cm3	Multiplying by one does not change a number.

How Do We Know?

ADDENDUM III

PRECISION TEACHING (PT)

SCORES, FREQUENCY TABLES

PRECISION TEACHING (PT) SCORES, FREQUENCY TABLES:

Note: Frequency $= \dfrac{\text{Counts}}{\text{minutes}} = \dfrac{\#\,\text{correct}}{\text{minutes}} = \dfrac{C}{t}$, to calculate the frequency the seconds should be converted to the decimal form of minutes.

Seconds	5	10	15	20	25	30	35	40	45	50	55	60
Minutes	0.08	0.17	0.25	0.33	0.42	0.5	0.58	0.67	0.75	0.84	0.92	1.0

CHAPTER 2, page 9: REAL NUMBER VALUE

Worksheet	Date	Questions	Number correct (C)	Time (min: sec)	Time (min) (t)	Frequency (C/t)
PT 1		17				
PT 2		16				
PT 3		16				

CHAPTER 3, page 21: PROPERTIES OF REAL NUMBERS

Worksheet	Date	Questions	Number correct (C)	Time (min: sec)	Time (min) (t)	Frequency (C/t)
PT 1		16				
PT 2		20				
PT 3		28				

CHAPTER 4, page 33: COMBINING SIGNED NUMBERS

Worksheet	Date	Questions	Number correct (C)	Time (min: sec)	Time (min) (t)	Frequency (C/t)
PT 1		14				
PT 2		13				
PT 3		15				

CHAPTER 5, page 45: MULTIPLICATION TABLES

Worksheet	Date	Questions	Number correct (C)	Time (min: sec)	Time (min) (t)	Frequency (C/t)
PT 1		28				
PT 2		39				
PT 3		39				
PT 4		30				
PT 5		30				

PRECISION TEACHING (PT) SCORES, FREQUENCY TABLES:

Note: Frequency $= \dfrac{\text{Counts}}{\text{minutes}} = \dfrac{\#\,\text{correct}}{\text{minutes}} = \dfrac{C}{t}$, to calculate the frequency the seconds should be converted to the decimal form of minutes.

Seconds	5	10	15	20	25	30	35	40	45	50	55	60
Minutes	0.08	0.17	0.25	0.33	0.42	0.5	0.58	0.67	0.75	0.84	0.92	1.0

CHAPTER 6, page 61: EQUIVALENT FRACTIONS

Worksheet	Date	Questions	Number correct (C)	Time (min: sec)	Time (min) (t)	Frequency (C/t)
PT 1		15				
PT 2		20				
PT 3		33				

CHAPTER 7, page 71: OPERATIONS WITH FRACTIONS

Worksheet	Date	Questions	Number correct (C)	Time (min: sec)	Time (min) (t)	Frequency (C/t)
PT 1		9				
PT 2		7				
PT 3		8				

CHAPTER 8, page 85: MULTIPLICATION AND DIVISION OF SIGNED NUMBERS

Worksheet	Date	Questions	Number correct (C)	Time (min: sec)	Time (min) (t)	Frequency (C/t)
PT 1		22				
PT 2		23				
PT 3		25				

CHAPTER 9 page 97: EXPONENTS

Worksheet	Date	Questions	Number correct (C)	Time (min: sec)	Time (min) (t)	Frequency (C/t)
PT 1		15				
PT 2		15				
PT 3		19				

PRECISION TEACHING (PT) SCORES, FREQUENCY TABLES:

Note: Frequency $= \dfrac{\text{Counts}}{\text{minutes}} = \dfrac{\#\,\text{correct}}{\text{minutes}} = \dfrac{C}{t}$, to calculate the frequency the seconds should be converted to the decimal form of minutes.

Seconds	5	10	15	20	25	30	35	40	45	50	55	60
Minutes	0.08	0.17	0.25	0.33	0.42	0.5	0.58	0.67	0.75	0.84	0.92	1.0

CHAPTER 10, page 109: PROPERTIES OF ZERO

Worksheet	Date	Questions	Number correct (C)	Time (min: sec)	Time (min) (t)	Frequency (C/t)
PT 1		10				
PT 2		13				
PT 3		13				

CHAPTER 11, page 119: PROPERTIES OF ONE

Worksheet	Date	Questions	Number correct (C)	Time (min: sec)	Time (min) (t)	Frequency (C/t)
PT 1		13				
PT 2		13				
PT 3		14				

CHAPTER 12, page 131: COORDINATE PLANE AND SLOPE

Worksheet	Date	Questions	Number correct (C)	Time (min: sec)	Time (min) (t)	Frequency (C/t)
PT 1		10				
PT 2		10				
PT 3		10				

CHAPTER 13, page 145: COMMUTATION AND DISTRIBUTION

Worksheet	Date	Questions	Number correct (C)	Time (min: sec)	Time (min) (t)	Frequency (C/t)
PT 1		12				
PT 2		14				
PT 3		14				

PRECISION TEACHING (PT) SCORES, FREQUENCY TABLES:

Note: Frequency $= \dfrac{\text{Counts}}{\text{minutes}} = \dfrac{\#\,\text{correct}}{\text{minutes}} = \dfrac{C}{t}$, to calculate the frequency the seconds should be converted to the decimal form of minutes.

Seconds	5	10	15	20	25	30	35	40	45	50	55	60
Minutes	0.08	0.17	0.25	0.33	0.42	0.5	0.58	0.67	0.75	0.84	0.92	1.0

CHAPTER 14, page 155: ORDER OF OPERATIONS

Worksheet	Date	Questions	Number correct (C)	Time (min: sec)	Time (min) (t)	Frequency (C/t)
PT 1		12				
PT 2		18				
PT 3		16				

CHAPTER 15, page 165: SYMBOLS

Worksheet	Date	Questions	Number correct (C)	Time (min: sec)	Time (min) (t)	Frequency (C/t)
PT 1		8				
PT 2		8				
PT 3		7				

CHAPTER 16, page 173: FACTORING AND GREATEST COMMON FACTOR

Worksheet	Date	Questions	Number correct (C)	Time (min: sec)	Time (min) (t)	Frequency (C/t)
PT 1		8				
PT 2		9				
PT 3		9				

CHAPTER 17, page 183: LIKE TERMS

Worksheet	Date	Questions	Number correct (C)	Time (min: sec)	Time (min) (t)	Frequency (C/t)
PT 1		13				
PT 2		14				
PT 3		14				

PRECISION TEACHING (PT) SCORES, FREQUENCY TABLES:

Note: Frequency $= \dfrac{\text{Counts}}{\text{minutes}} = \dfrac{\#\,\text{correct}}{\text{minutes}} = \dfrac{C}{t}$, to calculate the frequency the seconds should be converted to the decimal form of minutes.

Seconds	5	10	15	20	25	30	35	40	45	50	55	60
Minutes	0.08	0.17	0.25	0.33	0.42	0.5	0.58	0.67	0.75	0.84	0.92	1.0

CHAPTER 18, page 193: SOLVING EQUATIONS

Worksheet	Date	Questions	Number correct (C)	Time (min: sec)	Time (min) (t)	Frequency (C/t)
PT 1		16				
PT 2		17				
PT 3		19				

CHAPTER 19, page 205: VARIABLE

Worksheet	Date	Questions	Number correct (C)	Time (min: sec)	Time (min) (t)	Frequency (C/t)
PT 1		15				
PT 2		14				
PT 3		11				

CHAPTER 20, page 217: RATIONALE FOR SOLVING EQUATIONS

Worksheet	Date	Questions	Number correct (C)	Time (min: sec)	Time (min) (t)	Frequency (C/t)
PT 1		11				
PT 2		10				
PT 3		11				

CHAPTER 21, page 231: STRAIGHT LINES

Worksheet	Date	Questions	Number correct (C)	Time (min: sec)	Time (min) (t)	Frequency (C/t)
PT 1		8				
PT 2		9				
PT 3		11				
PT 4		12				
PT 5		16				
PT 6		16				

PRECISION TEACHING (PT) SCORES, FREQUENCY TABLES:

Note: Frequency $= \dfrac{\text{Counts}}{\text{minutes}} = \dfrac{\#\,\text{correct}}{\text{minutes}} = \dfrac{C}{t}$, to calculate the frequency the seconds should be converted to the decimal form of minutes.

Seconds	5	10	15	20	25	30	35	40	45	50	55	60
Minutes	0.08	0.17	0.25	0.33	0.42	0.5	0.58	0.67	0.75	0.84	0.92	1.0

ADDENDUM II, page 277: DECIMALS, MULTIPLICATION, AND DIVISION

Worksheet	Date	Questions	Number correct (C)	Time (min: sec)	Time (min) (t)	Frequency (C/t)
PT 1		11				
PT 2		14				
PT 3		11				

ADDENDUM II, page 293: PERCENT

Worksheet	Date	Questions	Number correct (C)	Time (min: sec)	Time (min) (t)	Frequency (C/t)
PT 1		11				
PT 2		15				
PT 3		17				
PT 4		15				
PT 5		18				
PT 6		22				

ADDENDUM III, page 313: CONVERSION FACTORS- DIMENSIONAL ANALYSIS

Worksheet	Date	Questions	Number correct (C)	Time (min: sec)	Time (min) (t)	Frequency (C/t)
PT 1		14				
PT 2		13				
PT 3		16				

LESSON NOTES

HOW DO WE KNOW?
GLOSSARY

As Humpty Dumpty teaches, "When I use a word it means just what I choose it to mean - nothing more nor less." (Through the Looking Glass, Lewis Carroll).

Definitions: Most definitions are adapted from Webster's New World Dictionary, some from The Laidlaw Glossary of Arithmetical-Mathematical Terms by Bernard H. Gundlach, occasionally from personal intuition and sometimes, sheer silliness.

Definition – A statement of the limits or nature of a word or word group or a sign or symbol.

Absolute – Perfect, complete, positive, not doubted, not relative.

Absolute value (| |) – Magnitude, value or size of a number, without a sign, neither positive nor negative.

Addition (+) – Combining things or numbers.

Additive Inverse – The sum of a number and its additive inverse is zero.

Additive Property of Equality – The same quantity can be added to both sides of an equation and not change the truth of the equation.

Algebra – The science that deals with the last three letters of the alphabet.

Algorithm – Any special way of solving a mathematical problem.

Alliteration – the repetition of initial consonant sounds in two or more neighboring words or syllables.

Analogy – Resemblance in some particulars between things otherwise unlike.

Angle (∠) – The space or shape made by the intersection of two straight lines. At this level, usually measured in degrees (°). On coordinate graph paper, usually measured counterclockwise from the x-axis.

Antecedent – A preceding event, condition or cause.

Arbitrary – Based on one's preference or whim.

Arc – Any part of a curve, especially a circle.

Area (A) – A measurement of the surface of figure, measured in square units of length.

Associative Property of Multiplication – Changing the groupings does not change the product of multiplication. Example: a(bc) = ab(c).

Assume – To take for granted, supposition, arrogance; to believe to be true without proof.

Assumption – A fact or statement taken for granted.

Axiom – A statement universally accepted as true.

Axis – A central line around which things are evenly arranged.

Base – The number that is raised to an exponent.
Example: in x^3 , x is a base.

Best Fit Straight Line – A line which estimates (guesses at) the best line which characterizes the cohesion of the confluence and correlates the consanguinity and concurrence of the data points. It is not the line that directly connects the points.

Circumference (c) – The line bounding a circle; the length of that line.

Cite – To mention by way of example, proof, etc.

Coefficient – A multiplier of a variable or unknown quantity; a number written in front of a variable, as 6 in 6x.

Combine – To join into one using some defined pattern or rule.

Common – Belong to or shared by all.

Commutative Property of Addition – Changing the order of addition does not matter. Example: a + b = b + a. (Subtraction is not commutative.)

Commutative Property of Multiplication – Changing the order of multiplication does not matter. Example: abc = bca = cab = acb = bac = cba
(Division is not commutative.)

Commute – To change or exchange; to interchange.

Compass – An instrument with two pivoted legs, for drawing circles.

Complex – Composed of two or more parts.

How Do We Know?

Complex fraction – A fraction with a fraction or a mixed number in the numerator (top) or denominator (bottom) or both.

Example: $\dfrac{\dfrac{3}{4}}{\dfrac{1}{2}}$

Composite number – A whole number that has factors other than 1 and itself.

Constant of Proportionality (k) – An unchanging constant that relates the value of two variables.

Example: $c \propto d$ and $c = kd$ and $k = \dfrac{c}{d}$

(See: Symbol of Proportionality)

Constraints – Prevent the occurrence of change except in a particular manner or direction.

Contrary – Opposite in nature order, etc.

Conundrum – A riddle whose answer is often a pun; any puzzling problem.
Example: see definition of paradox.

Converse – Reversed in position, order, etc.

Conversion Factor – A ratio with the value of 1 that can be used to change the name of a quantity.

Convert – To exchange for something equal in value.

Decimal Equivalent – The form of a fraction obtained by dividing a numerator by a denominator, as from a calculator.
Example: $\dfrac{3}{4} = 3 \div 4 = 0.75$

Deduction – Reasoning from the general to the specific.

Deductive Reasoning – Reasoning that uses logic based on rules and definitions to establish principles.

Degree (°) – A unit of measure for angles and arcs; 1/360 of a circle.

Defined – To determine the limits or nature of; to describe exactly.

Delta (Δ) – A change, positive or negative in the value of a variable; often used to describe a change from one condition to another, Example: $\Delta x = x_2 - x_1$

Denominator – The term below the line in a fraction.

Density – A way of describing the mass of a volume of matter, typically in chemistry it is measured in g/cm³. Density $= \dfrac{mass}{volume}$, $D = \dfrac{m}{v}$

Dialectic – A logical test of ideas for validity.

Dimension – Any measurable extent.

Distribute – to spread out.

Distributive Property of Multiplication – Multiplication spreads out over addition and subtraction. Example: $a(b + c) = ab + ac$

Dividend – The part of a fraction that is above the line (numerator); the part that is to be divided in a division problem.

Division (/, –, ÷, $\overline{)}$) – The inverse of multiplication; dividing by a number is the same as multiplying by the reciprocal of that number.
Examples: $a/b = \dfrac{a}{b} = a \div b = b\overline{)a} = a\left(\dfrac{1}{b}\right)$

Division Property of Equality – The same quantity (except zero) can be divided into both sides of an equation and not change the truth of the equation.

Divisor – The number by which a dividend is divided; the bottom number of a fraction (denominator).

Dogmatic – Asserting without proof, positive or arrogant in stating opinion.

Empirical – Based on experiment or evidence.

Equation – A mathematical sentence stating the equality between two quantities, the sentence may be true or false; contains an = sign.

Equivalent – Equal in quantity or meaning.

Equivalent Fractions – Ratios that have the same value but have different bottom numbers (denominators).

Equivalent Quantities – Quantities defined as being equivalent. For example: 1 meter = 100 centimeters, 1 yard = 3 feet, 1 pound = 16 ounces, 12 inches = 1 foot *etc.*

***Etc.* (abbreviation for etcetera)** – And others, and so forth, *etc.*

Evaluate – To find the value or amount.

Exponent – A superscript after a number (base) indicates how many times the number (base) is taken as a factor.

Example: in x^3, the three is an exponent and x is a base.

Exponential Property of Equality – Both sides of an equation can be raised to the same power while maintaining the equality.

Expression – Mathematical symbol or symbols that show meaning.

Extent – The point, degree or limit over which something extends.

Factor – Any of the quantities which when multiplied together form a product. In the sentence $3(5) = 15$, the 3 and the 5 are factors of the product 15.

Fancy – Imagination when light, playful, etc.

Form of a Solution – An equation is considered solved when the variable is by itself on one side of the equation with a coefficient of +1, and the numbers or symbols that make the equation true on the other.

Fraction – My dictionary says "A numerical representation of two numbers whose quotient is to be determined". Your teacher might well argue irrational numbers need more defining. And that is a good thing. For now let us say a fraction is a number that has a numerator and a denominator. Remember, the fraction bar means the top (numerator) is divided by the bottom (denominator). Often the numerator represents a "part" and the bottom represents a "whole".

Fraction Bar (–) – Indicates division of the top number (numerator) by the bottom number (denominator).

Function – A thing that depends on and varies with something else. Sometimes a lower case y is used.

Generalization – To give a broad rather than a specific character to a principle.

Greater than (>) – Number on the left of the sign is larger. larger > smaller.

Identity Element of Addition and Subtraction – There exists an element 0, such that: $a + 0 = a$, and $a - 0 = a$.

Identity Element of Multiplication and Division – There exists an element 1, such that: $a \times 1 = a$, and $a \div 1 = a$.

Identity Property of Equality – If $a = b$ then $b = a$.

Imply – To indicate more than the words plainly say; to involve inference; not a direct statement.

Improper Fraction – A fraction whose top (numerator) is larger or of higher degree than its bottom (denominator).

Examples: $\dfrac{7}{2}$, or $\dfrac{2x^2}{3x}$

Induction – Reasoning from particular facts to general conclusions.
Example: If something is true in a few times, it will always be true.

Inductive reasoning – Reasoning based on experimental evidence; often referred to as empirical induction.

Infer – To derive a conclusion from facts or premises.

Intersect – To meet or cross.

Intercept – To cut off, or mark off, or mark off between two points.

Inverse, Invert – To turn upside down; to reverse the order. For numbers, this inverse is often thought of as a reciprocal. Example: The inverse of x is 1/x.

Inverse of Addition – Subtraction; often used to remove numbers when solving equations.
Example: +5 – 5 = 0.

Inverse of Division – Multiplication; a process of undoing division.

Example: $5(\dfrac{x}{5}) = x$

Inverse of Exponentiation – Taking a root.

Example: $\sqrt{x^2} = x$

Inverse of Multiplication – Division; a process of undoing multiplication.
Example: 5 x ÷ 5 = x

Inverse of Subtraction – Addition; often used to remove numbers when solving equations.
Example: –5 + 5 = 0

Irrational Number – Non-terminating, non-repeating decimal number; a number that cannot be expressed as a quotient of two integers.

Example: π and $\sqrt{2}$

Justification – To show to be right; to supply grounds for; the reasons for.

Law – The rules of conduct established by an authority; a sequence of natural events occurring with unvarying uniformity; the statement of such a sequence.

Least Common Multiple (LCM) – The LCM of two numbers is the smallest number that is a multiple of both. The LCM of 3 and 5 is 15. The LCM of 4 and 6 is 12.

Length – Distance between two points, often measured in centimeters (cm).

Less than (<) – Number on the left of the sign is smaller. smaller < larger.

Let – To assign (arbitrary assumption).

Like – Having the same characteristics; equal.

Like Terms – Terms where the variable portions of the expression are alike.

Limit – The point, line, etc. at which something ends.

Line – A thin threadlike mark; a row of things, as of number points across a page.

Log (logarithm) – Exponent.

Logic – As Tweedledee teaches, 'Contrariwise, if it was so, it might be; and if it were so, it would be; but as it isn't, it ain't. That's logic.'

Logical – What is expected by the workings of cause and effect.

Mass (m) – The amount of matter. In chemistry mass will usually be measured in grams.

Magnitude – Greatness of size, importance.

Mathematical Induction – A concept introduced by G. Peano (1858-1930) to define the number system. A simplistic summation of Mathematical Induction might suggest that: If a statement about integers is true for some integer m and it is possible to show that from the statement for an integer n+ 1 follows from the statement for n, then the statement holds for all integers n greater than or equal to m. It has been proven by formal mathematical logic. Formal mathematical logic is often referred to as deductive reasoning.

Mathematics – The science of quantity, shapes and arrangement s of objects.

Metaphor – A figure of speech in which a word or phrase literally meaning one kind of object or idea is used in place of another to suggest a likeness or analogy between them (Example: *Cheeks are roses*).

Mixed number – A number that has a part that is an integer and a part that is a fraction.
Example: $2\frac{1}{3}$

Multiplication (X, ( ), x, •, a vertical line "|") – The process of finding the quantity, obtained by adding a specified quantity to itself a specified number of times. It is often easier than addition, if groups of things are counted.
Example: for three groups of five, 3(5) = 5+5+5 =15.

Multiplicative Inverse – The number that gives a product of one when multiplied times another number.
Example: $\dfrac{1}{xy}$ (xy) = 1. $\dfrac{1}{xy}$ is the multiplicative inverse of xy.

Multiplicative Property of Equality – The same quantity can be multiplied times both sides of an equation and not change the truth of the equation.

Natural numbers – The number 1 or any number obtained by continually adding 1 to this number.

Negative – 1. Opposite to or lacking in that which is positive.
2. *In Mathematics*, designating a quantity less than zero, or one to be subtracted.
3. *In Electricity*, the place in a battery that has an excess of electrons.
4. The point of view that opposes the positive.

Negative exponent – Negative exponents indicate reciprocals.
Example: $7^{-2} = \dfrac{1}{7^2}$

Negative (–) numbers – Numbers less than 0, decreasing in value as the numbers get larger. Every real positive number has an opposite that is a real negative number.

Notation – The use of signs and symbols to represent words.

Nothing – A thing that does not exist.

Numerator – The term above the line in a fraction .

Numerical – Something involving or expressed in numbers.

One – The first of the counting numbers; the identity element of multiplication and division.

Opposite – In a contrary direction; the sum of a number and its opposite is zero.

Opposite Numbers – The opposite of a number is the number that is the same distance from zero on the number line, but in the opposite direction. Sometimes the term additive inverse is used to describe an opposite.
Example: the opposite of -3 is +3.

Order – A definite plan; system.

Order of Operations – The order in which operations are performed in order to evaluate expressions; acronym PEMDAS (parenthesis, exponents, multiplication and division, addition and subtraction).

Origin – The source; the intersection of the x-axis and the y-axis; the point (0,0).

Paradox – 2MDs

pi (π) – The symbol designating the ratio of the circumference of a circle to its diameter.
$$\pi = \frac{\text{circumference}}{\text{diameter}}$$

Percent (%) – In, to, or for every hundred.

Percent Number – In the percent ratio, we are going to call the number over 100 the percent number. Example: $\frac{1}{2} = \frac{50}{100} = 50\%$. The 50 is the percent number. (Humpty Dumpty would be proud of this definition!)

Positive – 1.   Showing agreement; affirmative.
        2.   *In Mathematics*, greater than zero.
        3.   *In Electricity*, having a deficiency of electrons.
        4.   Overconfident or dogmatic.

Positive (+) numbers – Numbers greater than 0, increasing in value as the numbers get larger. If no sign is written, assume there is a + in front of the number.

Pragmatic – Practical; testing the validity of all concepts by their practical results.

Premise – A proposition antecedently supposed or proved as a proposition as a basis for argument or inference; specifically either of the first two propositions of a syllogism from which the conclusion is drawn.

Prime factors – Factors of a whole number that are prime numbers. The prime factors of 6 are 2 and 3.

Prime numbers – A whole number that can be evenly divided by no other whole number other than itself and 1.
Examples of prime numbers: 2, 3, 5, 7, 11, 13.

Product – The result obtained when multiplying two or more quantities together.

Proof – Evidence that establishes the truth of something.

Proper Fraction – Any number that can be written as a ratio of real numbers that have a value between 1 and 0 and 0 and -1.

Property – A characteristic or attribute.

Proportion – An equation stating the equality of two ratios.

Prove – To establish by experience or trial to be true.

Quantity – A number or symbol expressing a thing that can be measured.

Quotient – The quantity obtained when one number is divided by another.

Radius (r) – Any straight line from the center of a circle to the periphery (circumference).

Raising to an exponent - Writing a number with a superscript indicates how many times the number (base) is multiplied times itself. Example: $x^3 = xxx$, 3 is an exponent.

Raising to the zero power – By definition, any number (except zero) raised to the zero power is 1.

Ratio ($-, \div, /, :$) – A comparison of two numbers by division.

Rational number – A number that can be expressed as a ratio, where the two numbers are integers (whole numbers).

Rationalizing a denominator – Removing an irrational number from the denominator (bottom number) of a fraction.

Example: $\dfrac{1}{\sqrt{3}} = \dfrac{1}{\sqrt{3}} \times \dfrac{\sqrt{3}}{\sqrt{3}} = \dfrac{\sqrt{3}}{\sqrt{3} \cdot \sqrt{3}} = \dfrac{\sqrt{3}}{\sqrt{3 \cdot 3}} = \dfrac{\sqrt{3}}{\sqrt{3^2}} = \dfrac{\sqrt{3}}{3}$

Real Numbers – All the positive and negative numbers on the number line including the rational numbers, the irrational numbers and zero.

Reason – The ability to think, draw conclusions to think logically, to argue or infer.

Reciprocal – One of a pair of numbers $\left(\text{as } 7, \dfrac{1}{7} \right)$ whose product is 1, $\left(7 \times \dfrac{1}{7} = 1 \right)$. Often the word inverse is used. Often a negative exponent is used to indicate a reciprocal, $7^{-1} = \dfrac{1}{7}$, $7^{-2} = \dfrac{1}{7^2}$. The product of a number and its reciprocal is 1.

Relative – Meaningful only in relationship (cold to hot).

Relatively Prime – Two whole numbers are relatively prime when their only common factor is 1. Example: 5 and 4 are relatively prime.

Rise – Change in the vertical direction (Δy). $\Delta y = y_2 - y_1$.

Root – A quantity that when multiplied by itself a specified number of times, produces a given quantity. The root of an equation is a value for the variable that makes the equation a true statement; a solution.

Rule – An established regulation or guide for conduct, procedure or usage.

Run – Change in the horizontal direction (Δx). $\Delta x = x_2 - x_1$.

Semantics – The study of the changes and development of the meaning of words.

Simile – A figure of speech comparing two unlike things that are often introduced by like or as (Example: *cheeks like roses*).

Simplify – To make simpler or less complex.

Simplistic – Simplified; usually implying that it is simplified too much.

Slope (m) – m = rise/run, $\dfrac{\text{change in y}}{\text{change in x}} = \dfrac{\Delta y}{\Delta x} = \dfrac{y_2 - y_1}{x_2 - x_1}$, where (x_1, y_1) and (x_2, y_2) represent an ordered pair of coordinates, indicating points in the plane.

Slope intercept form of an equation – When a linear equation is solved for y, it is in the form $y = mx + b$; m, the coefficient of x, is the slope and b is the y intercept (where the line crosses the y-axis).

Slope of any line parallel to the y-axis – Undefined because $\Delta x = x_2 - x_1 = 0$ and division by 0 is not permitted.

Solution – If a mathematical equation contains a variable, a value for the variable that makes the sentence true is called a solution. Sometimes the word root is used for solution. Example: In the equation $3x = 6$, $x = 2$ is a solution, it makes the equation a true statement.

Solving Process – In general the solving process reverses the normal order of operations (PEMDAS); addition and subtraction are reversed first and multiplication or division second and dealing with exponents last.

Straight – Having the same direction throughout its length; not crooked or bent.

Substitute – To put in place of another. We will assume that the number system allows us to substitute numbers for letters and letters for numbers. This assumption will usually imply constraints on the substitution. We will assume that if quantities are defined as equal, the number system allows us to substitute the symbols and the numbers for the quantities interchangeably. This assumption will often imply constraints on the substitution. This assumption is essential for the Transitive Property of Equality: If $a = b$ and $b = c$, then $a = c$.

Substitution – Using a number for a variable or using a variable for a number. We will assume that if quantities are defined as equal, the number system allows us to substitute the symbols and the numbers for the quantities interchangeably.

Substitution Assumption – If quantities are defined as equal, they may be substituted for each other.

Subtraction (–) – Finding the difference between things or numbers; sometimes thinking "take away" is useful.

Subtractive Property of Equality – The same quantity can be subtracted from both sides of an equation and not change the truth of the equation.

Supposition – To consider as a possibility. (Right there in the dictionary between supporter-athletic and suppository.)

Syllogism – A deductive scheme of a formal argument consisting of a major and a minor premise and a conclusion.

Symbol of Proportionality (∝ or "= k") – A symbol indicating a relationship between two variables.

Tangent – A line touching a curved surface at one point, but not intersecting it.

Terms – Each quantity in an algebraic expression.

Transitive Property of Equality – Things equal to the same thing are equal to each other. Example: If a = b and b = c, then a = c.

Truth – Sincerity, honesty, conformity with fact, reality, actual existence.

Undefined – The opposite of defined; not possible to describe exactly.

Unit of Measure – A quantity that is used as a standard of measurement or exchange.

Value – A numerical quantity assigned or computed.

Validity – Based on evidence or sound reasoning.

Variable – A letter or symbol that stands for a number that can be changed; often x, y and z are used to denote a variable.

Vertex – The point of intersection of the two sides of an angle.

Whim – A sudden fancy.

x-axis – The horizontal line on a graph, usually indicating an independent variable; the line $y = 0$.

y-axis – The vertical line on a graph, usually indicating a dependent variable; the line x = 0.

y-intercept – The point where a line crosses the y–axis; the value of the expression when x = 0.

Zero – The sum of a number and its opposite is zero; the point marked 0 from which quantities are reckoned on a graduated scale; nothing. Zero is a real number.

LESSON NOTES

How Do We Know?

<u>S</u>AY <u>A</u>LL <u>F</u>AST A <u>M</u>INUTE <u>E</u>VERY <u>D</u>AY <u>S</u>HUFFLED

SAFMEDS

Flash cards. The **Precision Teaching** program terms the use of flash cards as <u>S</u>ay <u>A</u>ll <u>F</u>ast a <u>M</u>inute <u>E</u>very <u>D</u>ay <u>S</u>huffled (SAFMEDS). Students go through the cards for a minute and plot the number of correct responses every day on graph paper. (Standard Celeration Chart)

See www.ralphmagoun.com for downloadable, printable business-card-size SAFMEDS.

BIBLIOGRAPHY

Carroll, Lewis, *Through the Looking Glass*.

Celeration.org, The home page of The Standard Celeration Society for an extensive list of references for Precision Teaching.

Chi, Michelene T. H., Miriam Bassok, Matthew W. Lewis, Peter Reimann and Robert Glaser (1989), Self-explanations and How Students Study and Use Examples in Learning to Solve Problems. *Cognitive Science* 13,145-182.

Einstein, *What I Believe*, (1930).

Fawcett, Harold P., *The Nature of Proof*, NCTM Thirteenth Yearbook, (1938).

Gundlach, Bernard H., *The Laidlaw Glossary of Arithmetical-Mathematical Terms* (1961).

Keedy and Bittinger, *Basic Mathematics*, 6th edition, Addison Wesley Publishing (1992).

Lindsley, O. R. (1990). Precision Teaching. By teachers for children, *Teaching Exceptional Children*, Spring, 10-15.

The Private Eye Project, *The Private Eye - (5X) Looking / Thinking by Analogy*.

West, Richard P., K. Richard Young, Fred Spooner (1990), Precision Teaching, An Introduction, *Teaching Exceptional Children*, Spring, 4-9.

White, Owen Roberts (1986). Precision Teaching – Precision Learning, *Exceptional Children*, Vol. 52, No. 6, 522 – 534.

RALPH E. MAGOUN

In his youth Ralph felt that his contribution to life would be as a research biochemist. He holds a BS Degree in chemistry from Louisiana State University (Geaux Tigers) and a MS Degree in biochemistry from Purdue University, and worked in industry for several years. It dawned on him that most peoples' difficulties in life arise from attitudes and that attitudes are choices. As an analytical biochemist using numbers was rather easy and enjoyable for him. He observed that most people seemed to have a real fear and dislike for mathematics and though they had the knowledge of the principals of math they could not put them together to solve problems. He began a quest to write an algebra book that would teach students that manipulating numbers and variables could be fun and enable them to make a new choice about how they felt about mathematics. This adventure resulted in <u>How Do We Know? Yes, You Can Learn Algebra!</u>. Ralph believes that the empowerment students acquire from accomplishment is what education should be about.

Ralph has taught in schools from the jungles of North Borneo to jungles of South Florida. He is certified as a teacher in Louisiana, California and Florida in science and mathematics.